D1564527

Teaching Ethics

Teaching Ethics

Instructional Models, Methods, and Modalities for University Studies

Edited by Daniel E. Wueste

Series Edited by Dominic P. Scibilia

ROWMAN & LITTLEFIELD
Lanham • Boulder • New York • London

Published by Rowman & Littlefield
An imprint of The Rowman & Littlefield Publishing Group, Inc.
4501 Forbes Boulevard, Suite 200, Lanham, Maryland 20706
www.rowman.com

86-90 Paul Street, London EC2A 4NE, United Kingdom

British Library Cataloguing in Publication Information Available

Library of Congress Cataloging-in-Publication Data

Names: Wueste, Daniel E., editor.
Title: Teaching ethics : instructional models, methods, and modalities for university
    studies / edited by Daniel E. Wueste.
Other titles: Teaching ethics (Rowman and Littlefield, Inc.)
Description: Lanham : Rowman & Littlefield, [2021] | Series: Teaching ethics across the
    American educational experience | Includes bibliographical references.
Identifiers: LCCN 2021020024 (print) | LCCN 2021020025 (ebook) |
    ISBN 9781475846720 (cloth) | ISBN 9781475846737 (paperback) |
    ISBN 9781475846744 (ebook)
Subjects: LCSH: Ethics—Study and teaching (Higher)—United States.
Classification: LCC BJ66 .T434 2021 (print) | LCC BJ66 (ebook) | DDC 170.71—dc23
LC record available at https://lccn.loc.gov/2021020024
LC ebook record available at https://lccn.loc.gov/2021020025

♾️™ The paper used in this publication meets the minimum requirements of American National Standard for Information Sciences—Permanence of Paper for Printed Library Materials, ANSI/NISO Z39.48-1992.

Contents

The Series Preface

What is the American social compact on education? From Jefferson's vision of a public education that forms and informs a democratic citizenry to the call from Betsy DeVos, the Trump administration's secretary of education, to ease church-state regulations regarding education, proposing $5 billion of public money to fund private and religious education (as a means of providing fair access to better schools), the current state of our national educational narrative is often framed by claims in conflict or claims that public education is deficient.

So much of the debate regarding the American educational experience since 1987 has focused on deficiencies—what students cannot do. Many works by commentators like Rudolf Flesch (1986), Allan Bloom (1987), and Erika Christakis (*The Atlantic* 2017) critically observe that students cannot read or write, or are unable to distinguish right from wrong, or that the trends in national public educational policy encourage a dystopian view of public schools.

In response to the conflicting claims about education in America, pedagogues propose whole curricula, design lessons, and implement assessments framed with SMART Goals, Backward Curriculum Design, Summative or Formative measurements of learning, and Professional Learning Communities as antidotes for what ails schools from kindergarten through graduate schools.

The last thirty years in American education feel like an extended autumn. The debaters and conversation partners look too often like people witnessing the sepia hues of the American public educational experience—as if it has been dying. Caught in the melancholy that sometimes accompanies autumn, catching us up in a deep appreciation for the beauty of the season and the advent of death, we miss the seeding that is occurring. Our children in public schools as much as in independent or religious schools are indeed learning to read, write, reason critically, create, and know right from wrong—imagine morally.

Insight into the state of our national educational narrative, the social compact we have with our children regarding their education and with each other regarding the forming and informing of democratic citizens, rises from the witness of the patriots who teach, especially ethics.

Teaching Ethics across the American Educational Experience gives us pause to consider the moral seeding underway throughout American schools. Indeed, students are learning how to distinguish right from wrong, to engage reason, emotion, and imagination when acting as moral agents. During the spring of 2018, Tom Koerner, senior executive editor at Rowman & Littlefield, encouraged me to raise the witnesses whose words and works provide evidence of effective learning, of the seeding of the moral imagination for future citizens.

MARCH 14, 2018

It has been a month since the shootings and killing of seventeen adults and students at Marjory Stoneman Douglas High School in Parkland, Florida. The front page of the *New York Times* frames the infancy narrative of the student social movement #NeverAgain. Like many student movements from around the world (from Colombia, Mexico City, Taiwan, and to the call for public education in Valparaiso, Chile), Parkland High School students call for social change.

Broadcast news services witness the national growth of #NeverAgain as the Parkland students call for a national walkout from school at 10 a.m. today for a seventeen-minute memorial to those who died on February 14. Online and television cameras broadcast pictures of students and adults from Parkland, Atlanta, Decatur, Washington, D.C., and New York City. As the central, mountain, and Pacific time zones reach 10 a.m., from Chicago and Littleton, Colorado to Idaho and Santa Monica, California, they walk out from classes with and without administrative permission.

Adolescents soon to break in on adulthood express ideas like civic responsibility, social reform, political will, civil disobedience, constitutional rights in conflict, and legislative change. They announce their advent as voters. How did those young citizens arrive at moments of political engagement? What stirred their social and moral imaginations—seeing visions of a good society in contrast to their experiences of a flawed society? How did they cultivate abilities to assess critically the functions and dysfunctions within our American political systems?

Someone designed and implemented educational experiences that proved to be effective learning moments in social ethics. The evidence for effective learning in that student movement is not measured by a test score; rather, the evidence comes in the students' applications of their moral imaginations to social questions. Look at how they act, at what they do. As their moral imaginations provoke civic engagement, students become the sort of citizens that advocates for public education from Jefferson to Dewey to Weingarten hope would graduate from American schools.

MARCH 14, 2019

There are teachers from kindergarten through senior year of high school, from undergraduate classrooms to postgraduate professional seminars and corporate committees who design and implement ethics instruction and assess the effectiveness of learning ethics. Those teachers have been responding consistently since the late 1980s to the caustic criticism that a moral vacuum exists in American schools: that Johnny and Jane cannot tell right from wrong as well as read.

Teaching Ethics across the American Educational Experience celebrates the commitment of educators who teach ethics. The contributors in each of the five books in this series take time to write about how students are learning ethics—how instructors teach ethics. It is an unusual writing for teachers. Few preschool and K–12 teachers receive the time to reflect critically on and write about instruction, especially teaching ethics. The demand for scholarship in higher learning rarely considers works seated in a critical reflection on instructional design and implementation.

In Teaching Ethics across the American Educational Experience, teachers take the time to consider ethical instruction and its effectiveness. They present models for ethics instruction and learning from kindergarten through professional life. Lesson plans, integrative plans across a school's curriculum, templates for implementation and means of learning assessment populate five teacher-friendly, student-centered, practical monographs. The series' goals encourage teachers to pause and in that critical contemplative space consider integrating ethics into their American students' educational experiences.

These five books call readers to respond to our witness—the instructional experiences that invite students to be citizens carrying out the American experiment. Teaching Ethics across the American Educational Experience offers the witness of administrators, teachers, parents, the teachers of teachers, and students that will stir moral imaginations to design and implement learning ethics, to open effectively American hearts, souls and minds. We raise a witness to the current state of our national educational social compact.

Brian Gatens, superintendent of The Emerson Public Schools District in New Jersey (Emerson, New Jersey), opens, in *Integrating Social and Emotional Learning: The Importance of Knowing Our Children, Knowing Ourselves*, a literary space wherein administrators and teachers model integrating ethics instruction within a social-emotional learning framework—education attending to the whole child.

In *The Ethics of Digital Literacy: Developing Knowledge and Skills across Grade Levels*, Kristen Hawley Turner (Drew University) convenes a community of educators from elementary school through graduate educational studies for dynamic conversations on the ethical dimensions of teaching digital literacy.

Jane Bleasdale and Julie Sullivan's (University of San Francisco) monograph, *Social Conscience and Responsibility: Teaching the Common Good in Secondary Education*, invites middle and high school teachers to offer models of teaching ethics (stirring self and social awareness that leads to civic agency) in public and independent high schools.

Daniel E. Wueste (Clemson University), in *Teaching Ethics: Instructional Models, Methods and Modalities for University Studies*, gathers a symposium of university faculty (many of whom are members of the Society for Ethics across the Curriculum) proposing models for teaching ethics integrating cognition and conation—teaching moral judgment involving the whole person.

Philip Scibilia (medical humanist) and Dominic P. Scibilia call together graduate school professionals who, in *Transforming Healthcare Education: Applied Lessons Leading to Deeper Moral Reflection*, offer prescient instructional models for teaching narrative ethics within a medical humanist praxis across healthcare curricula.

Dominic P. Scibilia

Foreword

The evolution of modern organizations in most disciplines allows individuals to do things they were never able to do before; and thus, it constantly raises ethical issues we have never encountered before. Perhaps for each individual, the challenges presented by an ethical problem may seem new and often singular unless that individual has some preparation to analyze the problem, a broader context in which to formulate a solution, and the support of other voices in following decisions of conscience. *Teaching Ethics: Instructional Models, Methods, and Modalities for Undergraduate Studies* in the series Teaching Ethics across the American Educational Experience (2021) reaches across disciplines to invite faculty and students to engage in relevant and shifting ethics discussions.

As educators we are seeking to prepare students to comprehend, analyze, and resolve ethical problems, both for the betterment of their lives and the society. Responding to the expansion and developments in our fields requires scrutinizing the ways we teach those who are preparing for the future outside the academy.

This volume's chapters reach across disciplines and challenge all of us to strengthen our intellectual commitment to and knowledge of ethics and ethical practices. Fulfilling our commitment includes an understanding of and appreciation for fundamental moral concepts, principles, or theories as well as skill in moral reasoning and practical judgment. The importance of stimulating our moral imagination is vital in helping to build ethical frameworks that can guide our ethical decisions.

Inherently dialectic, the authors encourage faculty to learn from each other and from their students as they engage in discussions of ethics within and across the curriculum. Ethics is a vehicle that moves well through any discipline, and the various contributors encourage educators to discover how ethical content can fit within each program. Many students come to our classrooms believing they fully understand their moral choices and behavior. A goal of ethics across the educational experience is to help students understand there is typically more than one answer to an ethical problem, and that if they analyze the circumstances carefully, they can often find more solutions than the ones that may be readily apparent.

Much of our understanding of contemporary American interdisciplinary ethics education can be attributed to the Hastings Center's work, beginning in 1969. At this time, many institutions of higher education were considering the need for students to have ethics as part of their wide-ranging educational experiences.

During the late 1970s, the Hastings Center organized a large gathering of educators from various disciplines to discuss what goals might be appropriate in teaching ethics in higher education. A consensus emerged that has inspired many of us in developing courses, workshops, and programs in practical and professional ethics. In a summary recommendation on the state of ethics education in American higher education, the group states:

> A "higher education" that does not foster, support, and implement an examination of the moral life will fail its own purposes, the needs of its students, and the welfare of society. The university offers a unique context for a careful examination of moral claims and moral purposes. We ask only that such an examination be made formal and explicit, and that sufficient imagination, energy, and resources be invested in the teaching of ethics that its importance will become manifest, both within and outside the university. (Callahan and Bok 1980, 300)

The Hastings Center work demonstrates how the extension of the study of ethics across the curriculum can build bridges and foster understanding across the various disciplines. As these scholars predicted, ethics touches every facet of organizational life. They stress that moral sensitivity and awareness are not only vital to each discipline.

Like the earlier work of the Hastings scholars, authors in this volume demonstrate the importance of merging ethics with disciplinary issues. Integrating ethics into various curricula creatively builds from Hasting's work. Chapters suggest various methods of incorporating ethics across the curriculum including case studies, critical thinking thought experiments, and the development and study of codes of ethics. Each faculty member should be willing to assist students in developing the foundation for their professional moral choices.

Our failure to prepare our students to recognize ethical problems in their professions, and thus our failure to prepare them to think critically about determining what ought to be done regarding such ethical incidents, presents a national problem of massive proportions.

The work in ethics across the curriculum seeks to change this. Responding to this problem requires changing the very way we teach those who will become the professionals upon whom we depend for the structures and infrastructures of our lives. In 1990, I began my work in Ethics across the Curriculum. This included bringing ethics into courses by assisting a broad contingent of faculty from almost every discipline on campus. In this program we prepared students to comprehend, analyze, and resolve ethical problems in their professions, both for the betterment of their lives and of society.

As this program continues today, we encourage our students to carefully study the harms associated with choices others have made as well as potential harms caused by decisions they could make in the future. Beneficence is also vital in the understanding of ethics within the disciplines. Studying how employees can "do good" with a field of study or a profession is part of the healthy development of the industry as well as a career.

In my more than thirty-five years of work in ethics and ethics across the curriculum, I have found some of the following goals assist in strengthening ethical understanding. First, faculty can expand the moral sensitivity of students by helping them examine the nature of their ethical assumptions. Second, it is important to continually increase understanding of current ethical problems within the professions for both students and faculty. Third, faculty can help students to carefully examine appropriate facts and develop decision-making strategies for resolving ethical issues. A fourth goal is to find methods to help students realize that moral values are not merely subjective opinions (Englehardt).

When the students we are training in these disciplines leave our colleges, universities, and schools, they should be prepared to think critically about the ethical issues they will encounter as professionals. Some of the complex ethical issues that will cross their desks may involve issues of trust, honesty, harm, fairness, respect, rights, and responsibilities. These are of central importance to the ethics across the curriculum framework for our faculty and students.

And *Teaching Ethics: Instructional Models, Methods, and Modalities for Undergraduate Studies* does well to put into praxis those four goals, becoming both persons and professionals with moral reason, affection, intuition, and imagination.

Elaine E. Englehardt, PhD
President, Society for Ethics across the Curriculum
Distinguished Professor of Ethics
Professor of Philosophy
Utah Valley University

REFERENCES

Callahan, D. and S. Bok, eds. 1980. *Ethics Teaching in Higher Education.* New York: The Hastings Center.

Englehardt, E. and M. Pritchard. 2019 *Ethics across the Curriculum, Pedagogical Perspectives.* The Netherlands: Springer, 2018.

Introduction

Daniel E. Wueste

Although the history of moral philosophy (moral psychology too) presents cognition and conation as competitors for pride of place with respect to ethical judgment, it is best to treat them as allies, as elements of human personality that are in play in the process of making ethical judgments. At any rate, so far as teaching ethics is concerned, such an approach is strongly indicated, because success is more likely when instructors can prevent disconnects that breed indifference or disregard of moral considerations.

Many such disconnects can be avoided, if teachers and students approach their work together with clear-eyed awareness that ethical judgments are made by *persons* who are not disinterested reasoners, devoid of passions or somehow effectively cut off from them, but individuals whose constitution (makeup, character) needs to be taken into account. A salient feature of the models, methods, and modalities discussed in the chapters of this book is that they do that.

The first section, "Setting the Philosophical Context," sets the stage by discussing the indirect model championed by sociologists and social psychologists in the mid-1970s. One of the most attractive features of this model, according to advocates, is that moral development would not require special methods or courses devoted to the teaching of ethics and values. Although the model fails to deliver on its promise of moral development, discussion of the reasons for its failure, and its shift away from cognition to conation, directs attention to critical elements for the success of direct models, methods, and modalities in teaching ethical judgment.

The second section, "Persons as Moral Agents," consists of three chapters that address the meaning of people as moral agents. Burroughs, Borden, and Cooley approach the study and application of ethics in ways that are attuned to the whole person, directing attention to context and moral thinking that

1

involves reason, emotion, intuition, and imagination. The contexts are personal, promoting a deeper awareness of oneself as a moral agent and social, revealing the necessity for the praxes of dialogue and reflection in responsible moral engagement as well as recognition, and analysis of the impact of socialized influences such as bias, ethnocentrism, or the reflexive relativism common among undergraduates.

In the third section, "Ethical Leaders," three chapters by Dufresne and Steingard, Luckman and Gunsalus, and Kretz focus attention on ethical leadership. The person/leader as an agent of social change receives special attention. It is significant that in each case it emerges clearly that ethics is not merely a supplement to or a secondary discipline that adds a welcome but inessential component to a more essential discipline.

That observation is noteworthy not least because the existence of professional codes of ethics, which arise from professional experience, or corporate codes and value statements may suggest otherwise. Yet, these quasi-legislative products, no less than positive law, are properly subject to moral scrutiny, which may either confirm or deny the validity of the obligations, permissions, or rights they purport to create.

In the fourth section, "Moral Reasoning: Instructional Methods," two chapters by Croskery and Preti invite attention to instructional models that are especially attentive to moral reasoning. Biasucci opens for the reader a critical consideration of the tools, technique, and the trappings of moral reasoning from a psychological perspective, for example, reflecting on cognitive biases such as "framing" and the impact of one's socialization revealed in the research of behavioral economics.

Daniel E. Wueste, PhD, Professor of
Philosophy at Clemson University

Section 1

SETTING THE PHILOSOPHICAL CONTEXT

Dominic P. Scibilia

Daniel E. Wueste charges those who teach ethical judgment to envision how cognition and conation deepen teaching ethics, learning how to make moral judgments. The shortcoming in the directions set out in Indirect Instructional Models stresses learning how to make moral judgments from the exemplars of those in authority—for example, a student's professor—or from the normative structures within social structures like the academy. The flaw in that instructional shortcoming is the antagonistic, some might posit dismissive, preference for reason over affection, or cognition over conation, in the process of making moral judgments. Learning moral judgment is far more complex than looking up the rules or appealing to reason.

Chapter 1

Cognition and Conation

A Potent Alliance in Teaching Ethical Judgment

Daniel E. Wueste

Although the indirect model fails to deliver on its promise of moral development, the reasons for its failure, examined here, and its shift away from cognition to conation invite attention to critical elements for the success of direct models, methods, and modalities in teaching ethical judgment.

INTRODUCTION

At roughly the midpoint in his book *Universities in the Marketplace*, Derek Bok, past president of Harvard University and former dean of the Harvard Law School, notes that "[h]elping to develop virtue and build character have been central aims of education since the time of Plato and Aristotle. After years of neglect," he says,

> universities everywhere have rediscovered the need to prepare their students to grapple with the moral dilemmas they will face in their personal and professional lives. In colleges and professional schools alike, courses on practical ethics are now a common feature of the curriculum. (Bok, 109)

While granting that courses on practical ethics may be valuable, Bok thinks undergraduates likely learn more about how to lead their lives from "the example set by those in positions of authority" (109). Prominent among these people, of course, are the professors they learn from in classrooms, lecture halls, laboratories, studios and seminar rooms, the vast majority of whom are not teaching ethics courses.

In the mid-1970s, the idea that such academic encounters could be founts of moral development was promoted by sociologist Martin Trow and others working in higher education studies. Trow dismissed the then fashionable view that higher education has little or no real impact on those who experience it and directed attention to the mechanisms of moral development in higher education and the forms such development might take (1976).

The mechanisms of moral development loomed large:

> We have a moral impact not only through what we teach—the content of our subjects and disciplines—but also through our ability to show how we come to know or believe what we do. There is a powerful morality implicit in the canons of verification, in our scholarly and scientific methods and procedures. (Trow, 22)

The Indirect Model

The operative idea here is that of normative structures. It is an idea championed, for example, by Robert K. Merton (1942) in his sociology of science and Lon L. Fuller (1964) in his jurisprudence. Normative structures have intuitive appeal for many in the academy and, indeed, have been argued and promoted by this author in more than one venue (Wueste, 2005, 2010, 2012). In the context of higher education, the idea is basically that, regardless of discipline, the scholarly/research enterprise depends for its viability and success on values and norms of practice that constitute a morality internal to the enterprise.

Expectations about what ought to be done are not imposed from above or outside the enterprise; rather, the purpose of the enterprise generates constraints on action that, if breached, undermine it, and, insofar as they are respected, largely explain its integrity. Richard Morill briefly summarizes the idea of an implicit morality of scholarly practice in his discussion of Trow's views as follows.

> The scholar is required to listen honestly and tolerantly to evidence from whatever the source, to entertain alternative points of view and negative evidence, to engage in self-judgment and self-criticism, and to abandon results that gratify the ego but are not true. Effective scholarship, then, depends upon allegiance to moral and intellectual values such as honesty, tolerance, respect, truth, rigor, and fairness. This distinctive set of values creates a moral community that makes it possible for science and scholarship to function and flourish. (1980: 32–33)

Jacob Bronowski, the British mathematician and historian perhaps best known as a champion of a humanistic approach to science, also promotes a morality implicit in scholarly practice. According to Bronowski, the very activity of trying to refine and enhance knowledge—of discovering "what is"—imposes on us certain norms of conduct. The prime condition for its success is a scrupulous rectitude of behavior, based on a set of values like truth, trust, dignity, dissent, and so on. (Derfer, 391-392)

Thinking in terms of rules governing scholarly/research practice, for more than a few folks, what comes to mind first may be the America Competes Act, which requires training in the responsible conduct of research supported by the National Science Foundation (http://www.nsf.gov/bfa/dias/policy/rcr .jsp).

Such training addresses several things, of course, but, with an eye to clarifying the "internal morality" idea, it will be helpful to consider falsification, fabrication, and plagiarism (FF&P), the three key elements in the Office of Research Integrity's definition of research misconduct (https://ori.hhs.gov/ definition-misconduct). The critical point is that the ethical unacceptability/ wrongness of falsification, fabrication, and plagiarism is not the result of a federal agency's definition of research misconduct; if there is a connection, it is the other way around. The internal morality of research prohibits these things because they undermine the research enterprise, which cannot achieve its aims let alone flourish, when they occur.

The idea, again, is that there is a morality internal to the scholarly/research enterprise—Morrill calls it an *academic ethic*—which "is a presupposition of scholarship, not its aim" (1980: 34). This *academic ethic* comprises values as criteria of choice and calls for deep commitment on the part of the person engaged in the academic enterprise; in practice this commitment is in fact essential. Accordingly, Morrill speaks of efforts on this front as aiming at the development of "what can only be called intellectual and moral virtues" (1980: 34). There is, then, a shift here "toward the conative [and] away from the narrowly cognitive" (1980: 34).

It is worth noting that with respect to the project of moral development, this marks a significant contrast with Lawrence Kohlberg, for whom moral education is principally and properly about cognition. Following Bronowski in focusing attention on the "activity of trying to refine and enhance knowledge" (Derfer, 391), which many would call the scientific or academic enterprise, the indirect model eschews a sharp distinction between cognition and conation.

Interestingly, Bronowski's rejection of a sharp distinction includes, yet extends beyond, the idea that scientific or academic practice has an internal morality—that values are an inherent condition of the practice (392)—as can be seen in his considered position that poetry and science are "inseparable" modes of knowledge (393-394, 402). Indeed, in "taking issue with the 'value free idea' . . . the insistence that there is no relation between the 'is's that science finds—the facts—and the 'oughts' that our conscience demands," he argues that the so-called "naturalistic fallacy," in particular as it is associated with G. E. Moore, is, in a word, "nonsense" (391).

The takeaway here is an intriguing suggestion: cognition and conation are allies instead of neighbors who, as it were, see one another on opposite sides of a river that separates them.

Like Derek Bok, advocates of the indirect model think that the teaching and learning of ethics is likely most effective if done indirectly, rather than in formal courses. They "do not suggest any special classroom methods or courses in values and ethics; their claim is that a sound education based on sound scholarship is itself a form of moral education" (Morrill, 34). Moral education and moral development are, then, epiphenomenal.

Trouble is, while the existence of this internal morality—the academic ethic—is hardly contentious, there is nothing here that assures moral education/development; at best it is indicative of potential for such development. Indeed, that there is anything more here is hard to square with the widespread misbehavior of researchers that led to the creation of the Office of Research Integrity to say nothing of the recent alarming increase in the number of retractions of published scientific research.

According to the journal *Nature*, in "the early 2000s, only about 30 retraction notices appeared annually" but in 2011, though "the total number of papers published [had] risen by only 44%, the Web of Science [was] on track to index more than 400" (Van Noorden, 26). This startling fact was followed by an observation to the effect that it's not all that bad, because although "the number of retraction notices had risen 10-fold," it appears "that only about half of them were for researcher misconduct" (27). Small comfort.

In 2015, the *New York Times* reported a retraction from the journal *Science* of a study about changing attitudes toward gay marriage. The retracted study, one of a *growing list* of retracted studies, received widespread attention. While many retractions receive little or no attention outside the scientific community, the *Times* noted that in "some instances, the studies that were clawed back made major waves in societal discussions of the issues they dealt with." A list of such retractions includes studies about vaccines and autism, cloning and human stem cells, cancer in rats and herbicides, pesticides and estrogen, as well as psychological studies that "generated considerable media attention," which were "based on falsified data and faked experiments" (Roston).

Such ethically sketchy behavior on the part of researchers strongly suggests that although intuitively attractive, the claim that moral development is an indirect consequence of observation of and participation in a practice governed by an internal morality is challenged rather than supported by the evidence. The appalling consistency of high rates of academic dishonesty among undergraduates and, perhaps especially, among graduate students constitutes a challenge to this claim as well.

The International Center for Academic Integrity (ICAI), which has studied trends in academic dishonesty for more than a decade, reports that about 68 percent of undergraduate students surveyed admit to cheating on tests or in written work. Forty-three percent of graduate students do the same. (Barthel, https ://www.theatlantic.com/education/archive/2016/04/how-to-stop-cheating-in-co llege/479037)

There is more to the story about academic dishonesty and research misconduct, much of which would lead us far afield. However, with these observations it should be clear that something more than what the indirect model provides is required to effectively address the ethical problems of academic dishonesty and research misconduct, or, better, to effectively promote academic and research integrity.

The claim that moral education/development is epiphenomenal and will occur naturally as teachers/scholars carry on with their work—meaning that there is no need for special classroom methods or courses in values and ethics—isn't merely lacking in empirical support, rather, the evidence strongly suggests that it is false. Still, it will be useful to ask why the indirect model fails.

The Indirect Model: A Diagnosis of Failure

The indirect model does not work for two reasons. First, it presupposes that faculty are positioned to be ethics mentors/role models without consciously undertaking the task, or that they have traits of character that one might hope will, as well as expect to, rub off on their students. The model eschews *teaching* in favor of what might be called *free-style mentoring* —where the expectation is that students will watch and replicate what they see; they will *walk the walk* they see their mentor walking (the mentor may be, but isn't necessarily identified as a mentor).

Such an approach will have results, because that is in fact a way in which we all learn. Indeed, this largely explains a parent's concern about who her children are running with (i.e., who their friends are), as well a manager's concern about messages conveyed implicitly by what she does, which may be taken as in some sense overriding explicit managerial direction (some such cases bring to mind the adage *Do as I say, not as I do*).

The critical point is that the results such a method delivers may not (and perhaps most often will not) be the desired results. Consider the crises in the arena of scientific research—where free-style mentoring supposedly imparted the norms of research ethics—leading to the rise of the (federal) Office of

Scientific Integrity, offices of research compliance at colleges and universities, and, with the America Competes Act (2007), legislatively mandated
instruction in the responsible conduct of research (https://www.congress.gov/
110/plaws/publ69/PLAW-110publ69.pdf Sec. 7009).

The second problem with this model is that it presupposes, wrongly, that
the faculty both know how to work their way, reliably and responsibly, to the
other side of an ethical challenge, and can effectively convey this knowledge
to others. Trouble is, so far as their understanding of ethics is concerned,
faculty are often quite like undergraduates, thinking, for example, that there
are no right answers to ethical questions; when queried what they mean, they
often reply that any answer is merely subjective or relative to culture (i.e.,
determined by conventional/customary norms that vary from place to place,
time to time, culture to culture).

They agree that the right answer, if there were one, would, of course, carry
the day; it would defeat any competitor in the way that truth triumphs over
falsity in science, for example. But with ethics, they think, the answers are all
equally good and, consequently, none are capable of carrying the day. Any
contest will end in a tie, and thus, the mantra, "Who's to say?" is heard from
faculty just as it is from undergraduates.

A key point in this connection is that the existence of more than one answer
to an ethical question does not mean that the answers are equally good, any
more than there being two sides to the story a parent hears from her children
means that the stories are equally good.

In ethics, as in science, some answers are *better* than others, in the sense
that they withstand critical scrutiny, or more precisely, because the evidence
and argument that support them are stronger than the evidence and argument
that support competing answers. While such answers are not final, they can be
embraced with confidence, which is what distinguishes and provides a war-
rant for treating them as right answers. This is not a novel idea. It is familiar
in the context of adjudication, for example, as well as science.

Here, one may be reminded of Aristotle's warning that one ought not
expect more in the way of surety/assurance than a discipline is capable of
providing. However, the move is not meant to in some sense apologize for
a regrettable lack respecting the surety/assurance one can reasonably expect
in ethics; it is, rather, to highlight the fact of parity with science, where it is
often assumed, wrongly, that the surety/assurance on offer is utterly different
(stronger/better) than that on offer in ethics.

Speaking of science, John Dewey puts the point succinctly: "From the
standpoint of scientific inquiry nothing is more fatal to its right to obtain
acceptance than a claim that its conclusions are final and hence incapable
of a development that is other than mere quantitative extension" (1948:
xvi).

Science, Dewey tells us, "is forced by its development to abandon the assumption of fixity and to recognize that what . . . is actually 'universal' [in it] is *process*" (1948: xiii). Yet, while science has walked away from fixity and universality as metaphysical conditions of truth and a failsafe prophylactic to epistemic chaos, morals stubbornly suppose that "immutable, extra-temporal principles, standards, norms, [and] ends [are] the only assured protection against moral chaos." In doing so, however, it can "no longer appeal to natural science for its support, nor expect to justify by science [an] exemption of morals (in practice and in theory) from considerations of time and place—that is, from processes of change" (xiii).

The second problem identified above is, in short, the existence of epistemic lacunae, among faculty generally, about ethics and ethics pedagogy. Professional development can provide a partial remedy for this problem, which could facilitate the teaching of ethics in a diverse collection of courses, which, in turn, could help colleges fulfill promises about the development of ethical judgment in the context of general education. It might also help in meeting the challenge of integrating ethics in programs that (a) have lock-step curricula and (b) have to meet accreditation demands respecting ethics instruction.

However, successful integration of ethics in programs with lock-step curricula is a multifaceted challenge that at best can be met only partially by means of professional development. After all, professional development in the teaching of ethics does not diminish curricular time demands in a discipline such as engineering. And with respect to general education, the clear and present danger is that ethics will be visited much as an exhibit in a museum, which can do little more than nothing to develop competency in ethical judgment. Although the box for the gen-ed competency can be checked, the promise will not to be kept.

The larger substantive challenge emerges with recognition of the desiderata of success in the project of developing ethical judgment, which is different than the project of teaching history or economics, for example; it is also, importantly, different than teaching moral philosophy.

While success in teaching moral philosophy does not entail development in students of an ability to recognize ethical issues and competence in the use of a method for addressing them systematically, reflectively, and responsibly, success in developing ethical judgment does. Put another way, the absence of a learning objective along the lines of, "students will be able to articulate and engage with an ethical issue in a systematic, reflective and responsible way," would not be a problem for a course in moral philosophy; the same cannot be said of a course that aims at the development of ethical judgment.

What is not immediately apparent is that success with that learning objective calls for something in addition to development of skill, for example, in the use of a method (in short, wherewithal), namely, awareness/sensitivity and commitment. These things are interdependent; the value of such skill, like that of a tool in a toolbox, is bound up with one's recognizing when it is apposite and one's having an interest in, to stick with analogy, building, or fixing something.

Curricular time demands in a discipline such as engineering are serious obstacles to the success of ethics integration efforts, even if faculty short-falls in knowledge about ethics and its pedagogy have been remediated by professional development. So too, the necessity of awareness/sensitivity and commitment in addition to wherewithal creates an obstacle to success in the development of ethical judgment by means of course modules or effective use of teachable moments in general education.

What is sought is more than can be achieved by these means. In this con-nection this author speaks from experience. For fifteen years, after which he stepped down and returned to the faculty, he directed an ethics institute that offered professional development seminars for faculty that were intended to prepare them to integrate ethics across the curriculum and help fulfill the gen-ed promise of competency in ethical judgment at Clemson University. Although the assessment measures did not mark the efforts a failure and con-tinuation of the program was justified by the limited success they revealed, institute leaders learned that genuine success in the development of ethical judgment calls for the setting and the time allotment of (at least) a regular 3-credit course.

Courses in Ethics: Exploring the Implications of the Indirect Model's Failings

It is important to recall that the normative structure Morrill calls an academic ethic comprises values as criteria of choice and calls for deep commitment on the part of those involved in the academic enterprise. That, indeed, is why he speaks of efforts on this front as aiming at the development of "what can only be called intellectual and moral virtues" (1980: 34). What we have learned about the indirect model can be reframed using this language.

If the aim is the development of intellectual and moral virtues or moral development, one would be making a serious mistake if they were to take the aim to be an epiphenomenon or the sort of thing that emerges effortlessly, that is, without concerted effort in its direction. Experience strongly suggests that concerted effort is required and that it should take the form of "special classroom methods or courses in values and ethics" (Morrill, 34).

Advocates of the indirect model deny this. They do so because, in their view, the indirect model is preferable to special methods or courses. Trouble is, the model they champion not only lacks evidential support, the available evidence regarding the indirect model points away from it. There is, however, another reason for reticence about courses in values and ethics, which is heard in other contexts as well, namely, that such courses would constitute indoctrination or an imposition of values.

But this reason smacks of paradox, because while such opposition is the upshot of an avowed commitment to value neutrality, that commitment itself is neither value neutral nor free of value-laden consequences. It is rather like the situation in which an instructor declines to share her own view on a topic during class discussion. Her choice evinces a judgment/belief that it would be *better* not to share her belief.

It will be useful to consider an example. A teacher's judgment that she ought not share her belief is, one may suppose, based on a pedagogical goal, say, cultivating critical acumen. An embrace of that goal speaks against any invitation to students to defer to authority, which is most likely what would happen if she were to share her belief, and so, with an eye to her goal, she declines to share it. Her hypothesis will be confirmed or not by experience, and that, in turn, will constitute the basis for a judgment as to whether her judgment was correct. Either way, declining to share her belief is not value neutral.

The reader may recall Derek Bok's observations that (a) "[h]elping to develop virtue and build character have been central aims of education since the time of Plato and Aristotle," and (b) "universities everywhere have rediscovered the need to prepare their students to grapple with the moral dilemmas they will face in their personal and professional lives" (109). His words capture well a pedagogical goal of ethics instruction that, like the teacher's goal in the example above, informs a judgment about how ethics should be taught: ethics should be taught in ways that prepare students to deal with the moral issues/problems they will come up against in the lives they will lead after graduation.

As considered earlier in the discussion of general education and professional development as a means to rectify lacunae in ethics knowledge and pedagogy among faculty, achievement of this goal calls for the development of awareness/sensitivity and commitment as well as wherewithal (i.e., skill in the use of a method, e.g., applying the principle of utility or the categorical imperative). Return, then, to another point which was made near the outset of the chapter: rather than ethics education being principally and properly about cognition, as Kohlberg believed it was, it is about both cognition and conation.

Since an example may be helpful in making this claim about the link between cognition and conation clearer, let's revisit briefly the subject of academic dishonesty. Extensive research conducted by Donald McCabe shows that "honor code schools have lower rates of cheating than other institutions by around a quarter, provided that [the] honor code was made a central part of campus culture." McCabe puts the point in a telling way: "The only reason I imagine students stop cheating is because they're being trusted" (Barthel, https://www.theatlantic.com/education/archive/2016/04/how-to-stop-cheating-in-college/479037/).

Being trusted is something one *feels*, like trepidation or hopefulness, for example. McCabe's point is that without this—that is, being, and thus feeling trusted—knowledge about what is and what is not permitted is often (too often) inefficacious. A student may have acquired the wherewithal to easily construct the syllogism, for example,

> Plagiarism is prohibited by the Academic Integrity code.
> Submitting a paper purchased at fastessay.com would constitute plagiarism.
> Therefore, submitting such a paper is prohibited the Academic Integrity code.

From which, by means of sound reasoning, the conclusion emerges that a proposed action would be wrong. Yet, so far as this goes, what the student will do remains an open question. Put another way, so far as the student's action is concerned, it's as if all one knows is the syllogism's mood and figure (AAA 1), which in this case constitutes certification of validity, but provides nothing that would or could prompt action, say, for example, one's judging that the conclusion is true. More is needed for that.

In this case, students need to know the content of the premises, which would allow for an assessment of their truth and thus position them to determine whether the argument is sound (and thus has—indeed, must have—a true conclusion). So too, with respect to action, the student needs something more than what the syllogism (reason) provides, in a word, motivation. If McCabe is right, the requisite motivation can be found in a student's being, and thus feeling, trusted, which, as he has it, is a salient feature of the culture at an honor code school.

At this juncture, one may be reminded of David Hume's famous statement about the place of passion (which would include emotions, feelings, and desires) in regard to moral action:

> We speak not strictly and philosophically when we talk of the combat of passion and of reason. Reason is, and ought only to be the slave of the passions, and can never pretend to any other office than to serve and obey them. (Hume, 2.3.3)

However, the point that tracks with the discussion above is somewhat less contentiously put by Hume when he says that "reason alone can never be a motive to any action of the will" (2.3.3).

In the context of this discussion, Hume's point about the impotence of reason alone, like McCabe's point about the power of trust, tracks with the shift seen earlier with the indirect model "toward the conative [and] away from the narrowly cognitive" (Morrill, 34) and suggests further that with an eye to success in the project of moral education teachers and students should treat cognition and conation as allies.

Taking this suggestion seriously, instructors will search for a way to engage with students that promotes a fecund sense of connection that can defeat the indifference that Hume associates with *reason alone* and generate commitment, which can, in turn, be a source of ethical motivation. Put another way, instructors will look for a model that helps students appreciate the very real sense in which who they are as persons is entwined with their ethical experience.

One challenge in this regard is appreciating sources of disconnection that can lead to indifference or disregard. Consider, for example, the disconnect students may feel in the face of morality's claim to universality and the concomitant requirement of impartiality. A brief discussion of this challenge as it emerges in Richard Wasserstrom's work on professional ethics and the moral dimensions of roles may be helpful.

Many, if not most, people believe that "it is right that [parents] do and should prefer the interests of their children over those of any or all other children in the world." According to Wasserstrom, however, this idea is "morally suspect" (Luban, 26). Why? Because understood rightly, morality is "essentially universalistic in reach and scope" and includes "at least a strong presumption of equality among all the members of the moral community, of the equal respect and treatment that is due to them, and of the impartiality that is morally due to a consideration of their individual needs and interests" (28-29).

In terms of "the most distinctively and unambiguously moral view," Wasserstrom writes, when the needs and interests "are of the same kind, there is presumptively, if not conclusively, no moral reason to prefer one person's interests over those of any others" (28-29).

So, for example, a lifeguard who saw on her right a young person floundering desperately in the water, and on her left her young daughter, also floundering desperately in the water, having to choose which way to turn, she would have *no moral reason* to prefer the needs and interests of her daughter to those of the other person. With the sole exception of a discussion among philosophers (where such things as the fact that the lifeguard would not be deliberating before choosing which way to turn, would be of little consequence because the case is a *thought experiment*), what this example reveals about the most distinctive and unambiguous moral view would be disquieting.

Thinking about roles—Wasserstrom invites attention to the role of a parent in a discussion of professional roles—in light of this understanding of morality, one might well worry as Virginia Held does that "there will be *more of a tendency than otherwise for no one to take any moral considerations into account*, and for responsibility to be even easier to evade than if different roles have more limited and specifiable obligations and expectations" (64 emphasis added).

The universalistic dimension of morality, which entails or at least brings with it a strong demand for impartiality, may be a source of difficulty in teaching ethics not only or primarily because it conflicts with the self-interestedness of many, if not most, students, or with their awareness of cultural differences, which often prompts a naïve ethical relativism, but because it suggests a disconnect with life as it is lived that undercuts a teacher's claim that what is being taught is applicable to and useful in dealing with life situations where one is committed to acting rightly and making a good faith effort to do so.

Mainstream moral philosophy is committed to the idea that moral questions about what ought to be done are to be decided on the basis of reasoned application of principle; in the mainstream account this occurs in a process that eschews emotion and thus excludes empathy and feelings of connection that would favor, for example, one's loved ones. As one text writer, Russ Shafer-Landau, puts it, according to traditional ethical theories morality is universal, impartial, and principled (i.e., its judgments follow from an absolute and fundamental principle), and is "primarily about doing justice (Kantianism), seeking mutual benefit (contractarianism), or impartial benevolence (utilitarianism)" (Shafer-Landau, 174, 176). The interests of those we love count, but no more than the interests of any other person (or sentient being).

There is quite a lot of grist here for a philosopher's mill, but for present purposes this point is key. A person is in fact partially constituted by his/her relationships. As Virginia Held says, "Our embeddedness in familial, social, and historical contexts is basic" (2006: 46). My colleague Todd May captures the point this way:

> I am bound to my kids, caught up with them in ways that I am not caught up with other people's kids. But it's more than that. My kids help mold me into the person I am. To be a father, and more to the point to be a father to these particular kids [May has three], creates me in certain ways that being a friend to them, or a father of others would not. (58)

Indeed, the relationship between, for example, father and son takes a part in making each of them who they are; each "is partially constituted by it" (59). A father's relationship to his children is not simply a matter of having certain obligations to them, as if they were "separate individuals that [he] happens to be surrounded by and so [has] to figure out what [he] owes to each" through reasoned application of abstract principle(s) (58).

Some philosophers might ask whether relationships of this sort can be properly accounted for in traditional moral philosophy, which demands equality (i.e., that each is counted equally or their interests are to be treated so) and impartiality, and assigns the task of moral decision-making to reason alone. And some other philosophers might say,

> Look, regardless of how that question is answered, while the existence of such a relationship may explain how a parent *feels*, it tells us nothing about what morally a parent should do; in that connection feelings are simply beside the point. A question about what morally ought to be done is a question about one's duty, about what one is morally obligated to do; such a question can only be answered through reasoned application of principle.

Still others, who pitch their tents with advocates of virtue ethics or the ethics of care, for example, might join the discussion by first arguing against their interlocutors' focus on duty. Again, there is quite a lot of grist for a philosopher's mill in May's discussion of his relationship to his kids. However, what's important for present purposes is the existence of the disconnect, which prompted reference to May's work, and the tendency it has to prompt a "dismissal of morality as hopelessly complicated, irrelevant or vague" (Held, 1984: 64) as something merely academic, in the sense that it would not be useful in one's life in the *real world*. Since such dismissal marks utter defeat in the project of ethical education, attention to and appreciation of its source is clearly indicated.

Earlier it was suggested that the source of the difficulty is a disconnect with life as it is lived. In the teaching of ethics, it appears that this may be explained in large part by the focus—a singular focus for those who follow Kohlberg or work in the mainstream tradition discussed briefly above—on cognition, in particular moral *reasoning*. Here, as elsewhere in this discussion, there are multiple points that invite philosophical inquiry and argument. We will have to decline the invitation, however, and instead focus narrowly on a common understanding of moral reasoning (Frankena, 2).

In his *Commentaries on the Law of England*, Sir William Blackstone describes a way of thinking in the law that mirrors one that has proved attractive in ethics as well. In both cases what makes it attractive is that reason does all the work, which means there is no place for and no reason to worry about the desires, foibles, eccentricities, or character flaws of the person who serves as reason's mouthpiece. Blackstone writes:

The judgment, though pronounced or awarded by the judges, is not their determination or sentence, but the determination and sentence of the *law*. It is the
conclusion that naturally and regularly follows from the premises of law and
fact. . . . [this] judgment or conclusion depends not therefore on the arbitrary
caprice of the judge, but on the settled and invariable principles of justice. (Vol.
3, 396)

Trouble is, as Oliver Wendell Holmes Jr. famously noted,

the actual life of the law has not been logic: it has been experience. The felt
necessities of the times, the prevalent moral and political theories, intuitions of
public policy, avowed or unconscious, even the prejudices which judges share
with their fellow-men, have had a good deal more to do than the syllogism in
determining the rules by which men should be governed. (Holmes 1881: 1)

The same can be said, *mutatis mutandis*, of ethics.

What leads to the embrace of logic/reason to the exclusion of what Hume
would call the passions? According to Holmes, it's that its "method and
form flatter that longing for certainty and for repose which is in every human
mind. But certainty generally is illusion, and repose is not the destiny of
man" (Holmes, 1920: 181). Holmes is speaking about the law, but here too,
as above, the same can be said of ethics.

What is perhaps most salutary in Holmes' observation is that it is realistic; it does not elide the human elements of the subject at hand. A judge is
not a disinterested reasoner, devoid of passions or somehow effectively cut
off from them as she makes judgments. She is *a person* whose constitution
(make-up, character) can scarcely be denied, if we are true to the subject of
our interest, namely, that she is making normative judgments. This is equally
true of each person who makes moral judgments.

Focusing narrowly on cognition, in the terms of Holmes' discussion,
on syllogistic reasoning, something of enormous importance is elided.
Consequently, the judge as seen here is a misrepresentation of the judge as
she is in fact. The partial capture of who she is allows for a misleading sense
of certainty, rather like what one has in dealing with syllogistic forms. As
explained, the abstraction that brings certainty does so because it lacks content; it is purely a matter of form. But without content (premises fleshed out
in a way that allows for an assessment of their truth), the certainty guaranteed
by form has no cash value.

This is what Hume is getting at when he says that "reason alone can never
be a motive to any action of the will" (Hume, 2.3.3). Speaking in terms of reason alone captures only a portion of any person, any would-be moral agent,
and, if Hume is right, the less potent part at that.

The attraction of logic/reason for Blackstone and others is that if it is doing all the work, one is immune to objections and accusations to the effect that one's decision is questionable because it is inconstant, being the upshot of feelings, desires, foibles, eccentricities, or character flaws. In this, though he does not put it this way, Blackstone is like someone looking for assurance of the sort commonly, though erroneously, associated with science. However, as we have seen, although it is widely thought that the surety/assurance on offer with science is utterly different (stronger/better) than that on offer in ethics, this is not in fact the case.

CONCLUSION

The allure of reason in this setting emerges from a quandary that is in the end unwarranted. In jurisprudence, it is bound up with a stark and frightening choice: reason or fiat, in ethics one source is an allegedly forced choice between absolutism and relativism. Dorothy Emmet speaks to this in an eloquent and helpful way in a chapter, "Moral Relativism," in her book *Rules, Roles, and Relations*:

> So, if we are asked summarily whether morality is "absolute" or "relative," it will not be possible to answer without making a good many distinctions. Particular moral rules may indeed make sense in the context of some kinds of social situation and not in others. But this does not imply an infinite diversity of morals, leaving us with only emotional preference or tradition to decide between them. Morality can be a matter of judgment. . . . Although judgment is guided by rules, it does not simply apply them automatically. Moral judgment remains problematic; *it is indeed possible that skill in making moral judgments can grow through facing the fact that they are problematic.* To face them responsibly is to approach them as *moral* problems, without special pleading or favour. It is also to face them as moral *problems* where the answer is not always given by just looking up the local book of rules. (108. Emphasis added)

REFERENCES

America Competes Act. 2007. https://www.congress.gov/110/plaws/publ69/PLAW-1 10publ69.pdf Sec. 7009.

Barthel, M. 2016. "How to Stop Cheating in College." https://www.theatlantic.com/ education/archive/2016/04/how-to-stop-cheating-in-college/479037/.

Blackstone, W. 1897. *Commentaries on the Law of England* (four volumes), ed., William Lewis, vol. 3. Philadelphia: Geo.T. Bisel Co. 1922.

Bok, D. 2003. *Universities in the Marketplace*. Princeton, NJ: Princeton University Press.

Derfer, G. 1974. "Science, Poetry and 'Human Specificity': An Interview with J. Bronowski." *The American Scholar* 43: 386–404.

Dewey, J. 1948 enlarged edition. *Reconstruction in Philosophy*. Boston: Beacon Press.

Emmet, D. 1966. *Rules, Roles and Relations*. Boston: Beacon Press.

Frankena, W. 1973. *Ethics*. Englewood Cliffs, NJ: Prentice Hall, Inc.

Fuller, L. 1969. *The Morality of Law* revised edition. New Haven: Yale University Press.

Held, V. 2006. *The Ethics of Care: Personal, Political, and Global*. Oxford: Oxford University Press.

———. 1984. "The Division of Moral Labor and the Role of the Lawyer," in Luban, D. ed. *The Good Lawyer Lawyers' Roles and Lawyers' Ethics*. Totowa, NJ: Rowman and Allanheld.

Holmes, O. W. Jr. 1920. Collected Legal Papers. New York: Harcourt Brace and Howe.

Holmes, O. W. Jr. 1881. The Common Law. https://www.gutenberg.org/files/2449/2449-h/2449-h.htm.

Hume, D. 1739. *A Treatise of Human Nature*. https://davidhume.org/texts/t/. https://davidhume.org/texts/t/2/3/3.

International Center for Academic Integrity, Statistics. https://academicintegrity.org/statistics/.

May, T. 2019. *A Decent Life, Morality for the Rest of Us*. Chicago: University of Chicago Press.

Merton, R.K. 1942. The Normative Structure of Science [1942]. https://www.panarchy.org/merton/science.html. Accessed February 22, 2020.

Morrill, R. 1980. *Teaching Values in College*. San Francisco, CA: Jossey-Bass Inc.

National Science Foundation. http://www.nsf.gov/bfa/dias/policy/rcr.jsp.

Plagiarism.org. "Plagiarism Facts and Stats." https://www.plagiarism.org/article/plagiarism-facts-and-stats.

Roston, M. 2015. "Retracted Scientific Studies: A Growing List," *The New York Times*, May 28, 2015. https://www.nytimes.com/interactive/2015/05/28/science/retractions-scientific-studies.html?_r=0. Accessed 22 February 2020.

Shafer-Landau, R. 2020. *A Concise Introduction to Ethics*. New York, NY: Oxford University Press.

Trow, M. 1976. "Higher Education and Moral Development," *AAUP Bulletin* 62: 20–27.

Van Noorden, R. 2011. "The Trouble with Retractions," *Nature* 478: 26–28. http://www.nature.com/news/2011/111005/pdf/478026a.pdf. Accessed 22 February 2020.

Wasserstrom, R. 1984. "Roles and Morality," in Luban, D. ed. *The Good Lawyer Lawyers' Roles and Lawyers' Ethics*. Totowa, NJ: Rowman and Allanheld.

Wueste, D. 2012. "RCR: Some Splendid Opportunities," *Teaching Ethics* 12(2).

——— 2012. "We Need to Talk about Institutional Integrity," Hale Ethics Series. Rochester, New York: RIT Press, 2012; ISBN: 978-1-933360-64-5. https://tigerprints.clemson.edu/cgi/viewcontent.cgi?article=1012&context=phil_pubs.

——— & Fishman, T. 2010. "The Customer Isn't Always Right: Limitations of Customer Service Approaches to Education, or Why Higher Education Is Not Burger King," *International Journal for Educational Integrity* 6(1) http://www.ojs.unisa.edu.au/index.php/IJEI/issue/current.

Section 2

PERSONS AS MORAL AGENTS: INSTRUCTIONAL MODELS

Dominic P. Scibilia

Michael Burroughs, Sandra Borden, and Dennis Cooley break open instructional models wherein students discover that they are and what it means to be moral actors.

Burroughs leads learning ethics with dialogue. Whether dialogue follows the practices of Dewey or Freire, teaching and learning ethics advances students' mindfulness of the roles that social and emotional experiences play in making decisions. Feelings, intentions, intuition, and imagination shape with a significance equal to reason students' ethical judgments and actions.

Borden turns attention to studies abroad wherein student and dialogue-centered learning challenge student ethnocentricity and ethical relativism. Structured student reflection and comparative analysis of social context stir a mindfulness of how oneself and other selves form ethical judgments. Dialogue with educational companions from diverse social and emotional contexts enhances one's mindfulness of persons as moral agents and the complexity of ethical judgments.

Cooley advances teaching ethics beyond the ideal of human beings as rational and self-interested actors through a model for learning ethics wherein emotions, intentions, intuition, and imagination interplay with reason—all occurring within people as they are rather than as they ought to be.

In the chapters that follow, teaching ethical judgment involving cognition and conation leads students into a mindfulness of their moral agency.

Chapter 2

Dialogue and Ethics in the Classroom

Michael D. Burroughs

This chapter focuses on the central role of *dialogue* in ethics education, as both a key pedagogical strategy and ethical imperative in our work with students. The chapter begins with historical and conceptual foundations for dialogue-based education and then turns to the uses of dialogue in the university classroom for the purposes of ethics education. This section will include reflections on lessons from early childhood pedagogy that, in turn, can serve as essential features of ethics education practice in postsecondary education.

INTRODUCTION

Ethics education has, historically, been a prominent part of the mission of American higher education. Education in nineteenth-century American colleges and universities was motivated, in significant part, by the belief that knowledge, morality, and civic action are *mutually reinforcing* and *thoroughly interconnected* in preparing students for life (Colby, Ehrlich, Beaumont, and Stephens 26).

The aims of higher education are now more diverse and include a greater focus on vocational education, faculty research, and scientific investigation. Nonetheless, ethics education still has an important role in postsecondary learning. One need only consider the vast array of ethical misconduct faced in institutions of higher learning—ranging from cheating and plagiarism to sexual harassment and discrimination—and, also, in professional life, to understand the continuing need for ethics education.

Nonetheless, ethics is not always a prominent feature of course offerings in institutions of higher learning. In many cases, ethics training is limited to specific departments and/or institutes within a university or is considered the domain of Human Resources. Given the far-reaching importance of ethics, there is a need, as James F. Keenan puts it, to "develop a culture of awareness among faculty, staff, administration, and students that for a university to flourish, it needs to recognize the integral, constitutive role of ethics in the formation of a flourishing community" (6-7).

Fortunately, there are numerous possibilities for creating and supporting this *flourishing community*. For example, and while diverse in their orientation, ethics institutes, philosophy departments, Ethics Across the Curriculum (EAC) programs, and other dynamic programming can make ethics education a prominent feature of undergraduate education and across university life, more generally.

But what are best practices for introducing ethics in higher education? While providing an exhaustive answer to this question is beyond the scope of a single chapter, we can consider productive approaches to ethics education for use across different contexts in our own institutions and as applied to diverse disciplinary settings. This chapter will present a case for leading with *dialogue*—understood as a method for engaging students in vital and motivated discussion of ethical issues—as a key element of ethics education in the classroom.

To that end, discussion in this chapter begins with selected historical and conceptual foundations for dialogical education, focusing, briefly, on philosophies of education as developed by John Dewey and Paulo Freire. Building on this foundation, the chapter turns to examples of dialogue-based lessons and activities for the purposes of ethics education. This section will include practical reflections on lessons from early childhood pedagogy that, in turn, can serve as essential features of ethics education practice in postsecondary education.

DIALOGUE-BASED EDUCATION: A BRIEF HISTORY

John Dewey and "Vital" Experience in Education

As educators, John Dewey's philosophy of education provides us with a motivational foundation to seek an "intimate and necessary relation between the processes of actual experience and education" (*Experience and Education* 20). Dewey's commitment to the relationship between students' lived experience and educational practice derives, in part, from his belief that students learn more effectively when they are *active*, as opposed to *passive*, in classrooms.

For Dewey, students are more active participants in learning when these experiences possess a *vital* quality, one that is felt within students' own interests, concerns, and inner motivations. As Dewey notes:

An ounce of experience is better than a ton of theory simply because it is only in experience that any theory has vital and verifiable significance. An experience, a very humble experience, is capable of generating and carrying any amount of theory (or intellectual content), but a theory apart from an experience cannot be definitely grasped even as theory. It tends to become a mere verbal formula, a set of catchwords. (*Democracy and Education* 80)

For Dewey, then, there is an *organic connection* between effective processes of learning and personal experience and, thus, the teacher's expertise alone—whether relating to ethics, science, history, or any other subject—is not, by itself, a sufficient basis for successful education (*Experience and Education* 25).

The connection between student learning and experience is made relevant for ethics education, explicitly, in Dewey's *Moral Principles in Education*. In this chapter, Dewey makes an important distinction between *moral ideas*—ideas that impact ethical motivation and take effect in student conduct—and *ideas about morality*, or, ideas presented, often abstractly, on moral topics (e.g., honesty, character, etc.) in classroom moral instruction (2). The key idea here is to distinguish forms of ethics education that are capable of motivating ethical behavior in students both within and beyond the classroom. As Dewey writes:

If a pupil learns things from books simply in connection with school lessons and for the sake of reciting what he has learned when called upon, then knowledge will have effect upon some conduct – namely upon that of reproducing statements at the demand of others. There is nothing surprising that such "knowledge" should not have much influence in the life out of school. (*Democracy and Education* 194)

In order to create a vital moral education, the educator must be aware not only of the curriculum at hand but also her students' attitudes, needs, interests, and capacities. The educator must focus on how to unite productively these conditions, internal to the student, with external considerations relating to the curriculum and educational outcomes.

Paulo Freire and Dialogical Education

Following Dewey, teaching ethics is not simply a matter of rote memorization of ethical theory or gaining the ability to restate correct answers to moral problems, but rather, aims at instilling a vital motivation to act ethically throughout one's life. As such, ethics education requires a unique and engaging pedagogical technique. In *Pedagogy of the Oppressed*, Paulo

Freire provides additional insight that can add to understanding of this approach.

Freire provides a distinction between two fundamentally different approaches to education. First, the *banking concept of education* involves approaching the student as a passive receptacle for information to be filled by the teacher (Freire 72). The students' primary task here is to memorize and replicate ideas passed on by the teacher. Education, Freire notes, "thus becomes an act of depositing, in which the students are the depositories and the teacher is the depositor" (72).

Second, Freire contrasts this mode of educating with what he calls *dialogical* or *problem-posing* education (79-81). This method of education involves creating a different relationship between teacher and student in the learning process. Most significantly, Freire argues that it is essential for the teacher to engage the student as a "critical co-investigator in dialogue with the teacher" (81). Freire writes:

> Through dialogue, the teacher-of-the-students and the students-of-the-teacher cease to exist and a new term emerges, teacher-student with students-teachers. The teacher is no longer merely the-one-who-teaches, but one who is himself taught in dialogue with the students, who in turn while being taught also teach. They become jointly responsible for a process in which all grow. (80)

This pedagogical relation views the student and teacher as partners in the learning process. The reformulation of teacher and student roles is key in that, first, it positions the student to be an active contributor to (as opposed to passive recipient of) the learning process. And, second, this change in roles re-forms what it means for a student to *know* or *learn*. In the banking concept, to learn was a passive process, a mere acceptance of a preformed idea or concept. But in the dialogical model, teacher and student learn, collectively, via *praxis* in which knowledge emerges "through invention and re-invention," through the mutual action and reflection of participants in the educational process (72, 79).

DIALOGUE AND ETHICS EDUCATION IN PRACTICE

Take stock of lessons learned from the previous brief turn into the philosophy of education. First, from Dewey, see the importance of practicing education in a way that is vital, aimed at engaging the interests, concerns, and primary experiences of students. Traditional knowledge and ethical concepts and arguments presented by the educator can set an important foundation for students but, ultimately, theory must be connected to students' engagement with their world and authentic experiences in order to be effective. Second, from Freire, to achieve this vital education, reconsider the roles of teacher and student in the learning process.

While the teacher maintains an important role in the classroom, the student, too, should be positioned as active in the learning process and treated as a *co-investigator* in defining and settling questions and outcomes.

One pedagogical approach for ethics education that supports the importance of student internal motivation and engagement is dialogue-based education. The work of contemporary education scholars affirms the pedagogical and social advantages of creating spaces in the classroom wherein students act as "participants in the production of their own knowledge" and as "active meaning makers" (Skidmore 506; Reznitskaya 448).

But how, specifically, are those insights related to the practice of ethics educators in the context of higher education?

Ethics engages with questions that are fundamental to the human condition, concerning good and evil, right and wrong, and how individuals ought to live their lives in community with others. Professional ethicists—from the utilitarian and care ethicist to the virtue ethicist and deontologist—put forward a diversity of answers to these questions. Regardless of which theoretical convictions one possesses, one implication from the discussion above is that an instructor should aim to develop in students dispositions to attend carefully to ethical issues, to reason in regard to their implications, and to carefully consider their own ethical conduct.

To learn ethics effectively requires students to engage in self-reflection, critical evaluation, and a willingness to take different perspectives into consideration. Teaching ethics successfully requires putting students in a position to develop the awareness and skills needed to make judgments about how to live well alongside others in the world. Dialogue-based education is, across numerous educational contexts, a key means for achieving these important aims.

DIALOGUE AND ETHICS: LESSONS FROM ELEMENTARY SCHOOL CLASSROOMS

Elementary school educators offer many instructional insights into authentic motivation for ethical life to educators involved in higher learning. At first glance, this claim might strike one as counter intuitive. After all, there are substantial developmental differences between young children and the adolescents and adults who enter university classrooms. Nonetheless, early childhood educators are on the front lines of ethics education and moral development and, in many cases, are highly skilled at utilizing the classroom as a vital and engaging space for students to learn important ethical lessons.

Ethics education in primary classrooms is not limited to the explicit lessons of the teacher but includes several indirect, yet, vital, *sociomoral* dimensions. The sociomoral environment is understood as the *entire network of interpersonal relationships in the classroom*, including child–teacher relationships, child–child relationships, adult–adult relationships, and classroom structure, rules, and norms (Hildebrandt and Zan 180). Early childhood educators are often expert at harnessing intrinsic social elements of classroom experience for the purposes of ethics education and development.

For example, alongside key relationships and first friendships, it is common for young children to experience conflict in early childhood classrooms. When these conflicts occur (e.g., over a mutually desired toy or an act of social exclusion from play), teachers often work to address the situation at hand through dialogue in the form of *scaffolding*, helping children to understand the action(s) they took, the consequences of the action(s), and its impact on others.

The key idea here is to use commonly occurring social and moral dynamics of the classroom to provide constructive and motivating lessons about key values—such as sharing, helping others, avoiding harm to oneself and others—and help to support and draw out skills for empathy and perspective-taking in young children.

In addition to scaffolding, early childhood educators use a variety of tools to stimulate children's thinking and dialogue about ethical issues. A prominent tool for this purpose is children's literature as there are a wealth of options with ethical themes (Wartenberg; Mohr Lone and Burroughs). These texts are productive in meeting students' interests and including them in dialogue about ethical issues ranging from empathy and perspective-taking to justice, fairness, and character development. In some cases, ethics lessons built around children's literature (e.g., see Wartenberg's "Teaching Children Philosophy" ethics book modules) can be used to create what is referred to as a Community of Inquiry (COI) with young children (Lipman).

In a COI, a teacher or facilitator, while sitting in a circle with students, will generally introduce a work of children's literature (or a different discussion prompt) and solicit questions and initial discussion from the group. As dialogue grows, students are encouraged to identify ethical and philosophical issues in the book and, also, to present their comments in the form of claims and responses to points raised by other students in the class. In early childhood classrooms, the COI could begin with student questions raised in relation to characters or problems within works of children's literature, or through discussion of artwork or an activity created by the class.

When working with older children, the COI could use other prompts, such as current events, films, or adapted philosophical texts. The fundamental aim in each case is to meet the interests and capacities of students to foster collaborative dialogue on a philosophical question, problem, or concept. Key to achieving this aim is the regard for students as active participants in the learning process, including, in many cases, choosing the themes and central questions for the COI from those initially raised by students and taking seriously their contributions for the learning process of both students and teacher.

ETHICS EDUCATION IN THE POSTSECONDARY CLASSROOM

Consider the context of a Professional Ethics course in higher education. Taught at many institutions of higher learning, these courses focus on helping students to cultivate ethical awareness as well as a variety of skills—critical thinking, ethical reasoning, and ethical imagination, among others—for understanding and addressing issues as relating to their future professional lives (Meyers; Mower). It is common for these courses to include students from vastly different disciplinary backgrounds, ranging from medicine, law, and computer science to education, social work, business, and criminal justice.

There are several practical elements of ethics training in a Professional Ethics course that can contribute to future professional life and, as such, these elements are important to introduce to students. For example, it is key for students to understand relevant codes of ethics so that they are aware of the ethical values and norms that are central to the history and contemporary practice of their chosen profession.

It is also helpful for students to learn about ethical exemplars (and, conversely, paradigmatic ethical failures) that can illustrate steps to follow (and to avoid) in professional life. By following the example of those who have come before them and who have excelled as ethical professionals they can, at least in some cases, learn important lessons without having to undergo the same trial-and-error(s).

But alongside these lessons—each of which can be introduced by the educator during a lecture or through pre-determined readings—it is important, perhaps fundamentally so, that students begin to take on an *identity* as an ethical professional. As Glen Miller writes:

> The ultimate task of ethics is to develop an integral view of one's self, which includes professional and personal dimensions, that is robust enough to develop over time, that is aware of professional expectations, including technical and ethical practices, that is inclined toward continued growth, and that results in thoughtful action. (92)

The ethical challenges our students will face as professionals will shift and evolve over time depending on their positions, relationships, and a wide range of contextual factors. One is in a better position to navigate these challenges (none of which can be captured in a single ethics course) if they understand their commitments as an ethical person and professional. Without the adoption of this ethical identity—a view of oneself as motivated to and capable of acting ethically—ethics education practices are in danger of being confined to the classroom, at risk of being forgotten at the end of class or semester and, thus, failing to translate into ethical action in the world.

Utilizing the classroom as a sociomoral environment is an excellent way to form this identity. Though certainly not exhaustive, one way to begin to do this is to provide structured opportunities for students to identify key ethical values that already animate and inform their decisions and, further, that are relevant for their development into excellent professionals in their chosen field(s). Ethics educators can begin this activity by asking each student to select and evaluate ethical values that are key to informing their lives and decisions as current or future professionals (see figure 2.1 for a list and instructions that can be used to facilitate this activity).

Next, students can be asked to form groups of three or four persons to share their value selections and explain why they chose each and, also, to explain how they have acted on these values, in concrete ways, in their lives. It is important, here, for students to not simply discuss ethical values in abstraction but, rather, to be clear on *why* they ranked values as they did and, also, how these values have animated their actions and decisions beyond the classroom, whether in major or relatively minor ways.

Following this initial discussion, students can be placed in groups of three or four with peers seeking to work in the same or similar professions. The instructor, then, asks these groups:

- From your "Most Important" lists, which three values are essential for performing excellent work in your future profession? Why?
- If you had to remove several values from your combined lists and identify only one as the *most* important for being an ethical professional in your field, which would you choose? Why?

The task is a sociomoral one that also focuses on identity formation. First, students must narrow down their lists and come to agreement through negotiation and dialogue. In this process, numerous lessons are possible on compromise, perspective-taking, and engaging in constructive dialogue especially in the midst of disagreement in cases in which there is no single *correct* answer (as is the case in so many of the ethical dilemmas professionals face).

Sort the following list of values in terms of their relative importance to professional life. Place each in one of the 3 columns. The order of the values *within* each column does not matter.

Values (15):	*Most Important (5):*
Courage	
Balance (in one's life)	
Curiosity	
Faith	
Honesty	
Integrity	*Important (5):*
Transparency	
Quality (Excellence)	
Compassion	
Loyalty	
Truth	
Wisdom	
Vision	*Least Important (5):*
Empathy	
Perseverance	

Figure 2.1   Selecting Values for Professional Life Adapted from The Good Project (Project Zero, Harvard University), https://www.thegoodproject.org/value-sort.

Second, students are, in a minor, yet, significant way, choosing and reaffirming ethical values as central to their identity and future lives as professionals.

Another activity that has the potential to place students in an active stance in ethics education involves the use of literature in the form of *case studies.* There is now a wealth of ethics case studies in text form and, also, freely available online for use in the classroom. Case studies can be particularly effective in that, for one, they can be chosen and tailored to focus on ethical issues and conflicts pertinent to student life or germane to a wide variety of professions, from conflicts of interest and paternalism to privacy and value trade-offs. (http://ethics.iit.edu/teaching/ethics-case-archive)

In addition, and referencing pedagogical lessons from above, case studies can be used in a way that provides a space for students to collaborate with each other and with their teacher in the learning process. Case study analysis can involve both teacher and students working to identify the ethical dimensions of a situation, evaluate alternatives for response, and define the best decision available in a hypothetical or real-world ethical dilemma.

There are many ways to organize the use of case studies and subsequent discussions. With some advance framing and guidance from the teacher students can be placed in position to conduct an ethical analysis of a case and, in turn, present this analysis to peers for further deliberation and dialogue. Case studies can be introduced at the start of a class session (e.g., by having the class read a case study together or in small groups) or assigned for reading prior to the relevant class session. An important element of success with using case studies is choosing a case that is engaging and relevant to the areas of focus for the class in question.

In addition, a best practice for successful use of case studies is to provide students with a framework for productively analyzing the ethical components of the case. That analysis, in turn, can be used to inform productive dialogue between students and with the instructor. Here is just one, non-exhaustive set of steps that can be used by students for purposes of ethical analysis in these discussions (see appendix for a sample case study analysis using these steps; also see Tuana and Wueste, referenced below, for additional resources for case study analysis):

- *What are the key facts?* Identify the facts that one will need to know in order to understand the central dimensions of the case: what has happened, who was involved, and what is at stake?
- *Who are the primary stakeholders?* An especially important subset of fact-finding: who or what is or will be impacted in the case and how severe (or minimal) will the impacts be?
- *What are the key ethical values?* What ethical values are informing the case at hand? Is there a conflict of values that students can identify and evaluate (say, between compassion and the demands of justice, between benefiting the greater good and respecting the rights of an individual, and so on)?
- *What are potential responses in the case at hand?* Given the problem at hand and the values identified as relevant to the case, what are potential responses one might take in order to arrive at the most ethical resolution possible?
- *What is the best, or most ethical, response in the case at hand?* After identifying a range of possible responses to the case, students can evaluate the merits of each and, ultimately, defend a particular response as most ethical given the problem at hand.

Case studies, coupled with a multitude of engaging resources (from film and podcasts to short stories and narratives), can make connections between ethics education and students' native interests. In addition, these approaches can be used to develop authentic dialogue on ethical values and challenges, increasing student motivation to consider ethical issues and their own role in responding to them.

CONCLUSION

This chapter has focused on the central role of *dialogue* in ethics education, as both a key pedagogical strategy and ethical imperative in our work with students. To demonstrate the significance of this pedagogical technique for ethics education, we considered its historical and conceptual roots in the work of two influential philosophers of education, John Dewey and Paulo Freire. In addition, we focused on forms of dialogue and student-centered teaching, more generally, that are effective in numerous ethics educational contexts, from primary to higher education settings. The use of dialogue through classroom activities can place students in an active role in ethics education and increase student engagement.

REFERENCES

Center for the Study of Ethics in the Professions. "Ethics Bowl Case Archive." Accessed December 26, 2019: http://ethics.iit.edu/teaching/ethics-case-archive.

Colby, Anne, et al. *Educating Citizens: Preparing America's Undergraduates for Lives of Moral and Civic Responsibility.* Josey-Bass, 2003.

Connolly, Peggy, et al. *Ethics in Action: A Case-Based Approach.* Wiley-Blackwell, 2009.

Dewey, John. *Democracy and Education.* Simon & Brown, 1916/2011.

Dewey, John. *Moral Principles in Education.* Southern Illinois University Press, 1900/1975.

Dewey, John. *Experience and Education.* Simon & Schuster, 1938/1997.

Freire, Paulo. *Pedagogy of the Oppressed.* Continuum, 1993.

Hildebrandt, Carolyn, and Betty Zan. 2014. "Constructivist Approaches to Moral Education in Early Childhood," *Handbook of Moral and Character Education* (2nd ed.), edited by Larry Nucci, Darcia Narvaez, and Tobias Krettenauer. Routledge, 2014, 180–197.

Keenan, James F. *University Ethics: How Colleges Can Build and Benefit from a Culture of Ethics.* Rowman & Littlefield, 2015.

Lipman, Matthew. *Thinking in Education.* Cambridge University Press, 2003.

Markkula Center for Applied Ethics. "Ethics Cases." Accessed December 26, 2019. https://www.scu.edu/ethics/ethics-resources/ethics-cases/.

Meyers, Christopher. "Ethics Theory and Ethics Practice." *Ethics Across the Curriculum: Pedagogical Perspectives,* edited by Elaine E. Englehardt and Michael S. Pritchard. Springer, 2018, 131–145.

Miller, Glen. "Aiming Professional Ethics Courses toward Identity Development." *Ethics Across the Curriculum: Pedagogical Perspectives*, edited by Elaine E. Englehardt and Michael S. Pritchard. Springer, 2018, 89–105.

Mohr Lone, Jana, and Michael D. Burroughs. *Philosophy in Education: Questioning and Dialogue in Schools.* Rowman & Littlefield, 2016.

Mower, Deborah S. "Increasing the Moral Sensitivity of Professionals." *Ethics Across the Curriculum: Pedagogical Perspectives*, edited by Elaine E. Englehardt and Michael S. Pritchard, Springer, 2018, 73–88.

Reznitskaya, Alina. "Dialogic Teaching: Rethinking Language Use During Literature Discussion." *The Reading Teacher*, vol. 65, no. 7, 2012, pp. 446–456.

The Good Project. "Value-Sort Activity." Accessed December 26, 2019: http://the goodproject.org/toolkits-curricula/the-goodwork-toolkit/value-sort-activity/.

Tuana, Nancy. "Conceptualizing Moral Literacy." *Journal of Educational Administration,* vol. 45, no. 4, 2007, pp. 364–378.

Wartenberg, Thomas. *Big Ideas for Little Kids: Teaching Philosophy Through Children's Literature*. Rowman & Littlefield, 2009.

Wartenberg, Thomas. "Teaching Children Philosophy." Accessed December 26, 2019: https://www.teachingchildrenphilosophy.org/Category/Ethics.

Wueste, Daniel E. "A Philosophical Yet User-friendly Framework for Ethical Decision Making in Critical Care Nursing." *Dimensions of Critical Care Nursing,* vol. 24, no. 2, pp. 70–79. DOI: 10.1097/00003465-200503000-00006.

APPENDIX: SAMPLE CASE STUDY ASSIGNMENT AND ANALYSIS

I. Assignment Steps

Part 1: Select a specific case study that raises important issues in professional ethics. The case should be one from the profession you are planning to enter (or one you are thinking about entering). The case can be based on a current or past ethical dilemma in your profession, hypothetical, or based on an already existing case study (see case study resources links below).

Part 2: Analyze the case study, answering each of the questions listed here:

- What are the key facts?
- Who are the primary stakeholders?
- What are the key ethical values?
- What are potential responses in the case at hand?

Part 3: Provide your own argument about what the ethical thing to do would be in this case. In other words: What is the best, or most ethical, response in the case at hand?

II. Selected Case Study Resources

- Ethics Bowl case archives (a wealth of cases for use on multiple fields and topics): http://ethics.iit.edu/teaching/ethics-case-archive
- Markkula Center for Ethics cases (a wealth of cases for use on multiple fields and topics): https://www.scu.edu/ethics/ethics-resources/ethics-cases/

III. Sample Case Study Analysis

Case: "Wells Fargo Banking Scandal" (Full text: https://www.scu.edu/ethics/focus-areas/business-ethics/resources/wells-fargo-banking-scandal/)

- What are the key facts?
  - "Cross-selling" became a major practice at Wells Fargo leading, ultimately, to the creation of over 2 million unauthorized customer accounts.
  - Immense pressure was placed on employees to meet sales quotas.
  - Many employees quit due to this pressure and unethical sales practices.
  - The Board of Directors commissioned an investigation that found cultural, structural, and leadership issues at the heart of the unethical conduct.
- Who are the primary stakeholders?
  - Wells Fargo customers (and banking customers, more broadly construed)
  - Wells Fargo employees (sales force)
  - Wells Fargo management
  - Wells Fargo Board of Directors
  - Wells Fargo CEO
  - Wells Fargo investors
- What are the key ethical values?
  - The ethical values most relevant here are those that were clearly violated, including:
    - *honesty* and *transparency* (avoiding deception of one's customers)
    - *leadership* (the need for a stronger example of dedication to ethics and integrity at management and supervision levels)
    - *compassion* (the need to be attentive to the needs, health, and ethical identities of one's employees)
  - In addition, there is a value tension here between *loyalty* and *integrity*. It is likely that some employees felt tensions between their own sense that creating fraudulent accounts is unethical (and should be reported) versus the desire to be a "good" employee and remain loyal to the company

- What are potential responses in the case at hand?
  - A primary response needs to attend to the formation of an *ethical culture*, a commitment to foregrounding ethical values and work systems alongside financial goals.
  - A primary response includes both holding key actors *morally responsible* while also learning from the Wells Fargo case to inform better work cultures and practices going forward, including changing incentive structures and encouraging ethical leadership in the organization.

Planning Notes:

- Students can work through this case analysis individually, in small groups, or, to illustrate this method of analysis, this can be done as a whole class with the teacher as guide.
- The teacher can also assign different elements of the analysis to specific groups (as in, Group 1 will outline the *key facts*, Group 2 will outline the *primary stakeholders*, etc.).
- An advantage of doing this analysis is that each student will have a connection to the case in question and should (based on what they wrote in their analysis) have an insight to contribute in class dialogue about the ethical dimensions and resolution of the case.
- Following this analysis, students can be prompted to discuss the final part of the activity (Part 3) regarding developing an argument as to the best, most ethical, response or resolution to the case in question.

Chapter 3

Study Abroad Strategies for Bringing Home the Complexity of Moral Judgments

Sandra L. Borden

This chapter demonstrates the distinctive opportunities presented by studying ethics abroad for challenging both ethnocentrism and relativism. Instructors can expect to learn about particular pedagogical strategies to interrogate these stances, including the use of experiential learning, structured reflection, and comparative analysis.

INTRODUCTION

When confronted with cultural difference, college students may approach ethics ethnocentrically, assuming that their own culture's conventional morality should be universalized, or relativistically, in which case they see moral standards as nothing more than local biases. Disrupting students' unquestioned assumptions can be challenging in the ethics classroom, as is eliciting empathy for people who are not like themselves. Yet these are necessary to think rigorously about complex ethical situations and to give commensurate consideration to all the stakeholders in a decision.

For many, college is the first time they encounter perspectives different from those with which they grew up. Students may resolve the resulting cognitive dissonance by doubling down on their preexisting assumptions or, instead, by settling for a *live and let live* stance. They are especially reluctant to pass judgment on an unfamiliar culture. To be clear, respect for difference is an important goal of college education. But there is a difference between appreciating the fact of moral disagreement among different cultures (cultural relativism) and reducing moral judgments to subjective preferences (ethical relativism).

Ethical relativism goes beyond recognizing that cultures differ in regard to what they think is ethical to claim that what they *think* is ethical also *should* be. In other words, the relativist claims that cultures have different ideas about what is ethical, not because of conceptual differences or disagreements about relevant facts (in other words, rational explanations). Rather, cultures have different ideas about what is ethical because it is truly the case that what is ethical for one culture is not ethical for another, even if their situations are similar and we could erase any relevant conceptual and factual disagreements.

Ethical relativism seems like a tolerant stance, and it is, to the extent that it deflates ethnocentrism—the belief that the values of one's own culture are superior to those of all other cultures. However, equating ethics with prevailing opinion or standard practice actually devalues other cultures by making their values appear totally arbitrary and irrational.

Ethics classes expose students to experiences and ideas that challenge ethnocentrism and ethical relativism. Because of its intensity (Kiely, 2005), study abroad is particularly good at helping students cross "developmental thresholds" (Stuart, 2012, 63). Indeed the well-known *W* pattern of cultural adjustment most study abroad students learn about before departure charts the ups and downs of adjusting to a new culture and integrating this knowledge into one's life back home. Study abroad literally rewires students' brains (Fischer, 2013).

The rest of this chapter discusses particular pedagogical strategies to interrogate ethnocentrism and ethical relativism when teaching ethics abroad. Examples are taken from three cycles of a comparative media ethics course set in London. The course offers upper-division students a chance to study, in depth, one foreign media system with important similarities to and differences from the U.S. system, with a focus on their implications for media ethics.

Even though the chapter will use examples from a media ethics class, the highlighted strategies may be applied across the curriculum and, at least to some extent, in traditional classroom settings. The learning objectives for the class included the following:

1. Demonstrate awareness and understanding of differences and commonalities between media ethics in the United States and United Kingdom.
2. Demonstrate ability to critically reflect on national identity and to articulate the role of the media in constructing that identity.
3. Demonstrate ability to integrate experiences and reflections abroad using writing and speaking as tools for acquiring (not just displaying) knowledge.

CHECKING YOUR ASSUMPTIONS AT THE GATE

All of us wear *cultural glasses* that color how we see the world. Study abroad provides a distinct occasion for noticing those glasses. The resulting awareness softens students' cultural assumptions and helps them to be open to considering other perspectives. For those who are used to being part of a majority culture at home, studying abroad takes them out of their (privileged) comfort zone. Here's a quote from one of the Caucasian students who completed the London course in 2015:

> Being in the position where you looked like the outsider really opened my eyes. Whether it was from my loud American voice on the subway, the amount of time it took me to give cashiers change, or openly taking embarrassing tourist *SnapChats* near St. Paul's Cathedral and The Tower Bridge, I always felt like I was standing out. This feeling allowed me to step into the shoes of others.

For minority students, conversely, spending time in London has been liberating. Here is another quote, from an African-American woman:

> I remember walking down the street and seeing so many black women and men, people that looked like me, as the faces of brands and products. It was a tad heart breaking to realize how stereotypical *black* felt in the United States and how normal I was feeling in London. . . . I felt less labeled as a black person, but more fitting in as just a person. The feeling was indescribable as the weight I did not know I had been carrying around with me was being lifted.

As an international, English-speaking media capital, London is the perfect *textbook* for U.S. students to explore media in another historical, political, and cultural milieu. Nevertheless, British media are similar enough to what students already know that they can use their media literacy skills right away and engage difference critically, rather than treating it as mere exotica.

The course specifically focuses on traditional media, including the press, film, television and advertising. However, the course also pays attention to what is called *ambient* media, including landscapes, monuments, museum exhibits, and royal pageantry. Doing so aimed to develop an appreciation of both contemporary and historical perspectives on what we think of as *media ethics*. The catch: The students are only abroad for two weeks.

Given that there is not time to develop abstract philosophical understandings of media ethics, the course introduces students to a parsimonious model for grounding media responsibilities and then relies on experiential learning to make the model come to life.

CONCEPTUAL FRAMEWORK FOR
STRUCTURING MORAL DISAGREEMENT

The course focuses on responsibilities originating in the media's social functions, the promises made by media occupations, and the personal commitments of individual media professionals (Elliott, 1986). This structure established a logical basis for moral difference: Media everywhere have common sources of responsibilities, while the specific content of those responsibilities may vary depending on local context.

For example, the media's social functions are not the same in every media system and, therefore, what they are expected to do to carry out those functions will not be the same either. To illustrate, both the U.S. and the U.K. political systems are *majoritarian* ones: *Catch-all* parties compete in *winner-takes-all* elections. In majoritarian systems, the media typically exhibit *internal pluralism*; that is, each title attempts to produce *balanced* content rather than have a recognizable political orientation. This is true in the United States, where objectivity remains the norm for mainstream newspapers. As media theorists Hallin and Mancini (2004, 51) noted, "Where catch-all parties predominate, it makes sense that catch-all media should also develop."

But not in the United Kingdom. Despite having a majoritarian system, the British news media share with the Continent's *consensus* democracies the characteristic of *external pluralism*; that is, particular media are identified with particular social groups and advocate for their political interests. Consequently, *bias* violates a responsibility of U.S. newspapers but not of U.K. newspapers. In case students wondered how seriously journalists from the two countries consider this difference, a London-based CBS correspondent was blunt in his disdain for *The Guardian's* liberal bent. As one student from 2015 recalled:

> It was mentioned that we had visited *The Guardian* and when he heard this a puzzled look came across his face. He stated, "*The Guardian* is an interesting place to learn about ethics," and then proceeded to comment on their lack of ethics.

EXPERIENTIAL TESTING OF THE FRAMEWORK

The visit to the CBS London Bureau illustrates the hands-on approach while students are abroad. They heard and saw different perspectives on what is (and is not) ethical in the media and how (or if) media should be held to ethical standards. The academic program takes advantage of hot topics in the United Kingdom at the moment and gives students access to experts who have been personally involved in some of those topics. This strategy takes maximum advantage of studying off campus and helps make the material relevant and engaging.

The ethics code of the body that regulates most of the print titles in the United Kingdom – the Independent Press Standards Organisation (IPSO)— provides a ready point of comparison with ethical standards professed by U.S. journalists. Students get to visit the regulator and hear about its code and complaint procedures; both are much stricter and more binding than anything ever tried in the United States.

Students are highly sympathetic with the regulator's approach—until they visit with some of its critics: a woman whose private communications were hacked by journalists, the ethics chair of the National Union of Journalists, who notes that the code was written by and for editors who often bully journalists into doing unethical things. Or the author who was trying to start up an alternative regulator because he thought the Independent Press Standards Organisation was too beholden to the industry—as did most Brits (he eventually succeeded). Suddenly a system that seemed strict by U.S. standards comes off as seriously defective.

As one student from 2014 put it, referencing the Independent Press Standards Organisation's predecessor, the Press Complaints Commission (PCC):

> When the class visited the PCC, it seemed clear that the commission strictly followed the Editor's Code of Practice that set up sixteen guidelines ranging from accuracy to payment of criminals that journalists were expected to follow while interviewing and publishing news stories. However, after hearing what our speakers had to say as well as seeing what some newspapers got away with publishing, it became quite clear that the PCC only jumps in when cases meet specific infractions.

Learning the historical and legal background of U.K. press regulation, and being exposed to different perspectives about the merits of recent developments, help students to critically evaluate that system on its own cultural terms.

Students also are able to critically evaluate that system in comparison to the United States. They are able to appreciate the significant overlap between the ethics code of the Society of Professional Journalists in the United States and the U.K.'s Editors Code of Practice. They also note the U.K. code's distinctive inclusions (e.g., the permissibility of partisanship in newspapers, the emphasis on journalist harassment post-Diana) and exclusions (nothing on fairness, source anonymity or conflict of interest).

Finally, exposure to thoughtful media practitioners who intentionally incorporate ethics into their personal and organizational conceptions of excellent work provides helpful exemplars for students poised to enter the job market.

Here is a (2015) student's reflection on the class visit with a CBS foreign correspondent and a producer based in London:

> When we began talking to the crisis reporters, I had an epiphany. They get to travel the world, report on real things that are happening in the world, and impact people's lives while doing it. Most people say they don't watch the news because they don't want to hear bad news. But bad news is what is happening every day in our world. I want to talk about actual problems the world is having and not what color the Kardashians dyed their hair this week.

Here is a student from 2014 writing on the class visit to Isobar, a digital marketing agency:

> Mark, whose focus is branding, gave us a lecture on global marketing. At one point, we examined the effectiveness of a Coca-Cola commercial attempting to break down tensions between Pakistan and India. Our class was moved deeply by the idea that world peace was as easy as sharing a soda. Mark's question as to what right Coca-Cola had to claim they could ignite world peace was shocking. He felt that the commercial exploited its consumer and used human emotion for profit. By bringing to the table a hidden agenda, he gave credibility to Isobar's ability to market by caring about the consumer.

STRUCTURED REFLECTION TO
PROCESS EXPERIENCES

These quotes are the outcome of a process of reflection. Without reflection to help students process their feelings and thoughts, experiential learning is ineffective. However, the structure of reflection matters.

Research into intercultural learning shows that students will be uncritical of their home culture's conventional morality if the curriculum focuses solely on commonalities between the home and host cultures (in other words, tending toward ethnocentrism). If, conversely, their studies dwell only on differences, students will tend to be uncritical of the host culture's conventional morality (in other words, tending toward relativism) (Medina-Lopez-Portillo & Salonen, 2012).

By reflecting on both commonalities and differences, students can generate competent intercultural comparisons that can help them appreciate underlying continuities in ethical standards across media systems, as well as local understandings that are inextricably (and rationally) linked to each system's particular intellectual and cultural history.

Micro-assignments help students to process and learn from their experiences abroad as they are feeling and observing them. Because the assignments are frequent, students have a chance to capture the intensity of their immediate experiences as well as to see how their understanding develops over time. For example, students can revisit earlier assignments and integrate their insights into later ones. Or they can consolidate their insights for formal development in a summative reflection paper or essay exam. The London course has used a couple of variations, though there are numerous possibilities.

ADD A LITTLE SALT

One assignment was an adaptation of Schaetti, Ramsey, and Watanabe's (2008, 131–145) *Critical Moment Dialogue* questions that the instructor called *SALT*; this assignment helped students process their cultural and media *aha* moments abroad as a group during class. The *SALT* acronym was based on the idea that salt both adds flavor and preserves.

Intentional writing helps us remember the *flavor* of fleeting experiences, while thoughtful reflection preserves the insights these experiences yield. The acronym helped students structure their writing:

- **S** (Something's up): Describe the circumstances that gave rise to the *something's up*.
- **A** (Attention): Share the judgment/emotion/sensation you attend to during your reflection.
- **L** (Learning): Discuss what you learned after doing some research.
- **T** (Take-away): Share the take-away from this experience for your intercultural competence.

The requirement to research encourages students to approach difference with the attitude that it is intelligible with some effort. For example, during one particular year, students were required to use this format to keep a photo journal. One student noticed how few trash cans there are on London streets; when she found one, she snapped a picture. But she did not stop there. She looked into this phenomenon and discovered the reason.

The Irish Republican Army, a paramilitary movement in favor of a reunited Irish republic, planted bombs in London trash bins during the 1990s. So British authorities have removed many metal trash cans to cut down on the risk of unseen bombs that could result in exploding shrapnel This led to a class discussion of the U.K. experience with terrorism during the Northern Ireland conflict that ended in 1998 with the Good Friday Agreement and how that experience feeds into contemporary worries about terrorism since the Al-Qaeda-inspired suicide bombings on London's public transportation system in 2005.

With that reflection, the students learned a little history and, more important, became aware of both how the British experience of terrorism converges with that of the U.S. after the 9/11 attacks, but also how it diverges and why. That is a lot of mileage out of a casual photo and a short writing assignment.

An Analytical Take on Journaling

Adapting to a new culture can be overwhelming. Reflective writing can slow things down so students can assimilate their experiences. It also encourages students to find some alone time to *catch up with themselves*, something that can be challenging in a fast-paced study abroad program in which students spend so much time with each other. Another take on structured reflection that has been successful in the London program is an adaptation of Wagner and Magistrale's (2000, 41–58) analytical notebook tool.

This tool encourages students to "to write analytically about culture" (Wagner & Magistrale, 2000, 43), which means going beyond personal impressions to develop working theories, based on students' evolving understanding of British media and British culture, and to explain the similarities and differences they encountered while in the United Kingdom.

As well as attentiveness to the little details that throw people off in a different culture, this kind of writing also asks students to process the theoretical knowledge gained from lectures, presentations, and tours. One of their tasks is *to connect the dots* among these various sources of knowledge so that their experiences might become more meaningful in the long term. In other words, students are gaining intercultural competence through writing, not just displaying verbally that competence.

Several entries focus on national identity as a social construction in which the media play an important role with ethically significant implications (see appendix A for sample prompts). National identity is ripe for exploration while abroad because U.S. American citizens may not think critically about this identity until and unless they are in the minority and have to articulate this identity to others who do not share it.

Students who took the class in 2017 were able to successfully reflect on this theme using as examples everything from a multicultural production of *Twelfth Night* at the Globe Theatre and the omission of British soldiers of color from the movie *Dunkirk*, to the worshipful marketing of Shakespeare's Birthplace and the funhouse sensibility of heritage tourism at Warwick Castle. They did this through a series of notebook assignments.

For the take-home final exam, students were encouraged to review and synthesize their notebook entries and relate them explicitly to their experiences abroad and to the formal course curriculum (readings, speakers, excursions, etc.).

For example, a graduate student writing on representations of *British* identity and their ethical implications, returned to notebook entries she had written after a day trip to Oxford and the *Twelfth Night* performance (which featured a drag queen, disco music, and other nontraditional elements). Comparing the awe she felt when touring Oxford University, with its impressive roster of important writers and other intellectuals, she wrote about the Pitt Rivers Museum of Anthropology:

> I became aware that the artifacts were not shown out of respect for cultures around our diverse world, but rather goods that were *collected* by adventurous British explorers, exclusively white males, were graciously donated from private collections after the men had passed away. This was a crushing blow to my expectations for this museum and an upsetting realization of what is often proudly presented as mainstream British identity based in *achievements* of the past.

In contrast, the Shakespeare play, with its diverse cast and characters, was a revelation: "This representation of multicultural and dynamic British identity, still deeply entrenched in classical British roots, rang true and felt right to me, to put it simply," she wrote.

Unfortunately, the student noted that representations of Britishness following the Pitt Rivers model were more common than those following the *Twelfth Night* model. Besides their inaccuracy, monolithic representations of *Britishness* are ethically problematic, she wrote, because they "create an 'us vs. them' climate" that "retards progress and cultural and social innovation that can only come from an open, global flow of ideas."

An analytical notebook is more formal and polished than a personal journal (though less formal and polished than an academic paper). Students had eighteen required prompts, plus they were asked to write additional entries based on their evolving interests abroad (twenty-five minimum entries total). Students completed some entries in class, but they completed most outside of class.

Students were introduced to the assignment and practiced doing entries in class before departure. The instructor checked notebooks once before departure and once during students' time abroad. The instructor collected the notebooks for grading after returning to the United States. Grading focused on organization, quantity and quality of the entries (see appendix B).

Although having to do nearly daily entries made the days busier, all of the students demonstrated personal, professional and intercultural growth in their writing as the program progressed and were able to articulate the gains they had experienced as a result of the program by the end of the notebook. The last couple of entries abroad focused on processing their learning based on research into experiential learning:

There isn't enough room in your pack to take everything home with you physi-
cally. This may also be true mentally and emotionally. What would you like to
take with you? What would you like to leave behind? Explain. Write about an
expectation you had before your trip that turned out better than expected, and
also write about an expectation that did not turn out as well as expected. What
did you learn from these "expectation violations"?

Students did their last entry in class after departure; it was a reflection on a
letter each student had written to herself before the trip following this prompt:

Write a letter to yourself about what you hope to gain from this experience.
What expectations do you have for your personal growth during your time
overseas? What expectations do you have for your growth as a media producer
or consumer? Why/how do you think these expectations might be significant
for your future?

Here is the prompt they responded to in class:

Read the letter you wrote to yourself before you left the United States. Reflect
on how your goals were met or challenged. What have you learned? How will
you put what you learned into practice now that you're back home? Discuss
both your personal and media goals.

Many students have trouble engaging in self-introspection and reflection.
They benefit from this kind of scaffolding (e.g., specific prompts, sample
responses), as well as the opportunity to share their perspectives and hear
those of others. Additional sample prompts are included in appendix A, as
well as the instructions for the analytical notebook assignment (appendix B).

In addition to focused writing assignments, the instructor conducts regular
debriefings after tours and media organization visits to help students reflect
on their experiences in London. The students also participate in several
read-arounds of notebook entries to process shared experiences or to share
unique insights about topics of their choosing. Read-arounds refer simply to
students reading out loud from their notebooks. These are always announced
in advance of meetings so that students are prepared to share.

Sometimes everyone reads aloud the same entry to compare perspectives;
sometimes students are invited to read aloud an entry of their choice that is
particularly meaningful to them. The instructor asks for volunteers to start,
and the read-around continues until everyone has taken a turn. The instructor
may ask questions or invite student reactions to help students process what
they have read or heard. Speaking, in other words, is a way to learn, not just
present information for assessment purposes. As organizational theorist Karl

Weick (1995, 18) summarized the process of sensemaking: "How can I know what I think until I see what I say?"

COMPARATIVE ANALYSIS TO
CONSOLIDATE LEARNING

The last assignment in the United Kingdom is to work in pairs comparing the adjudication of an ethically problematic media case by the Washington News Council with the way in which it might have been decided by the U.K. newspaper industry's regulator. This assignment consists of a written report following the regulator's format and an in-class presentation (see appendix C). This assignment is the single most effective one for students to appreciate intercultural similarities and differences between U.S. and U.K. media. One of my students from 2015 wrote:

> Before the case ruling assignment, I understood in general that IPSO was designed to regulate newspapers, but after presenting a case to the class and having to explain how IPSO would have probably handled the situation, I have a much more detailed comprehension on how much control and influence the organization has in England. For example, IPSO can force a newspaper to write a correction and admit to being at fault, and it can also fine the company in more extreme cases.

The case comparison assignment challenges students to assess different views about the effectiveness and fairness of the United Kingdom's current press regulation and to critically apply these perspectives to their analysis of their assigned Washington News Council cases. In particular, their analyses highlighted the inability of the U.K. Editors' Code to deal with ethical problems not specified in the Code. They also developed sensitivity to different conceptions of freedom of expression and of public service. The same student wrote:

> Americans view the concept of being able to say whatever they like as a requirement, which is the polar opposite of England, who do not want its citizens to be controversial or provide inaccurate information when publishing articles in newspapers, and thus have regulations. The First Amendment strikes me as one of the leading factors as to why America is different than England, and without this media ethics class, I would have never realized how vital the First Amendment is to American culture.

As an added bonus, students developed a concrete sense of the trade-offs involved in making ethical evaluations using a code (as the U.K. regulator does), as opposed to a decision-making process that took as its starting point the grievances of injured stakeholders (as the Washington News Council operated). A code provides more structure, clarity and guidance—but less latitude and flexibility. This mode is typical of professional ethics, where professionals define their particular responsibilities in some detail to distinguish them from the general responsibilities that we all have.

Sometimes these rules are legally enforceable, as in the case of lawyers and other licensed professionals. Operating from predefined ethical categories and consequences for breaches can result in a narrower, legalistic decision—but also one that is more specific and predictive and, thus, more influential on future behavior. Thus, codes provide guidance for professionals and constraints on unethical conduct that protect clients and other stakeholders, including the wider society in which they practice.

When making decisions about ethics generally, in contrast, most of us operate more casuistically, proceeding from specific details (such as complaints) and working our way to more general ethical guidelines or principles. This *thicker* approach to ethics is harder to codify, however, and thus less easy to pass down or enforce.

PRACTICAL LIMITATIONS TO CONSIDER

Besides the time crunch involved in teaching a course lasting two to four weeks altogether, another practical limitation is that students are more tired and distracted than usual when they are abroad. These factors mean it is impractical to assign a heavy reading load or to bring students' conceptual and analytical capacities along as incrementally as you would in a typical semester.

The theoretical framework of necessity must be fairly basic. That being said, theoretical application is much more immediate and concrete. Instead of trying out theoretical assumptions on a hypothetical case study in class, students see these assumptions play out in real time in actual regulations and professional practices *in situ.*

The intensity that jump starts learning abroad can also be overwhelming at times, so students need support to cope with homesickness, culture shock, interpersonal conflict, and so on. This aspect of teaching abroad can end up consuming a good chunk of instructional time (already at a premium).

The temptation to cram too much into the available time is even greater abroad because this is a *ONCE-IN-A-LIFETIME OPPORTUNITY!* But it is worth slowing down to allow experiences to sink in and to encourage reflection. As happens on campus, experienced study abroad instructors often find that *less is more* when it comes to learning—and they gradually excise content to allow more time for application and processing.

Pacing is also important for teaching. Study abroad instructors typically have more contact hours with students in two weeks than they would have in an on-campus class all semester. This means that grading in a timely and effective way requires balancing. For example, performing notebook checks—while pedagogically essential—is rather hard to pull off in practice. The instructor herself is busy making final preparations for travel and, later on, is busy on the road coordinating logistical and social-emotional dynamics like schedules, preparing lectures, and counseling students.

One way to streamline notebook checks would be to accept and return assignments electronically rather than in a physical notebook, but Wi-Fi may be spotty or slow. Students are always surprised to find, for example, that the United Kingdom's broadband speed is considerably lower than that of the United States. Different digital regimes can affect instruction as well. For example, in 2017, some websites students needed to access for the comparative analysis assignment were unavailable due to emerging practices under the European Union's fairly recent implementation of the *right to be forgotten*. In some countries, access to electricity itself may be a problem.

In short, there are a number of practical obstacles that complicate teaching and learning about ethics abroad. Instructors should prepare for them as much as they can before travel, but, inevitably, surprises pop up that will require adjustment.

CONCLUSION: IMPLICATIONS FOR
TEACHING ETHICS ON CAMPUS CLASSES

Plopping students into a whole new culture for weeks or months disrupts their settled notions quickly and powerfully. That is why teaching ethics abroad can be an especially effective way to challenge both ethnocentrism and relativism. However, instructors must take care to provide some kind of conceptual framework to undergird experiential learning. For best results, they also need to provide carefully designed assignments to structure student reflection and to help students compare both similarities and differences between their home and host cultures.

College students who study abroad report that it is the most significant experience of their college years—more so than college friendships or their (other) coursework. And, if they are well done, short-term courses are just as transformative as long-term ones (Fischer, 2009). However, fewer than 10 percent of undergraduates take advantage of this opportunity, and there is some research that suggests that there are learning strategies that can yield similar benefits without a passport.

Such strategies include cross-cultural learning opportunities or *study away programs* within students' local communities or in domestic locations that present intercultural experiences, such as the U.S.-Mexico border (Fischer, 2015). Certainly, these options are worth exploring for teaching ethics in a wide variety of applied areas.

However, there are simpler ways of alienating students from the familiar to help them process moral complexity with more rigor in your classroom. And you can do it *this* semester. Strategies include role-playing and rich narratives from history or sci-fi that make them question their everyday assumptions.

One lesson from the experience of teaching abroad is that students get a lot from experiencing ethics through concrete interactions with people and organizations. Inviting guest speakers to class can be a powerful way to make what can seem to be theoretical discussions come alive. If these speakers come from another time zone or at least another culture, that enriches the discussion that much more (Skype!).

Maybe you cannot whisk your students off to London for two weeks, but you can schedule a field trip to an organization with reflective practitioners that can inspire your students to shape their career goals around ethical concerns. And, of course, one can intentionally introduce comparative elements in on-campus courses, such as the case ruling project in which students compared decisions by the Washington News Council in the United States and the Independent Press Standards Organisation in the United Kingdom. As long as adequate structures for comparison and reflection are part of the mix, some of the study-abroad strategies described here can be used to good effect at home.

REFERENCES

Boeyink, David E, and Sandra L. Borden. 2010. *Making Hard Choices in Journalism Ethics: Cases and Practice.* New York: Routledge.

Elliott, Deni. 1986. "Foundations for News Media Responsibility." In *Responsible Journalism,* edited by Deni Elliott, 32–44. Beverly Hills: Sage.

Fischer, Karin. 2015. "Why a Global Education Doesn't Have to Mean Going Abroad." *The Chronicle of Higher Education,* August 12, 2015. https://www-chronicle-com.libproxy.library.wmich.edu/article/Why-a-Global-Education/232311.

Fischer, Karin, 2013. "This is Your Brain on Study Abroad: The Experience Changes Lives and Neurons, a Scholar Says." *The Chronicle of Higher Education,* May 31, 2013. https://www-chronicle-com.libproxy.library.wmich.edu/article/This-Is-Your-Brain-on-Study/139543https://www-chronicle-com.libproxy.library.wmich.edu/article/This-Is-Your-Brain-on-Study/139543.

Fischer, Karin, 2009. "Short Study-Abroad Trips Can Have Lasting Effect, Research Suggests." *The Chronicle of Higher Education,* February 20, 2009. https://www-chronicle-com.libproxy.library.wmich.edu/article/Short-Study-Abroad-Trips-Can/1541.

Hallin, Daniel C., and Paolo Mancini, 2004. *Comparing Media Systems: Three Models of Media and Politics.* Cambridge, UK: Cambridge University Press.

Kiely, Richard, 2005. "A Transformative Learning Model for Service-Learning: A Longitudinal Case Study." *Michigan Journal of Community Service Learning*, 12, no. 1 (Fall): 5–22. Permanent link: http://quod.lib.umich.edu/m/mjcsl/3239521. 0012.101/1.

Medina-Lopez-Portillo, Adriana, and Riikka Salonen, 2012. "Developing a Global Learning and Living Community." In *Student Learning Abroad: What Our Students Are Learning, What They're Not and What We Can Do About It*, edited by Michael Vande Berg, R. Michael Paige and Kris Hemming Lou, 360–82. Sterling, VA: Stylus.

Schaetti, Barbara F., Sheila J. Ramsey and Gordon C. Watanabe. 2008. *Personal Leadership: Making a World of Difference: A Methodology of Two Principles and Practices*. Seattle, WA: FlyingKite Publications.

Stuart, Douglas K. "Taking Stage Development Theory Seriously: Implications for Study Abroad." In *Student Learning Abroad: What Our Students Are Learning, What They're Not and What We Can Do About It*, edited by Michael Vande Berg, R. Michael Paige and Kris Hemming Lou, 61–89. Sterling, VA: Stylus.

Wagner, Kenneth, and Tony Magistrale. 2000. *Writing Across Culture: An Introduction to Study Abroad and the Writing Process*. New York: Peter Lang.

Weick, Karl E. 1995. *Sensemaking in Organizations*. Foundations for Organizational Science Series. Thousand Oaks, CA: Sage.

APPENDIX A

Sample Analytic Notebook Prompts

Notebook assignment (in class): How do you think of your identity as a U.S. American? To what degree is your U.S. American identity shaped or reinforced by U.S. brands and media culture? How do you think Brits will see you as a U.S. American? To what degree do you think their perception of the U.S. is shaped by U.S. brands and media culture?

Notebook assignment (on your own): Put your media culture glasses on as you are touring London's sights. Take in the urban landscape, including the architecture and monuments. Think about these as mediums for communicating British identity. What are you invited to think about the British based on what's included in these mediums? What's left out?

Notebook assignment (on your own): Describe a British media artifact you have collected while abroad (e.g., magazine cover, brochure, picture, packaging, screen shot, swag) that you think represents national identity (British or U.S. American). What does this artifact communicate about national identity, and what are possible ethical implications? Bring your artifact to class.

Notebook assignment: How were your expectations of "Britishness" met today? How were they challenged? How does the overlapping of cultures over the centuries influence your conception of British identity? Is this complexity represented in the media?

Notebook assignment (on your own): How does the marketing of English heritage at Warwick Castle compare to the marketing of English heritage at Shakespeare's Birthplace and Shakespeare's Globe? How does this compare to the marketing of U.S. American heritage at sites such as Colonial Williamsburg or Greenfield Village in Dearborn? Is there any ethical tension between keeping things authentic and making things tourist-friendly? If so, why? If not, why not?

Notebook assignment (in class): How has your understanding of the United States' role in the world been affected by your international experience? How about your understanding of yourself as a U.S. American? What role do you think the media have in forming people's ideas about national identity? (You might want to look back at your (date) entry in class.)

APPENDIX B

Analytical Notebook Assignment

Writing (like speaking) can help you process your intercultural experiences in a way that connects your personal perspective to larger historical, political, cultural, and legal forces in a new place. For this program I am interested in how you understand media ethics generally, the role of the media in constructing national identity particularly, and your own self-discovery as a U.S. citizen, a student, and a future professional.

As Wagner and Magistrale (2000) noted, the goal of an analytical notebook is "to write analytically about culture" (43). That means you must go beyond personal impressions to develop working theories, based on your evolving understanding of British media and British culture to explain the similarities and differences you encounter while in the U.K. This involves attentiveness to the little details that throw you off on a daily basis. However, it also means processing the theoretical knowledge gained from lectures, presentations and tours. One of your tasks is to *connect the dots* among these various sources of knowledge so that your experiences become more meaningful in the long term.

Although you should take notes during lectures and presentations to use for the final exam, keep those separate from your analytical notebook.

Adapting to a new culture can be overwhelming. Keeping an analytical notebook can slow things down so that you can assimilate your experiences.

The writing in your notebook should be conversational—though it should be easily understood by me and your classmates. It can be speculative—as long as you keep striving to understand what confuses or surprises you. It can begin with your personal experience—you may doodle, attach photos, and make the notebook your own however you like—but it shouldn't end there. Think of your analytical notebook as something more formal and polished than a personal journal, but less formal and polished than an academic paper.

Your writing should be selective and focused–instead of trying to record everything, zero in on specific topics that you can explore in some depth. It should be exploratory—test your worldview and your working theories against your experiences and the perspectives of others. Revisit your entries to see how your perspective has changed over time (and write another entry!).

Most important, your writing should be reflective.

To accomplish these goals:

Give each entry a short title.
Date each entry.
Start with brainstorming. This can be a list or series of impressions.

Compose your entry by developing your initial thoughts and impressions in more depth. Add details about your observations, sensations and feelings. Formulate some working generalizations to explain your experience. Give reasons for your stand or your hunch.

Re-read your entry. Engage in self-exploration and critical reflection about what you've written. Add one or more sentences, exploring the truth revealed by your entry. What does your entry suggest about you, about the media, about nationality, about culture?

Each entry should be at minimum 1 page long.

To begin, set up your notebook: Number the pages in your notebook. Create a table of contents on the inside cover of your notebook (including page numbers). This will provide structure and focus to your analytical writing. Include the name of the program (Media Ethics in London, 2017) and your name and contact information should you misplace your notebook.

Table of Contents
Analytical Notebook, Media Ethics in London, 2017
Your name and contact information

There should be a chapter for *Notebook Assignments*. This is where you will write entries as assigned in the syllabus. Set aside at least one-third of the notebook for this chapter.

Create at least two additional chapters to suit your interests before travel. Some suggestions: *Reactions, Cultural Contrasts, Reversals & Realizations, Architecture, People and Stories.* See pp. 48–55 in Wagner & Magistrale (2000) for ideas. You can always add chapter headings in London.

Divide up the other 2/3 of the notebook according to the number of other chapters you will have.

There is a pocket in the notebook where you can put artifacts, such as pictures, clippings, wrappers, tickets, etc. Two of the required notebook assignments require you to collect media artifacts to share with the rest of the class.

The total number of entries (including the required notebook assignments) must equal no fewer than twenty-five; you can have more entries if you wish.

I must be able to read all the entries in the "Notebook Assignments" chapter. If there is an entry in other chapters you would rather I didn't read, cover it with paper, and I will respect the privacy of that entry.

Grading criteria: Here are the criteria I will use to grade the notebook as a whole (not each entry). Each criterion will be assessed with a "+" (above average), "√" (average) or "-" (below average):

(1) *Organization*
   - Notebook has prescribed table of contents
   - Notebook has prescribed chapter of Notebook Assignments
   - Notebook has at least two other chapters
   - Entries are dated
   - Entries have titles
(2) *Quantity of entries*
   - All required notebook assignments are included in the Notebook Assignments chapter
   - There are at least 25 entries total
   - Each entry is at least 1 page long
(3) *Quality of entries*
   - Entries focus on a specific topic
   - Entries are attentive to details
   - Entries are attentive to broader cultural context of observations and experiences
   - Required entries directly address prompts in the syllabus
   - Entries demonstrate reflection (can be reflected in topic choices as well as final lines of an entry)

Assignment adapted from Wagner and Magistrale (2000) and Taylor (1991).

APPENDIX C

Working in teams, you will come to a decision about a complaint originally made to the United States' Washington News Council using the Code and procedures of the United Kingdom's Independent Press Standards Organisation (IPSO).

1. *Written ruling*
   Each team will prepare and hand in a written ruling about their complaint using the format on the IPSO website (see examples of the format IPSO uses for its rulings). In addition, the ruling will include a section titled *Comparative Analysis* (see below). The description and analysis in the ruling should be thorough, logical and accurate (see grading criteria below). Cite any sources besides the Washington News Council and IPSO websites using the 6th edition of the *APA Style Guide to Electronic References*

2. *Press conference*
   Each team will report their findings during a mini press conference in class on July 18 concluding with questions from the "press pool." Each team will have 15 (minimum) to 20 minutes (maximum) for their press conference. This time includes at least 5 minutes for questions from "reporters." All group members should participate. This presentation should address the elements in the ruling, including any remedial action required. Include visuals (such as clips of the stories in question) that support the oral content (not the other way around). The rest of the class will act as reporters, asking questions about the ruling.

The cases:
Here are the complaints students have to choose from:

1. *Dr. Richard Wollert v. The Seattle Times*
2. *Leschi School Community v. KIRO7 Eyewitness News*
3. *Vitae Foundation v. KUOW 94.9*
4. *Midway Meats et al. v. KIRO7*

To prepare:
Research the facts of your assigned Washington News Council case. The Washington News Council's website is archived at https://web.archive.org/web/20170617202532/http://wanewscouncil.org/

Using the IPSO Editors' Code of Practice, identify relevant clauses and parts (if relevant)

Determine whether the complaint in your case should be upheld based on your understanding of the Code and its decisions in similar cases. Guidance

for understanding each clause in the Code can be found in The Editors'
Codebook.

For guidance on observing the spirit (as well as the letter) of the Code,
see pp. 8–10 of The Editors' Codebook. For guidance on the public interest
exception to certain Code clauses, see pp. 96–98 of the Codebook. For a sense
of the range of remedial actions that you can recommend in your report and
precedents set by previous IPSO rulings, check IPSO's previous rulings on
its searchable web page. You should strive to rule consistently with IPSO's
past practice. Here are details about IPSO's rules and regulations; possible
sanctions are explained on page 12. You might also want to see the guidance
on financial sanctions (How is IPSO Run?>Financial Sanctions Guidance).

Format for Your Report

Summary of complaint
    Decision of the Complaints Committee
    Complainant Name(s) v. Name of Media Organization

1. Summary of Complaint made to Washington News Council (1 paragraph):
    [Complainant Name] complained to the Washington News Council that
    [Media Organization] acted unethically in an (article or package) titled
    "[title of article or package or series]," published (or aired) on [date].
2. Describe article/package in question, elaborate on substance of com-
    plaint, summarize media organization's response in 5-9 numbered
    paragraphs.

Relevant Code Provisions

3. Copy from the IPSO Code the text of any and all relevant clauses (includ-
    ing Public Interest)

Findings of the Committee

4. Address each clause in relation to the details of the case, the arguments
    of the parties, the Editors' Codebook, and IPSO's rules and regulations
    in 4-10 numbered paragraphs. As part of your rationale, be sure to:
    *Explain why/why not a public interest exception to the relevant
    clause(s) is/is not justified if there is an asterisk by the clause/s.*
    *Make reference to a previous IPSO ruling dealing with one or more
    of the same clauses to show how your findings are consistent with IPSO
    practice.*

Conclusions

5. State clearly whether the complaint was upheld in one brief declarative sentence.

Remedial Action Required

6. State options available under IPSO regulations and specific actions the media organization is required to take in 2-4 numbered paragraphs if you decide to uphold the complaint. Explain your choice thoroughly. If the newspaper or station must publish/air a correction or adjudication, specify placement, headline and wording, whether it should be online as well as in print or on the air, how long it should be online and whether it should be archived. If the complaint is not upheld, enter "N/A" in this section. See past IPSO rulings for examples.

Comparative Analysis

7. Compare with resolution reached by Washington News Council; be specific. Comment on difference it would have/would not have made if Washington News Council had been working from the IPSO Code to make its determination and why (2-5 numbered paragraphs). Conversely, were there aspects of your case that were not captured by the IPSO Code?
8. The Washington News Council held public hearings on complaints, even allowing the public to "vote" online during the live streaming of its last hearing. IPSO deliberates about complaints behind closed doors. Comment on the difference public input would have made in in your decision and why. What is gained by deliberating in private? What is lost? (1-3 numbered paragraphs).

Grading criteria: You will be penalized for excessive APA style mistakes and excessive mechanical mistakes. As always be sure to give proper credit to all sources. This assignment will be given a joint grade. However, if any individual does not make a substantial (speaking) contribution to the presentation, he or she may receive a lower grade than his/her partner. Here are the criteria I will use to grade this assignment. Each criterion will be assessed with a "+" (above average), "√" (average) or "-" (below average):

(1) *Thoroughness*
   • Includes all required sections
   • Describes facts in enough detail to understand complaint, media response, adjudication and comparative analysis

- Supplies examples that are relevant, including specific reference to at least one previous IPSO ruling
- Resolution addresses all ethical issues mentioned in complaint

(2) *Accuracy and proficiency of application*
- Bases ruling on IPSO's Code and practice, including the Editors' Codebook, the public interest exception (if relevant), and IPSO rules and regulations
- Presents facts that are accurate and verified through cited sources
- Presents facts that are relevant
- Resolution recognizes perspectives of all parties
- Analysis goes beyond obvious observations

(3) *Reasoning*
- Interprets IPSO Code consistently with IPSO guidance and practice
- Recommends resolution that is practical and effective in achieving desired result
- Follows format used by IPSO rulings
- Supports claims through sound logic
- Uses visual elements that generate interest and support main points in ruling

Chapter 4

Teaching Ethics through Literature

Dennis Cooley

Effective instruction requires pragmatism instead of unrealistic idealism. Human morality/ethics does not work the way that computer programs function: the former requires a balance of emotions, feelings, and reason, whereas the other is pure reason. We are also able to use imagination to think of the way things ought to be rather than being trapped with how things are. Reason plays an essential role but emotion/feeling and imagination are essential partners; both are necessary to create the unitary moral thinking that makes us the moral agents we are. To teach ethics well requires that reason, emotion, and imagination are engaged.

INTRODUCTION

Effective ethics instruction is pragmatic. It first determines what morality is perceived to be, and then probes boundaries to discover what changes are possible and assigns probabilities to what it found. It then develops an ethics based on how ethics are possible for us, favors the more probable over the less likely, and finally works efficiently for a morally desirable, reasonable set of values and principles. Effective instruction determines, probes, discovers, assigns, and develops. Unfortunately, some standard ethics courses focus too narrowly, thereby missing essential elements of what students need to know to be better decision makers.

Most ethics classes begin with the basics of rational, moral decision-making for actions: values are the construction material and principles are the tools to put the material together in various, approved ways. Once memorized through practice on theoretical problems, such as case studies or professional objections, students then learn some decision procedure with carefully delineated steps to build a solution, much as a computer programmer designs a program to complete a task.

Expert instructors impart their information, and then condition students to use it by repetitious practice, much as mastery of symbolic logic is acquired. The goal here asks only that students are able to identify the rules and material, and then manipulate them successfully to show at least a nodding acquaintance with an ethical system. While learning these tools is an essential part of learning about ethics—and is the first section taught in this class incorporating ethics—something more is necessary.

Human morality/ethics does not work the way that logic in computer programs functions; mostly because human beings are not designed, mechanical systems. People *qua* reasonable, social animals are the products of evolution, socialization, and self-directed development; hence, they are more like patchwork, Frankenstein monsters in our thought processing than they are finely tuned machines. Reason has a necessary role, but emotion/feeling is its essential partner. Moreover, morality inherently incorporates imagination and creativity.

When human beings think about what they *should* do or be, then they are thinking about worlds that may or may not exist. If they exist, then individuals ask if they ought to continue to do so. If they do not and individuals have the power to make a change, then they acquire an obligation. Slavery existed—and repugnantly still does. It took creativity to imagine a world without slavery or one in which women are equal as persons to men, and then dream how to achieve such result. Being a moral agent requires human beings to be good critical *and* creative thinkers.

Incorporating literature in ethics classes has at least four major benefits. First, narratives help people build empathy, in addition to providing opportunities to use morality's values, principles, and decision procedures. Reading about others creates an image within the reader's mind about who the other is. That subjective construct, by necessity, is imbued with the feelings, desires, and characteristics of the reader's mental personality. By developing the capacity to create images of others within one's mind, she can empathize with real people in real situations.

Second, by stitching together the story's information, narratives help students develop complex ideas and arguments, as well as the skills to do so, both individually and in groups. First, through the reading of the literature itself, which requires memory, comprehension, anticipation, and imagination to bring the story to life. Second, students in groups talking about the material have to come to a collaborative consensus on what the work means, which values and principles are at play, what should be done, and why this is the case.

Third, literature is more effective in engaging students in the learning process than textbooks and case studies, which tend to appeal to reason alone—and often in a depressingly dry way. The latter might work for professional ethicists, but students and other laypeople, on the other hand, are unaccustomed to that communication style. They need something that engages their interest and maintains it. Literature can do this by prompting a desire to learn what happens to the fictional characters about whom they have come to care.

Most importantly, through literature, students are thinking about ethics in the way that human beings are suited and inclined to, that is, as emotional *and* rational creatures, rather than beings for whom reason is privileged beyond justification. They emotionally connect with and feel for the characters because the author and the students create a fictional reality that is based on real-world truths, and because they can see themselves in and identify with their mental constructs.

So instead of requiring those learning about ethics to use only a reasoning process that is distant from their experiences and emotional core, teaching ethics through literature incorporates what already exists, and then builds upon it in a way that flows from the existing edifice. In conjunction with a section on ethical theory, principles, and values which exposes students to the rational part of ethics, they have a fuller understanding of what ethics is and how it works in their decision-making and lives.

IMAGINATION, THE MORAL PARADIGM TEST, AND LITERATURE

Creating fictional characters based on reality and imagined reality is essential to ethics. It is also useful for teaching ethics, which should help students become better makers of moral decisions. *The Moral Paradigm Test*, for example, asks each student to identify an individual with whom she has a positive person-to-person relationship, and then improve that mental construct or picture of the other's character by changing its narrative until it becomes a moral paradigm of virtue and right action.

The idea here is to begin with a base mental image of a real admirable person with whom the student has a personal relationship, and then develop that image into a construct that will help the student distance herself a bit from embedded rationalizations most people automatically use, while considering the matter through the familiar eyes of someone she cares for and respects.

Developing the *Moral Paradigm* takes approximately 30–50 minutes of class time, but once it is done, the test can be used in class discussions and classwork for the rest of the semester. It is basically a form of the *Ideal Observer Standard*, but one that engages students in why morality is important and has the force it does, rather than being an exercise in theoretical, abstract reasoning. Using the steps below, each student is asked to write down on paper or their computers the following information:

1. Starting the conversation:
   a. In an online class: ask students to do the following on their own (i.e., without discussing it with others): Identify something they did at work or elsewhere that got them into trouble, but that they thought they were justified in doing. Basically, the goal is to think about a real incident in their lives rather than something theoretical. Their life-examples are more engaging for them, and they already know most of the details, so it is much easier and useful than a case-study.
   b. In a face-to-face class: an ethical question can be posed, such as is it morally permissible to make personal copies on company copiers when that has not been approved of by the managers or other relevant authorities? This approach has the benefit of everyone in the class being able to discuss the same topic and develop their arguments from their own thoughts and what they hear from others.

2. Have the students build an ethical justification for their position. Returning to the original life-example in which they did something that got them into trouble but they thought they were justified in doing, students are asked to defend why they acted as they did using the moral principles and values taught previously. For example, most people think little of making personal copies on company copiers, regardless of whether they have permission to do so. Students should be able to explain why it is morally permissible to use the company's resources in this manner, or not, if that is the decision they made previously. They can use some form of Consequentialism, Relativism, or Deontological theories. If in a face-to-face class, then the various arguments formulated are discussed in the class period.

3. After the justification is given, each student is asked to identity a person the student personally knows, believes to be a paradigm of morality, and wants to emulate in her life. This should take only a few minutes. The main issue is to help students understand who these people should be.

   The most effective way of getting a good result is to ask students who they admire and would like to emulate in their lives; this person should be someone with whom the student already has a personal relationship. Since the student feels this way toward the person, then the person must be someone whose character is worthy of being admired and emulated. It is helpful to the class for the instructor to ask a few volunteers to share who and why they picked the person they did, so that everyone can know what is required for this stage.

It is necessary to explain why the individual has to be a person the student has a personal relationship with. Mother Theresa and Martin Luther King are laudable individuals who deserve their status in society, but a student's emotional connection to them is not the result of a personal relationship. To get the *Moral Paradigm* to be a motivator for the student to think hard about ethical issues and then do what is good and right, there must be some sort of positive emotional bond between them. The student wants to please and not disappoint this individual because the latter is valued by the student, thereby providing a very strong emotional motivator to being ethical.

4. After carefully evaluating the actual person chosen by the student, the latter finds and eliminates any moral flaws the proto-paradigm has, where a moral flaw is one that will harm the chosen individual's ability to do the right thing or be who he or she should be.

    Providing several common examples is helpful so that students know what to identify and how to work this step.

    Being a workaholic is one flaw often used. Hard work, of course, is a virtue, but if working unreasonably interferes with other important commitments and relationships that need attention, then it can become excessive and a vice. If a person does not attend significant family events, such as birthdays, and fails to give support to children and others with whom they have significant personal relationships, then the work the person is doing might be causing an imbalance in the proto-paradigm's moral reasoning.

5. After the moral flaws are identified, then each is replaced with its corresponding virtue.

    A workaholic, for example, is turned into a hard worker with time for her family and other personal commitments. The result of the improvement exercise in step four is a virtuous ideal-real person, with whom the student has an emotional connection that provides appropriate motivation to do what is right and to be what one should be, i.e., a *Moral Paradigm*.

6. Where a great deal of imagination comes into play is when the student, in her own mind, asks *the Moral Paradigm* whether she has it right about her answer to the question in the real-life example (Steps 1 and 2). The student *tells* her *Moral Paradigm* what her decision is and all the relevant information she used in reaching that conclusion.

7. Still using her imagination and reason, the student decides what *the Moral Paradigm* would conclude. If the Moral Paradigm *tells* her that the conclusion is correct, then the student has selected a morally defensible solution. If the Moral Paradigm *tells* her that she has erred in her moral reasoning, and therefore thinks less of her, the student knows that she does not have a morally defensible solution. She returns to the

decision procedure to re-evaluate or discover relevant moral factors until she can convince her *Moral Paradigm* that her position is morally justified.

In one class, a student who had been making copies for her personal use explained that she no longer thought it permissible. When asked why, she stated that her *Moral Paradigm* was a version of her grandfather who would have said it was stealing. The student said that she had never seen what she was doing in that light until she *heard* what her grandfather would say about her activities. Other students have had the same experience when they realized what they were doing was wrong.

Even if students determined that they were justified in their actions and judgments according to their *Moral Paradigm*, they realized that there is value in looking at ethical issues from different perspectives because their decisions might actually be unjustified for a number of reasons. As their actual person disagreed with them from time to time, *the Moral Paradigm* based on that person will have the same feature.

Of course, *the Moral Paradigm* exists only in the student's imagination, so it is not a separate entity. But *the Moral Paradigm* is a creative and critical reasoning fiction that can separate students from their biases and rationalizations to have a more objective evaluation of the situation without losing the emotional and motivational connection to ethics. They want to satisfy *the Moral Paradigm*'s moral code; *the Moral Paradigm*'s moral code tends to be a more ideal version of the student's own. Creating and using the moral paradigm mental construct incorporates how ethics works, which is as a combination of emotions, feelings, and reason.

Designing, Implementing, and Assessing Literature's Impact in the Classroom/Training Session

If *the Moral Paradigm Test* sufficiently resolved all moral dilemmas and answered all ethical questions, then there would be no reason to add literature to the mix. The problem, though, is that the test cannot incorporate relevant diversity. That is, if the student has not been exposed to enough variety in opinion, situation, interaction, and so on, then he or she has no referent by which to create *a Moral Paradigm* that can fill in the gaps.

Just as someone cannot imagine what the color red is if they have been blind from birth, a person's imagination cannot create workable fictions out of nothing at all. To be able to think of what is not but could be, there has to be some information about what is from which to build. Understanding/ exposure to diversity is a source of information for the construction of a more useful *Moral Paradigm*.

Literature provides a pathway for a moral agent's moral imagination to incorporate external narratives that provide diversity in ideas, viewpoints, and so on, while maintaining the emotional connection that is required to do ethics well. Literature selections should marry the class' content and outcomes to the narrative. The organizing idea here is that there are multiple ways to get at a truth, and that that truth might have a number of components with varying complexity, degree, and existential reality.

Some pathways are through formal systems of reasoning, whereas others are through stories that generate certain emotional reactions. Each path introduces elements that the others cannot, but all are part of what makes us human. The most effective, holistic learning experience, hence, is through multiple approaches, that is through formal cognition and narratives that provide arguments appealing to human reason, emotions, or both. Evaluating good literature for what it is telling us about the human experience does this.

The literature selections themselves must be interesting enough to motivate reading, thinking, and conversation; this applies to both instructor and students. The language, story, and characteristics have to be accessible to those reading it, otherwise it merely turns out to be a frustrating experience that might set students against further forays in literature of any type.

This does not mean that the selections should be cartoonishly simplistic, such as *The Little Engine that Could*. Challenging work is necessary to develop higher level reasoning, creative skills, and the appropriate emotions. The easiest way for an instructor to make the selections is to remember what worked for him in his undergraduate classes. Another is to ask colleagues or fellow instructors in comparable institutions what has worked for them. No one should invent the wheel for these, especially since there is a wealth of resources based on experience.

Perhaps the best idea is to use literature that addresses problematic experiences, from which people learn in their everyday lives, and does this in a way that engages students' interest because they can relate to the story or characters. Such literature involves difficult subjects that make the student think about what the relevant issue and available evidence are, employ moral principles and values to sketch out a decision, test that decision with the understanding it might need alteration to better achieve the desired outcome—or be replaced altogether—and then assess the student work's success in terms of perceived desires, needs, and standards.

Sufficiently clear positions and arguments in the work are a must, but they have to be identifiable and written in a way that will generate a student's desire to think about them in a more abstract way, asking about the thesis, characters, and so on. In addition, these qualities are important because students have to develop a connection with the story line and the characters so that it becomes more authentic to them.

What cannot be emphasized enough is the instructor's interest in the work. Students can tell when an instructor is uninterested by her verbal and nonverbal cues, including tone. The literature is supposed to open a space for both reason and emotion to be engaged; if it is not working for the instructor, then it is unlikely to work for students. Even worse, if students were engaged—which means that they constructed the fictional characters, in part, from themselves, then they will feel betrayed by the instructor's lack of interest.

Even worse is that they feel disrespected by the instructor. What mattered to the student did not matter to the instructor, thereby implying that there was something wrong with the student's taste or values. To be bored by the story suggests that the instructor is bored by the students' personal narratives. In fact, even if the students are initially uninterested, instructor excitement can prompt students to engage more with the work because they become curious about what they are missing, or want to make the instructor happy with their interest

HOW TO TEACH SHORTER PIECES

The literature's subject matter must be appropriate, of course, but the story's length also needs to be considered. For training sessions and for people unaccustomed to reading, for formal analysis or merely for pleasure, short stories are best. James Thurber's *The Catbird Seat* is an excellent piece for several reasons, including helping students realize that they have unconscious biases that can affect their perception of reality and critical thinking.

Since the work is so short—approximately five pages—there is less need to provide reading questions to guide students through the work. Instead, students have the opportunity to develop their own interpretation and focus on what they desire. This approach lets them have power over their education, but perhaps more importantly, it puts some nascent groundwork in place for them to develop a process to analyze other pieces of literature.

After breaking the class into the groups of three to four (the size of the group is important because larger groups encourage free riders, whereas with groups smaller than three the answers will be too personally identifiable) the groundwork is set by having the groups come up with answers to the following basic questions: Who is Mr. Martin? Who is Mrs. Ulgine Barrows? What is the relationship between Mr. Martin and Mrs. Barrows? Why does Mr. Martin dislike Ms. Barrows? What is the story about? What happens in the end?

What's good about this approach is that the group as a whole is talking about the work (while peer pressure encourages students who think that they do not have to read the material before class to do so). In addition, the groups and class as a whole will begin with a shared consensus on these simple empirical facts, and the ice has been broken on speaking in front of the group.

There is an additional benefit: if a student has not read the material, then they will not feel too embarrassed in the group work. While they are not going to be especially valuable as contributors in the discussions, they will not be as stressed, and might even come up with an insight they are willing to share as the group converses.

It becomes more interesting in terms of analysis and engagement when more probing questions are posed for each group to answer:

a. Who is the good person? Why?
b. Who is the bad person? Why?
c. What does the good person try to do to the bad person? Is doing that morally right or wrong? Why?
d. Was justice served? Were all people affected by the action respected? Utility maximized?
e. What values are at play?
f. Is there some moral factor or issue we missed?

Not all of these questions should be used in a 50-minute class for several reasons including that it takes too much time out of the class, prevents the class as a whole from being able to have a conversation, and many students stop paying attention because of the lack of structure. However, it is a good idea to formulate all of the interesting questions beforehand, and then see where the class interest leads by asking the one or two questions the instructor thinks most important.

After the individual groups have done this work, it is time to have the class as a whole discuss the answers. For each question, a group spokesperson tells the rest of the class what the group determined. Each group is asked to provide their answers as the instructor goes around the room. The class as a whole begins to discuss what the consensus is for the answer.

One benefit here is that no individual student is responsible for the answer, especially if it turns out to be unjustified. Another is the exercise of understanding what others are saying, and then trying to work that into one's own to produce a coherent, plausible response. Finally, students feel comfortable challenging other's interpretations as they try to figure out what the author wanted them to think about with this particular set of characters doing these actions in this particular story.

To finish thinking about the story from multiple perspectives, then, it is essential to provide a challenge to the class' interpretation. The students are given an alternative reading that questions the standard interpretation of Mr. Martin being the hero. Suppose that Mr. Martin is the bad person and Mrs. Barrows is the victim, students in the class as a whole are asked: Is this a plausible interpretation? Why or why not?

Students are asked to think about the following questions: let us think about F & S, the company for which both Mrs. Barrows and Mr. Martin work:

1. If you were hired to run this company in today's economy/market, which problems identified in the story would you need to address? Which assets did you identify in the story?
2. Mr. Martin was going to murder Mrs. Barrows. Is this something that a good person would do or even think about doing?
3. What exactly is it that makes Mrs. Barrows deserving of being murdered or having her career ruined by Mr. Martin? Do victims have to be sympathetic to be victims?

Generally, the students begin to realize that the standard interpretation has serious flaws to it. When they begin to think more deeply what this would mean in the real world, it turns out that while they do not like Mr. Martin, Mrs. Barrows remains unsympathetic.

For the step that opposes the original consensus, the instructor has to be careful not to embarrass students by making this interpretation appear to be obvious. Students want to do well in class, and unnecessary challenges to their self-esteem make them think the instructor is out to get them, playing mind games to satisfy his ego, or showing that analyzing work is far more competitive than intellectually interesting.

The remainder of the class is talking to each other about what the *right* interpretation is. They figure out that competing interpretations can be acceptable because they are plausible and probable, while at the same time others are implausible.

More importantly, there is a discussion on how unconscious bias works. Do we have unconscious ideas of the proper place for women and men in business? That certain characteristics are assumed good for men but detrimental to women's characters if they have the bad luck to possess them, such as being aggressive or progressive? Students begin to question why they disliked Mrs. Barrows and rooted for Mr. Martin, when Mr. Martin was an employee who tried to prevent the company from becoming better organized, and far more importantly would have committed murder if a better plan had not come along.

HOW TO TEACH LONGER PIECES

If more class time is available, longer pieces, such as novels, work well. But even if there is time for longer works, it is strongly recommended to begin with a few short stories to develop students' memory, imagination, and analytic skills before taking on a much larger project that will test the mettle of people who are likely to be accustomed to reading texts and other short pieces. Small successes build patterns that enable larger successes by building confidence and the processes needed to effectively analyze literature.

Alice Walker's novel *The Color Purple* is an excellent resource for a variety of classes. In *Contemporary Moral Issues*, it gives insight into racism, sexism, social exclusion, and developed and developing world elitism through a lens of care ethics. *Introduction to Philosophy* classes benefit from the care ethics component, individual and group identity narratives, and a version of God that is much different from the one discussed in philosophy texts.

This God desires reciprocal care relationships with each person, rather than being an infinite being almost unintelligible to finite minds. Regardless of class, students care about Celie, Shug, and the others. Students see the characters' transformations based on their relationships and interactions, which makes them far more interested in learning about the story's philosophical aspects.

To make long literature work in a classroom or workshop, an instructor needs to facilitate readers' success. First, the expectation is that they will read the work twice: the first time to understand and the second to evaluate. Two readings are essential, especially since students are tested for content reading comprehension before any class discussion of the work.

Students are told to read the book first at least two weeks before, and again a few days before the class discusses it. The time between the two readings lets the material settle and the student think about it a bit before reading the work for the second time. The idea here is that big ideas developed over long works need to be slowly thought through, which requires a little bit at a time approach to building the information into the narratives students' use to have a comprehensive, evaluative view of the material.

Second, given that reading long fiction has become rarer than it used to be, and students want to know why they are doing what they are doing, while receiving some support with how to do it, reading questions should be prepared to focus students' attention on what to look for in the passages. Questions about more easily found ideas come first, with more important ones, such as about the thesis, being brought up later. The progression allows students to build small successes into bigger ones, rather than becoming frustrated and giving up because they are not immediately good at seeing the big picture. If their competence and confidence are built through the smaller tasks successfully completed, then larger ones are not as daunting.

Below are some of the guiding information and questions that can be provided to students through blackboard or other learning management system for their individual use when reading Walker's novel:

Walker's work is complex with many subtleties. There are elements of Walker's
ethical theory, which is a form of care ethics. It is clear that she thinks people
need help developing their full potential. Trace out how this is done by examining the relationships between Shug, Celie, and Mr. /Albert, or Mary Agnes/
Squeak, Harpo, and Sophia.

When reading the book, please keep the following questions in mind

On Race:

1. How do whites think about and act toward blacks in the American South?
2. How do whites think about and act toward blacks in the American North?
3. How do whites think about and act toward blacks in other countries?
4. How do blacks think about and act toward whites in other countries?
5. How do blacks think about and act toward whites in the American North?
6. How do blacks think about and act toward whites in the American South?
7. Are there general ideas/rules about how people think about race that you
   can derive from the previous questions?

The Big Questions:

a. Does Walker think that any race, gender, sex, or country is completely
   right on an issue?
b. Does Walker think that any race, gender, sex, or country is completely
   wrong on an issue?
c. What do the answers to 1 and 2 tell us?
d. What is Walker trying to tell us when she uses the imagery of quilting
   and sewing?
e. What is the main theme of the book? Focus on the differences and similarities between groups of people and individuals. What is Walker asking
   us to think about these?

By the end of the reading assignment, students will have their individual-
based responses to the questions above. Each student's answers serve as the
basis for group and class discussion.

Before doing any discussion, students are tested for reading comprehension
in class. The test is mostly to motivate students to read the work twice before
the class discussion, but it should also focus on what is important rather than
the trivial. A true–false or multiple-choice quiz using particular, significant
details that only those reading them would likely remember is recommended.
In *The Color Purple*, for example, knowing why Celie's biological father was
murdered is important to the story. It is best to base the questions for the test
on those provided earlier to guide their reading.

To be fair, and to avoid any perception that the quiz is designed to make it as difficult as possible for students, the questions are organized according to the work's sequential order. The idea here is that thinking about content in this way uses the narrative approach the student has in mind from reading the story. If the questions jump around in the work's chronology, then the narrative's benefit is lost, and it is harder for students to remember information they otherwise would be able to bring to mind.

Once again, the main part of class engagement is through discussion and group work. Lecturing tends to shut down thinking processes and creativity, as students become receptacles of information rather than active participants in creating information and thinking about it, its relationships, and implications. Morality requires engagement and practice.

Instead of telling them what to think, the class is broken into small groups to discuss one or more of the questions above. Generally, this should be three to four people at most because the point is to have everyone talk about what she or he thinks based on their individual responses to the questions but also to listen to what the others are saying (other reasons for this group size were noted earlier).

After an appropriate amount of time (which depends on the questions, e.g., Does Walker think that any race, gender, sex, or country is completely right on an issue?), groups are asked to have one of their members distill their findings into one or two sentences. Besides helping them learn how to build consensus in a group, this component encourages clarity, conciseness, and precision, which stands anyone well in their professional life. Each recorder then comes to the front board to write the group's sentence(s).

During the board recording process, students are asked to read the sentences on the board, and then find general themes, ideas, or other results. When they are doing that, they are asked to answer both what evidence is there for it, and how do the ideas fit together? These are questions that are useful for them to work on in order to move the larger conversation ahead but also to keep them engaged in the teaching process at hand, while they are not actively talking with each other in their groups.

After each recorder has submitted her or his group's finding, the instructor engages students by asking the class as a whole what the general conclusions are, and what information from the book supports them. The dialogue allows students to reengage individually and as a group with the narrative, by hearing other interpretations in conversation and subjecting them to analysis.

The instructor can direct attention to additional passages that add information, so that the class can refine their thoughts and conclusions in light of the new information. Also, the instructor should guide the conversation to passages that might be inconsistent with each other or the interpretation under discussion, which will force students to rethink and to inquire whether their findings require modification or rejection. The exercise is very useful for it teaches students one way to decide how to resolve issues: modify and explain how, or replace and explain why.

At the end of the discussion, the instructor summarizes what she thinks the main points are, and then asks the class whether they agree or whether there are other points that should be noted. This offer is rarely taken up by students, but they do appreciate being asked.

ASSESSMENT OF LITERATURE'S EFFECTIVENESS

Assessment of impact requires a variety of tools. First, student self-evaluation asks students whether they learned more about ethics from the literature or from the lectures. In general, students believe they have learned more the more that they are engaged through meaningful, successful class participation. Another question asked students to decide if one or the other method—lecture on ethical principles and values versus reading literature to see principles and values in use, and so on—is sufficient, or if a combination of the two leads to better understanding of what ethics is and why it is important in their professions and lives. If this question requires a sentence or paragraph written by the student to defend the answer, then there is at least qualitative evidence for the combination's effectiveness.

What has been informally found is that students think both are necessary, although they prefer the literature because it is not as rigid as learning the various moral principles and values through lectures. That being said, there is a recognition that one without the other would leave important information out that students need to help them make their ethical choices and build their arguments.

Additional assessment information can be obtained through writing assignments that require students to sit down and think about a question without resorting to outside sources. Students should be able to write a two-page paper stating a clear position on a moral issue and defend that position. The paper's evidence and arguments should make the paper's conclusion plausible and probable.

After the class lectures focusing on the theoretical groundworks of morality, including whichever moral principles the instructor believes useful—the various forms of consequentialism, deontological theories, and virtue ethics, a paper assignment is given that requires the application of at least one of them to a real-world example. "As a manager, is it morally permissible to hire a friend?" is an example of a topic for such a writing assignment.

After the literature section is completed, a second paper of application to a real-world example is assigned. Again, the formatting, purpose, and so on of the paper is for each student to be able to write a clear, concise, precise paper on an ethical issue that does not use outside sources.

To see if progress in ethical reasoning has been made, comparisons between the first and second assignments are made. Three papers from each possible grade—A through F—are selected from the first assignment. Using the student names, their second papers are collected and collated with their first efforts. The assessment consists of comparing the two papers against each other to see if the second has greater understanding of the human element involved, as well as additional stakeholders being identified.

Basically, the check is to see if each student has moved from the more abstract to a more informed, thoughtful response that incorporates an understanding that there are real people with real needs and desires being affected by the action. One way to measure this is by how many stakeholders are identified, and if their needs and desires are taken more thoughtfully into account. Another is to see if the students exhibit more ethical sensitivity when making their case.

A final possibility is to see if the students use more ethical sensitivity when making their case. This is characterized by placing greater emphasis on how the actions will impact stakeholders' wellbeing—often identified as happiness, flourishing, relationships, pleasure, pain, and so on—than it is on trying merely to add up quantitative amounts of costs and benefits.

In addition, the agent's relationships with others and what and why duties are entailed no longer seem contractual, but a recognition that real relationships have emotions and care involved, as well as being relevant to what one is permitted to do. For example, posit a question about the student as company manager hiring a friend who is laidback versus a better qualified candidate who is often labeled as abrasive focuses on the relationships between the individuals involved, including how an abrasive employee will interact with other employees.

They start to realize that we cannot evaluate someone on mere credentials, but that the best qualified might be someone who can work with others. Prior to the literature introduction, students tended to favor hiring the better qualified without thinking of any other implications involved. They still tend to do so, but they now write about those implications.

CONCLUSION

There is an apocryphal story that the United States' space program spent a small fortune trying to develop a pen that would write on missions without gravity. The Soviets, it is said, solved the same problem by providing pencils to their cosmonauts. Although factually wrong in many ways, the legitimate point is that commonsense dictates that we work wisely with what we have instead of trying to force what we have to fit our idealizations of reality.

The apocryphal story as a fiction brought that point home in a way that reason alone did not. Why? Because people are not the rational, self-interested creatures they have been made out to be by classical ethicists. Instead, they are messy combinations of emotions, feelings, and reason created through biological and social forces, and their own decisions. If we want them to be better people doing the right thing more often, we have to approach teaching ethics to them as they are rather than as they would be in an ideal world.

ETHICAL LEADERS: INSTRUCTIONAL MODELS

Dominic P. Scibilia

The chapters in section 3 invite readers into instructional models about ethics and social agency. The student-centered learning experiences affirm the vitality and moral difference that teaching ethics breaks open for students as they apply reason, affection, intention, intuition, and imagination in the formulation of ethical judgments.

Ronald Dufresne and David Steingard introduce Saint Joseph's University's undergraduate program Leadership, Ethics, and Organizational Sustainability (LEO). Students develop into leaders who see business as an opportunity for doing social good. In chapter 5, Dufresne and Steingard focus instructional attention on the senior capstone course called Applied Sustainable Leadership in which students integrate reason, affection, intuition, and moral imagination in the formation of social ethical judgments.

The context of the capstone, which is important to keep in mind, is a live client consulting project. Dufresne and Steingard lay out a method wherein students immersed in triple bottom-line thinking as well as a holistic approach to informed decision-making reframe the *winner-take-all competitive* business relationship between the elements of people, planet, and profit into a *synergistically complementary* business relationship.

In chapter 6, Elizabeth A. Luckman and C. K. Gunsalus recognize the significance for students of learning how to develop into social moral agents from failed ethical experiences. The formation of foundational leaders and organizational citizens calls for deep moral and social contextual awareness and reflective ethical decision-making. Luckman and Gunsalus open to the reader an instructional method framed by behavioral ethics which liberates students from a linear and rational thought process.

There are in the instructional praxis of this chapter realizations that moral judgment is more conative than cognitive, that the absence of awareness or a superficial awareness of biases prevents foundational leaders and organizational citizens from acting consistently with their values.

Lisa Kretz's instructional methodology in chapter 7 confirms that forming ethical judgment calls for practice. And the discussion of the ethics and social change major at her university offers a liberating affirmation of the dynamic of emotion in moral decision-making. Recognizing and forming judgments that lead to personal and social transformation requires more than a rational analysis of individual and systemic oppression; deep mindfulness of emotions like empathy and hope as dynamic moral sources positions students to become individuals able to work for substantial social change.

Chapter 5

Teaching Applied Ethics and Triple Bottom-Line Leadership with an Integrated Undergraduate Capstone Course

Ronald L. Dufresne and David S. Steingard

At Saint Joseph's University in Philadelphia, the Leadership, Ethics, and Organizational Sustainability (LEO) major and minor employ an integrative approach to developing undergraduate students as ethical leaders who use business as a force for good. To do so, the LEO program requires courses in each of the three areas of focus—business ethics, leadership, and sustainability—as well as a senior capstone course called Applied Sustainable Leadership. This chapter describes how the capstone course integrates the key ethical lessons from the program using a live client consulting project.

INTRODUCTION

The program-level objective of the LEO major and minor is to develop *thoughtful, ethically grounded, and broad-minded leaders who enable businesses to serve the common good, which encompasses the need for developing shared value that generates sustainable profit, provides for human well-being, and consciously stewards natural resources.* Each of the required courses contributes to the students' ethical development and prepares them for the complexity of the senior capstone course. This, in turn, prepares them for the complexity of being ethical leaders after graduation.

The underlying ethical framework for the program is normative in nature, guiding students to view their leadership growth through the lens of how they *ought* to act. The main ethical perspectives the students learn are utilitarian and rights-based theoretical lenses. Utilitarianism considers aggregate welfare among a mix of competing human and environmental stakeholder interests, commonly referred to as *the greatest good for the greatest number*. As an ethical theory, utilitarianism aims to insure that all stakeholders enjoy at least a minimum of benefits and suffer no harm, while increasing net benefits for all.

To guarantee that benefits and harms are not unduly distributed in utilitarianism, the complementary rights-based theory specifies more precisely the basic rights to which humans and the environment are ethically entitled, and the commensurate duties others have to support these rights. This framework of substantive ethical analysis and decision-making provides a crucial normative framework undergirding the triple bottom-line (pertaining to people, planet, and profit), multi-stakeholder, and purpose-driven approaches throughout the LEO program and culminating in the capstone.

Before describing the integrative capstone course, consider the ways each of the three core classes in the LEO program expand the students' ethical understanding.

ETHICS IN THE THREE CORE COURSES

Students typically take the required business ethics course, *Business, Stakeholders, and Ethics*, during their sophomore or junior year. The course learning objectives function at four levels: (1) comprehension of the substantive, philosophically based ethical theories discussed above (utilitarianism and rights-based theoretical lenses); (2) understanding of contemporary applications of ethical theory to current, topical cases in business ethics (e.g., marketing, finance, governance, sustainability); (3) application of these theories to a systematic ethical decision-making framework for cases in business ethics; and (4) applying course learning to students' own ethical decision-making self-leadership development, consonant with the *Perspectives on Leadership* course detailed here.

The course employs different pedagogical modes to deliver on these learning objectives. The first several weeks of the course dive deeply into the content-heavy nature of the background material on philosophical ethics. Through interactive class lecture-dialogues, students learn the material, critically interrogate it, and apply it to ethical issues in business.

Students apply a customized six-step ethical decision-making framework to current issues in business ethics. This framework incorporates identifying ethical and strategic issues, outlining stakeholder rights and duties, generating viable decision alternatives, and arguing for one alternative that is ethically superior and upholds the triple bottom-line perspective enfolded throughout the LEO curriculum. This framework is incorporated throughout lectures, team presentations, and two individual exams. Ultimately and ideally, students will internalize the basic concepts and tools of the framework to use in their personal and professional decision-making.

As a final demonstration of learning, each student writes a paper and presents to the class a reflective self-analysis of what they learned in the class and how it has impacted them. Here, students make connections between this substantive course, overall LEO program knowledge, and their own orientations about what it means to be an ethical business leader. Students regularly report how the course provides concepts and arguments to seriously engage business ethics—to *voice* their perspectives with both reason and passion—one of the overall curricular objectives of LEO.

Students are also required to take a leadership course called *Perspectives on Leadership*. This course entails both learning essential leadership theories and engaging in personal leadership development. The leadership theories include classic concepts such as trait theory (i.e., which attributes distinguish more effective leaders), behavioral theory (i.e., how leaders engage in task and relationship behaviors), leader-member exchange theory (i.e., attending to the need for high-quality relationships between a leader and a follower), and situational theory (i.e., how leaders need to adjust their style depending on the needs of the follower).

The course also covers more contemporary theories that make the ethics of leadership more explicit. For example, transformational leadership theory argues leaders should develop a deep connection with followers by pursuing a lofty, inspirational goal. Servant leadership theory normatively states the role of the leader is to care for the well-being and growth needs of others, while challenging them to serve their communities. Authentic leadership theory entails leading with a clear ethical compass and listening to the concerns of others.

A core personal leadership skill developed in the course is the ability to engage in cognitive and emotional perspective-taking. This entails understanding how someone else sees an issue or a situation and the emotional intelligence required to know how they are feeling. This skill is required for effective communication, since one must understand the other's worldview before sharing information with them, and for collaborative effort, since one must know what motivates the other before moving forward. Finally, taking the other's perspective also helps leaders assess the impact of their decisions, thereby improving the awareness of the consequences of one's decisions.

The last of the three required core courses is *Organizational Sustainability*. Central to this course is the United Nations' Brundtland Commission's definition of sustainability as "meet[ing] the needs of the present without compromising the ability of future generations to meet

their own needs" (United Nations 1987, Part 1 No. 27). This broad definition covers all resources employed by organizations, including human,
financial, and environmental resources. Students conduct case studies of
for-profit companies—such as Patagonia—that focus on sustainability as
a strategic goal, as well as case studies of what happens when companies
neglect to lead sustainably—such as chemical companies that dump waste
into public water supplies.

Organizational Sustainability is built upon utilitarian and rights-based
perspectives on ethics, as students use these perspectives to analyze the quality of companies' sustainability decisions and to make normative statements
regarding how companies ought to prioritize sustainability. A critical component of the course is the distinction between *needs* and *wants* for various
stakeholders, since the essence of sustainability is ensuring the fulfillment
of future *needs* by not exhausting human and environmental capital through
satisfying unnecessary *wants* in the present.

The central assignment of this course is a systems analysis of a contemporary sustainability-related issue of the students' choosing. For example, students may choose to study fishing in the Northern Atlantic Ocean, exploring
the issue of the sustainability of the fishery as well as the effects on fishing
communities, the biosphere, and the carbon footprint of alternative sources
of dietary protein. To evaluate the effects of various regulatory responses,
students employ utilitarian and rights-based perspectives on ethics.

THE INTEGRATIVE CAPSTONE COURSE IN
APPLIED SUSTAINABLE LEADERSHIP

Seniors in the LEO program, after taking the three core courses described
above, enroll in the *Applied Sustainable Leadership* capstone course. Just
as in architecture, the capstone builds upon the lower blocks and holds the
entire structure together; the curricular capstone integrates the core components into a unified whole. The heart of the *Applied Sustainability Leadership*
integrative course is a live-client consulting project built around the *B
Impact Assessment (BIA)* used in the *B Corps certification process* and the
Aim2Flourish appreciative inquiry innovation storytelling platform.

As an integrative course, the intent and design of *Applied Sustainable
Leadership* help students see connections among the three core courses and
how these connections relate to the larger world around them. Since these
are students on the cusp of graduation, this experience prepares them to
become ethical leaders in the complex, multi-stakeholder world they are
about to enter.

Overview of B Corps

B Corps are companies, certified by the nonprofit *B Lab* (based near Philadelphia, PA, with offices globally), that provide evidence of having positive environmental and social impacts. To qualify for *B Corp* certification, companies need to earn a passing score on the *BIA*, which is a free, comprehensive, approximately 200-question tool that captures practices in the domains of governance, workers, community, environment, and customers. *B Lab* has tailored the assessment depending on the company's size, sector, and geographic market in order to gain an appropriate perspective on each company's impact.

The *BIA* is built on a normative—albeit implicit—ethical framework regarding which practices make positive impacts. The *B Lab*'s independent *Standards Advisory Council*, which consists of sustainability experts, thought leaders, and business executives, determines the areas on which the *BIA* should focus and how many points to reward for each specific practice. The Council reviews and updates the *BIA* every three years.

Within the *BIA*, the *governance* area includes a variety of practices and asks if the company being assessed includes its commitment to a social or environmental mission in its formal documents, if the company regularly makes its financial information transparent to employees, and if managers are evaluated based on meeting social or environmental objectives. The *worker* section includes questions about how well employees are compensated, if they are supported with continuing education, and if there is a formal commitment to worker diversity, health, and safety.

The *BIA*'s *community* section asks about, among other things, if the company assesses the social and environmental performance of their suppliers, the inclusion of underrepresented communities in the ranks of management, and if workers receive paid time off for community service. The *environment* area includes questions about waste management and energy and water usage. A company may also earn points in the *customer* area if its product or service directly serves an underrepresented community.

The *BIA* is premised on an appreciative inquiry perspective, in that companies only gain points for positive practices and do not lose points for negative practices. Beyond the *BIA*, there is a verification check that would capture any seriously harmful practices that would offset the positive impact captured in the assessment. The normative ethical assumption is that when companies consider stakeholders such as workers, community, and the environment through formal, codified approaches and actual practices, the result will be increased utility for those stakeholders and greater protection of their rights.

If the company earns eighty or more points on the *BIA*, they may then choose to pursue certification as a *B Corp* and join the ranks of the over 3,000 certified *B Corps* (some well-known *B Corps* are Patagonia, Ben & Jerry's, and Seventh Generation). After *B Lab* audits and verifies the score, companies then pay an annual fee (which scales with the level of the company's revenues) and commit to codifying its obligation to social and environmental stakeholders in their incorporating documents. *B Impact Reports* of certified companies are publicly displayed on the https://bcorporation.net/ website, making the social and environmental performance of *certified B Corps* transparent, standardized, and comparable. Even companies that do not pursue certification will still benefit from using the *BIA* to determine their social and environmental impact.

Using B Corps in the Integrated Capstone Course

In the *Applied Sustainable Leadership* course, teams of four to six students contract with a local company and guide them through the *BIA* process. The significant milestones of the project include determining terms of the engagement, gathering all documentation required to complete the *BIA*, benchmarking the company against existing *B Corps* and other best-in-class companies, and developing specific and actionable recommendations to improve impact.

The *B Impact* project is big and ambiguous. Students engage in significant leadership to enlist the partner company's help to complete the project during the constrained time frame of an academic semester. The partner companies have varied levels of formalization and record-keeping, and their operational demands result in varied degrees of time that can be committed to the project. Furthermore, the partner companies range from those who are curious about their *BIA* score to those who are fully committed to pursuing *B Corp certification* after completing the *BIA* with the students. The project's ambiguity provides students a realistic preview of the complex work they will be doing soon after graduation.

The first step for the students to undertake is securing a local business partner. These partners tend to have a brand that in some ways communicates their commitment to social or environmental causes. For example, students have discovered and then contacted such small businesses as a café that hires previously incarcerated people, a food producer that uses a buy one/give one model to support local food shelves, a coffee roaster who travels to Africa to share best environmental practices, and a clothing producer that upcycles used clothes into new fashion items.

Students commonly find their partner companies either through personal contacts (such as companies that students have previously frequented) or through web searches. One additional valuable resource students use are directories of companies that identify themselves as being sustainable, ethical, or otherwise *good* companies (e.g., *the Sustainable Business Network* in

Philadelphia). Once potential companies are identified, students engage in business development work, which entails visiting, calling, or emailing to request partnership.

When establishing the partnership relationship, the students frame the project as a mutually beneficial opportunity. The partner company receives no-charge project management support to complete the *BIA* and benchmarking information about similar companies, while the students gain the opportunity to learn about how leaders of local companies make decisions to advance their social and environmental missions while still pursuing financial profitability.

The next step in the project is to draw up a contract with the business partner. The contract, which is practical rather than legal in nature, establishes mutual expectations regarding responsibilities and deadlines. This step ensures the partner company is aware, for example, of the course requirements and their deadlines. Sometimes the partner company is concerned about the confidentiality of their data to be entered into the *BIA*, so the contract may also include a nondisclosure agreement preventing the students from sharing information learned through the project. Finally, the contract also makes explicit who the project lead is at the partner company.

The next step, which entails considerable work, is to complete the *BIA*. As noted above, the *BIA* consists of approximately 200 questions, covering the areas of governance, workers, community, environment, and customers. During this step, students work as project managers, supporting the project lead in completing the assessment. This work requires significant leadership to keep the partner company on track.

It is during the completion of the *BIA* that students gain the clearest understanding of the normative ethics underlying the certification process. For example, when exploring the *workers* section of the assessment, students see both the utilitarian and rights-based perspectives in practice. Companies that share profits through such means as generous pay and benefits embody the ideal of maximizing utility for employee stakeholders, rather than only the owners. Also, companies that provide mechanisms for employee voice demonstrate a commitment to supporting their right to self-determination and workplace participation.

The following step of the process is to engage in benchmarking work. Students conduct benchmarking research to determine what companies similar to the partner companies (including both *certified B Corps and non-B Corps*) do to amplify their social and environmental impact. This is the type of work that most small businesses tend not to have time to undertake, so learning best practices from the field represents a distinct benefit that partner companies receive.

Between completing the *BIA* and benchmarking work, students gain the experience of seeing which seemingly beneficial practices might *not* earn impact points. Commonly, these practices take the form of things companies do for which metrics are difficult to find. For example, in the case of the small clothing designer who upcycles used men's clothes into new women's fashion, it proves difficult to measure the environmental impact of clothes diverted from landfills. Analyzing such practices through the utilitarian and rights-based lenses reinforces how sometimes it is difficult to measure what matters most.

The final step of the project is for students to formulate recommendations for the partner companies. *B Lab* offers practical advice for improving impact in every area of the assessment. Whether the partner company passed the eighty-point threshold or not, every company could benefit from adopting practices to enhance their social and environmental impacts. The key challenge for the students is to grapple with the practicality of their suggestions. Given limited time and resources, companies cannot adopt all best practices at once. Where, then, should they start? And why?

Formulating recommendations challenges the students to think critically and make principled recommendations for why one good may be better than another good—for example, should the company invest resources to train and develop workers or install energy-saving technology? Here again, students gain practice applying the ethical lenses used throughout the *LEO* program. If there are multiple paths to earning five more points on the assessment, which path is likelier to improve the overall performance of the company while considering ethical duties to various stakeholders?

The project brings together the lessons learned from the core courses described above, all with a focus on *real-world* application. From the business ethics class, students apply the ethical lenses to determine how and why the business practices serve the common good. From the leadership class, students practice taking the perspective of the business leader as they formulate recommendations and help establish lofty, inspirational goals. From the sustainability class, students apply the systems approach to determine which sustainability-related recommendations are most feasible.

Furthermore, through this project, students learn the importance of companies' maintaining data that indicate positive impact. It is not, for example, enough for a company to *say* they treat employees well; they need to maintain evidence to *show* they treat employees well. Formally adopting stakeholder-sensitive practices and sharing them regularly with internal and external stakeholders is far better than engaging in them in ad hoc, intermittent ways.

Aim2Flourish Case Study

As an additional way to capture the lessons learned from the partner company, students explore how their company's strengths align with the *United Nations' SDGs*. The *SDGs* are seventeen global goals adopted by UN member-states in 2015 in order to enhance human and ecological thriving worldwide. The SDGs cover such areas as eliminating poverty and food insecurity; supporting quality education, gender equality, decent work, and economic growth; and protecting the environment.

To connect the lessons learned from the partner companies with the *SDGs*, students write a case study (called an *Innovation Story*) to be published by *Aim2Flourish*. The *Aim2Flourish* platform embraces *Appreciative Inquiry* to accentuate the positive impacts businesses are making. Students, through their work with the partner company, learn how the company's operations work to fulfill one or more of the *SDGs* and capture these lessons in a positive-impact case study that is eventually published on the *AIM2Flourish* website (https://aim2flourish.com/).

For example, a recent team of students partnered with TerraCycle for the *Applied Sustainable Leadership* capstone course. TerraCycle works to recycle materials and products most recycling operations are unable to process. After completing the *B Corp* project, the students conducted an in-depth interview with a TerraCycle leader, learning about how their work supports the *SDGs* pertaining to sustainable communities and responsible consumption. The students then wrote and published a case study to highlight this positive story. This story was published by *Aim2Flourish* and earned the *2019 Flourish Prize* for being an exemplary story of a business promoting responsible consumption and production https://aim2flourish.com/2019-flourish-prizes.

ASSESSING THE EFFECTIVENESS OF THE INTEGRATIVE CURRICULUM AND CAPSTONE

Experience with eight years of the *LEO* program, capstone course, and live field application with local companies suggests that such integrated pedagogy increases learning outcomes for academic programs. As an example, throughout the LEO undergraduate major and minor program, students learn a variety of perspectives on business ethics and ethical leadership. They gain experience conducting structured ethical analysis of current events, exploring their own roles as ethical leaders, and viewing stakeholders through a sustainability and systems-theory lens. Each core course in the program has learning objectives and assignments that support the students' ethical development.

The *Applied Sustainable Leadership* integrated capstone course brings together the lessons developed in the core courses. The learning objectives of the capstone course include:

• students learn how to assess the positive impact made by a local company,
• students learn how to conduct benchmarking of best-in-class practices,

- students learn how to make practical recommendations to improve business impact, and
- students engage in *Appreciative Inquiry* to connect business practices to the *United Nations' Sustainable Development Goals* (SDGs) by using the *Aim2Flourish* platform.

By completing the *B Impact project* and writing the *Aim2Flourish case study*, students grapple with the complex challenges faced by companies committed to social and environmental impact. This applied, real-time project allows students to see, in practice, how utilitarian and rights-based decisions serve stakeholders such as workers, the local community, and the environment.

Students have responded very positively to the program design and the capstone course. There have been ten iterations of the *Applied Sustainable Leadership* course over the past eight years, and the average overall student evaluation of the course is approximately 4.9 on a five-point scale. This is despite the considerable frustration that comes along with doing an applied, field-based project that hinges on the cooperation of external partners. Students value the experience and learning of working with actual companies in the context of enhancing triple bottom-line impact.

In individual reflection papers, students routinely report how their experience with the *LEO* curriculum and capstone course deepens their awareness of stakeholders and teaches them how to make utilitarian and rights-based arguments in both their personal and professional lives. For example, they critique the *maximizing shareholder wealth* worldview seen in other parts of their business education as lacking in attending to the utility experienced by and the rights of other stakeholders. They narrate how they decide between job offers because one potential employer more actively considers the rights of employees than the other potential employer. Other students describe how they are taking public transportation since the utility of having the freedom of movement of driving their own car is offset by the utility gained by generating less greenhouse gas in the environment.

Evidence of the effectiveness of the curriculum and capstone course can be seen in the experiences and stories of recent graduates. A recent survey of the alumni of the *LEO* program provides evidence that the graduates gain a better understanding of stakeholders and applied ethics, keener insight into their own personal ethical practices, and a normative belief in business as an agent of common good. These alumni, despite holding college degree entry-level positions, are applying the lessons from the program in creative and meaningful ways. For example, alumni cite the *Applied Sustainable Leadership* course as helping them:

- As a seafood buyer for an online grocery company, convince a manager that sustainability of seafood should be a criterion for choosing which fish to source.
- As a new employee, convince a manager that performing community service projects as a team would both help others and serve as a team bonding exercise.
- As a rotational program participant at a large supermarket chain, develop a food recovery initiative that serves unsellable food at local soup kitchens, all while saving $2 million in reduced landfill charges.
- As a junior account manager at a cosmetics company, propose an initiative to use reusable/refillable bottles for shampoo.

In all of these examples, former students apply the multi-stakeholder, ethical perspectives developed through the *LEO* program. They display their ability to navigate the complexities of contemporary business while attending to the triple bottom-line of people, planet, and profit. The three core courses and the capstone course develop in students the ability to make real-world business decisions that embody thoughtful, applied ethics.

Pedagogical Implications for Integrating Ethical Leadership and Sustainability

One unforeseen, but welcome, set of insights from the *LEO* program and capstone revolve around how this type of pedagogical approach can perhaps inform ethically grounded education more generally. Two of these insights are detailed here in turn.

First, providing a transformative educational experience to foster ethical leadership, in a business school context or otherwise, requires a potent admixture of three elements: content knowledge, self-development, and applied experience. *Content knowledge*, traditional academic theory and analysis, provides the necessary intellectual background to power the ethical decision-making processes students learn. Without a substantive understanding of philosophical ethics and moral reasoning, students would be woefully ill-equipped to engage the type of rigorous, principle-based discernment endemic to ethical and effective decision-making in professional life.

Yet, even with highly honed skills of ethical decision-making, professional decision-makers may not, quite paradoxically, ultimately deliver ethical and effective decisions in organizations. *Cognitively understanding* the most defensible ethical position about a decision does not automatically correlate with the *empowered execution* of that decision. More simply, knowing the right thing to do does not always translate into doing it. To increase the probability that well-reasoned ethical decisions will be implemented by decision-makers, the *personal developmental level* of the decision-maker is key. Self-aware, morally mature, and purpose-driven professional decision-makers are much more likely to courageously champion taking the higher moral ground in organizational life.

To catalyze these intellectual and character dimensions for ethical leadership, it is prudential to provide a living-learning laboratory in which to apply and practice ethical decision-making. Whether through company consultations, service learning, internships, or other field-based learning experiences, providing students the opportunity to apply what they have learned is paramount. For pedagogical purposes, strategically and intentionally developing students in these areas is fundamentally important to them eventually having the inner fortitude and character to make decisions and lead others toward a higher good.

Second, achieving some mastery with the triple bottom-line concept is critical to cultivating ethical leadership, regardless of the type of curriculum or higher education environment (e.g., business, other professional schools, liberal arts). Triple bottom-line thinking and informed decision-making require judicious consideration of competing forces in all organizations and management contexts: ethical elements concerning human flourishing (people), impacts on the natural environment (planet), and financial performance (profit) are always in competition.

CONCLUSION

Profit considerations tend to overshadow—and sometimes obviate—the judicious consideration of human and environmental concerns in organizational decision-making. This cultural and historic dynamic pervades all sectors, including business, government, education, and nonprofit organizations. Pressure to advance economic interests in organizations, oftentimes at the expense of human and environment stakeholders, is unfortunately an unconscious and ubiquitous norm in professional decision-making. Triple bottom-line thinking and informed decision-making challenge this norm by reframing the purported *winner-take-all competitive* relationship between the elements of people, planet, and profit, into a *synergistically complementary* relationship.

If pedagogy can deliver some command of triple bottom-line concepts, then students are more likely to operationalize better ethical and sustainable decisions in their professional lives. Combined with powerful content knowledge, keen self-leadership, and the triple bottom-line mindset, promoting the type of *LEO* program learning goals discussed in this chapter to any discipline is a worthy goal of any higher educational pursuit in any discipline.

REFERENCES

United Nations, World Commission on Environment and Development, *Our Common Future,* (1987) accessible at http://www.un-documents.net/our-common -future.pdf.

Chapter 6

Teaching Reflective Decision-Making

Exercises for Navigating Ethical Dilemmas

Elizabeth A. Luckman and C. K. Gunsalus

This chapter offers educational exercises, based on recent research and easily incorporated into a variety of classroom contexts, that instructors can use to help students develop skills for reflective and thoughtful choices when making decisions with ethical implications.

INTRODUCTION

How do faculty help students navigate a world in which ethical failures, large and small, seem pervasive? Daily, we are bombarded with examples of corporate and individual misdeeds: consumer privacy violations, flawed products, fake news, fraudulent research, embellished resumes, manipulated financial data, sexual harassment and uncivil behavior, and more. Today's students face hard choices. The skills and character required to manage ethical dilemmas effectively demands practice to build positive habits related to ethical decision-making.

Beyond personal development, employers seek to hire those who are equipped with the professional and social skills necessary to navigate work life: organizations (whether industry or academia) that recruit from the undergraduate population consistently say that students are coming to them unprepared to be successful employees, let alone great leaders or team-members (Petrone 2019; Bauer-Wolf 2018). Further, in a research study that asked 195 leaders around the world to rank the top leadership competencies, 67 percent identified *high ethical and moral standards* as a foundational leadership quality (Giles 2016).

Educators are being called upon to develop organizational citizens who can be trusted to lead teams and organizations of all types to both ethical and effective outcomes (Chamorro-Premuzic and Frankiewicz 2019; Minnis, Abebe, and Elmuti 2005). Universities must do more to prepare their students for the real demands of professional life, and one piece of that is helping students to develop the necessary social and interpersonal skills that influence these ethical and effective outcomes.

Being aware of unethical behavior and knowing what to do about it are important leadership skills (Bazerman and Sezer 2016). This includes the ability to make reflective and thoughtful decisions with ethical implications. Navigating the ethical dilemmas inherent in organizations requires well-developed moral awareness and reflective decision-making.

The methods described in this chapter are based on research in behavioral ethics, adult learning theories, and leadership development, and provide educational tools that can be used together or separately to engage students in learning. The pedagogical framework offers development in social and moral awareness and decision-making, and scaffolds student learning to produce more ethical and effective leaders.

Although the focus here is on undergraduate education, this approach has been successfully used from high school through executive education across a wide range of fields and settings, including research, business, law, education, medicine, engineering, and beyond.

RESEARCH BACKGROUND

Behavioral Ethics

The study of ethics is rooted in the discipline of philosophy, and over time, significant thought has been devoted to theories of ethics and morality. From a philosophical perspective, ethical issues are presented and debated to evaluate how different lenses provide different understandings of actions and their moral implications. While fundamental to the study of applied ethics, theories alone are not always helpful in settings seeking applied solutions, especially in professions including medicine, law, and business. Research shows that training in normative philosophical ethical theories does not necessarily decrease unethical behavior (e.g., Schwitzgebel 2009).

Current work, specifically in psychology, focuses on the social and cognitive aspects of decision-making in choices with ethical implications. The earliest psychological research on the process of ethical decision-making posited a linear and rational thought process for evaluating decisions based on their ethical implications (Kohlberg 1981; Rest 1986). Many of the earlier models of ethical decision-making are rooted in the idea that there is some form of awareness of the morality of the situation, followed by judgment, intention, and behavior (Rest 1986; Treviño 1990; Jones 1991).

When researchers began to realize that people do not necessarily follow a rational, evaluative process when making decisions, there was a *revolution* in psychology (Slovic, Fischhoff, and Lichtenstein 1977; Einhorn and Hogarth 1981). Herbert Simon is typically credited with the discovery of *bounded rationality* (Simon 1955, 1978), a concept that suggests economic rational models of decision-making are not aligned with real human judgment due to cognitive biases, frames, and heuristics.

This idea that rational thinking can be bounded by cognitive frames was extended to moral psychology. Jonathan Haidt and colleagues argued that the psychology of morality was not motivated by a linear and rational thought process, but rather by intuition or *gut responses* that people have when facing morally charged situations (Haidt 2001; Haidt, Koller, and Dias 1993). Their research suggests that when an issue is moral in nature, our cognitive responses are both emotional and intuitive; the process of going through the evaluation and rationalization of that immediate reaction is the downstream effect.

Rational choices can be anything but rational in nature. The idea that moral decision-making is based on intuition instead of rationality, combined with the work in behavioral decision theory, supports the idea that decision-making in the face of an ethical dilemma is subject to the same frames and biases as decision-making in other circumstances (Kern and Chugh 2009; Bazerman and Gino 2012; Chugh, Bazerman, and Banaji 2005).

We now have a more nuanced appreciation that issues of morality are more intuitive, and that people are blinded by biases that may prevent them from acting in alignment with their values, along with a deeper understanding of the psychology of ethical decision-making. Ethical decision-making is not as simple as having knowledge of one or more philosophical frameworks, selecting one to evaluate the situation, and then deciding.

Ethics Education

To be effective, therefore, ethics education requires more than a philosophical understanding of ethical dilemmas or knowledge of the law: it requires building habits related to awareness and decision-making. Research in ethics education has demonstrated that thinking philosophically about ethical dilemmas is insufficient to prepare for confronting them in reality (De Los Reyes, Kim, and Weaver 2017), largely because it is not possible to imagine all of the boundaries and biases that may cloud judgment.

Teaching ethics effectively requires that students engage with ethical dilemmas and practice how they might deal with them, which is at the heart of behavioral ethics (Prentice 2014; Arce and Gentile 2015). Best practices for teaching ethics include keeping the cases themselves short with easily remembered details, relevant to the real-life experiences of the students, with a systematic decision-making process offered (Mumford et al. 2007, 2008). For example, in one study, self-report measures of ethical decision-making improved in doctoral students after they worked through case studies with ethical issues, including identifying their biases and approaching the case through a problem-solving lens (Mumford et al. 2008). Ethics education that is embedded in the context of the learner improves self-reported measures of moral awareness (May and Luth 2013).

Exercises

These exercises are predicated on the assumptions that most people are not out to make unethical decisions, and that unethical decision-making is often a result of individual and situational forces that influence people's thinking in ways that encourage them to deviate from ethical thought processes. The exercises can be used together or separately, and iteratively or as one-time activities, though we believe they are more effective when used repeatedly over time. The description of each exercise includes information about the underlying pedagogy affiliated with it.

After helping students to understand their own values and then to learn to identify the cognitive biases that can influence the decision-making process, the students then have the opportunity to practice working through potential ethical dilemmas that they are likely to face. Together, these exercises are designed to develop and build habits that interrupt biased thinking that can lead to unethical decision-making.

The pedagogical approach begins with values articulation and identification, provides a framework for understanding and identifying the barriers to ethical decision-making, then offers a way to practice thinking through ethical dilemmas. Through this suite of approaches, students can explore their own perspectives and cognitive frames, increase their moral awareness, and engage in more ethical decision-making.

ARTICULATING AND UNDERSTANDING VALUES

People are egocentric, so an engaging starting place is to get students to think about themselves. The first exercise focuses on the role of values in driving behavior and helps students explore and articulate their own values. There are various approaches to using this exercise. Generally, the goal is for students to take away two key insights: (1) that they can simultaneously hold conflicting values and will occasionally have to make decisions that pit one against another, and (2) that values are only values if they are willing to act on them—and that, sometimes, that means sacrificing for them.

Individual Values Identification: One introductory approach is to use a pencil and paper exercise, asking each individual student to write down the five to seven values they believe they hold most strongly. Generally, the younger the group, the more likely they are to need examples of what *values* means, either in the introduction to the exercise or incorporated as a list into a worksheet.

Invite students to reflect (bullet points, an essay, a journal, a conversation) on how they *live* their values (*walk their talk*). A sample worksheet for students needing priming can be seen in table 6.1. Examples can also be provided through a short introduction, slides, chalk talk, and so on.

Self-Concept: It can be effective to pair this with a quick exercise asking students to write down a sentence encapsulating what they want people to say about them at the end of their careers—what reputation do they want to build in working with others? (An interesting thought question to drop in at some point is to ask students what reputations they are already building among their peer groups.) Ask them to write by hand, explaining that writing uses different neural pathways than just thinking about something or typing on a computer (Mueller and Oppenheimer 2014; Smoker, Murphy, and Rockwell 2009). Ask them to save their sentence for the last day of class, or seal into

Table 6.1   Values Worksheet

List two people you personally know who you respect and admire, and think about what kind of values they model with their behavior:	
Read through this list of values and circle FIVE that guide your life:	
Achievement	Change and variety
Friendships	Independence
Physical challenge	Community
Status	Inner harmony
Money	Integrity
Excellence	Religion
Nature	Competition
Excitement	Reputation
Fame	Country
Growth	Security
Pleasure	Self-respect
Adventure	Deciseveness
Having a family	Leadership
Power and authority	Wisdom
Affection	Honesty
Helping other people	Helping society
Write about the kind of person that you want people to say you are at the end of your career.	

Source: Authors Luckman and Gunsalus Product.

envelopes and collect for return later; this can be a powerful additional activity if incorporated into the last session where it is referenced in a capstone conversation.

Values Conflicts: This can be a good time to present examples where values may conflict and ask students to think through how they might choose one value over another. Offer a simple example, like working with a group to order a pizza. If the student values fairness, perhaps each person gets to pick a topping—pepperoni, mushrooms, and onions. If the student values loyalty, and knows that one person refuses to eat mushrooms, that student now has a conflict of values. The choice they make indicates which value means the most to them in that situation.

Providing examples of simple, low-stakes, everyday values conflict sets the foundation for understanding the concept of ethical dilemmas. Conflicts of loyalties are particularly engaging to students and are also difficult to facilitate, so entry-level discussions are best run with simple examples, saving more fundamental conflicts—confidentiality at work over sharing information that would benefit a friend, family over honesty, and so on—for later when students have a deeper understanding.

Cohort Values: Once students are comfortable identifying their own values, this exercise can be extended to have them create a common set of *group* values. This works best when there is a cohesive group in the room (like a cohort, classroom, or workshop). With their own five to seven values, they work with a partner to create a shared list of five to seven common values. Next, the dyad works in a larger group (perhaps three to five people) to create another shared list, another five to seven values. Finally, the groups work together as a whole unit, narrowing down to the top five to seven values for the cohort or classroom.

This exercise not only encourages conversations around values and what values are important, introducing students to values they had not considered; it also serves to demonstrate how commonly held certain values are. This exercise can be used to create a set of ground rules about how classroom discussions will be conducted around difficult topics, or as an identifying credo for a group.

As an example, the authors recently ran this exercise in a group of about 150 first-year student athletes. After the first two rounds in which students identified their own values and then worked with partners, they moved around the room to have successively larger group conversations until there were six groups. Each group provided their list of five values, which were displayed at the front of the room. In discussion with the entire cohort, similar answers were condensed. The final five values were hard work, family and friends, loyalty, success, and integrity (with a bonus sixth value of focus). The cohort adopted this, branding them as *our class*. Student engagement was high, and the final values were then passed along to the athletic administrators and coaches as the *group identity* of that class of athletes.

INTRODUCING BIASES: CAREER TRAGEDIES

After the focus on self, the next step is to raise moral awareness by introducing individual and situational elements that can influence unintentional unethical behavior, or ethical blindness. Ethical blindness refers to the cognitive biases that can lead to ethical lapses (Sezer, Gino, and Bazerman 2015). Research has shown that individuals are biased toward themselves, whether that means maintaining a perception of the self as ethical (Mazar, Amir, and Ariely 2008) or simply protection of one's own work and status (Wade-Benzoni, Tenbrunsel, and Bazerman 1996).

Individual decision-making is also influenced by goals (Schweitzer, Ordóñez, and Douma 2004), power dynamics (Dubois, Rucker, and Galinsky 2015), and group pressure (Pascual-Ezama et al. 2015). All of these affect rational and ethical cognitive processes, so improving ethical decision-making starts with helping students appreciate how these factors affect them.

The TRAGEDIES

A framework called TRAGEDIES (Gunsalus and Robinson 2018), an acronym based on its components, integrates individual biases and environmental pressures that can lead individuals to make decisions that do not align with their personal ethical values. The framework can be introduced relatively quickly, with an example of each that can be as short as a sentence: it is easily grasped and if examples are chosen that are relevant to the audience, remembered. An illustration of the TRAGEDIES framework can be found in figure 6.1.

Identifying with TRAGEDIES

Once the TRAGEDIES have been introduced, the next step is to have students practice identifying TRAGEDIES in a variety of situations. Present different scenarios and ask students to identify potential TRAGEDIES that could exist in that situation—and undermine effective decision-making. Start with an example that is easily identifiable: having one more cookie or serving of dessert when trying to watch calories. They might identify *Temptation* because it looks so good, *Rationalization* because it's *just one*, *Group or Authority Pressure* if the person who made it or the group is urging you to

 🏆	*Temptation*	"Copying my friend's paper from last year would help me get that A so my parents will let me go on the spring break trip."
⚙	*Rationalization*	"I worked really hard on the last group project, and I deserve to not have to put so much time in on this one."
 📈	*Ambition*	"We are going to get this project done no matter what it takes."
🛡	*Group and Authority Pressure*	"The RA's instructions don't exactly match the dorm rules, but she is in charge of our floor…"
 🤚	*Entitlement*	"I've worked so hard on this paper, I deserve to fudge the results a bit so I can make sure I get an A."
 🎭	*Deception*	"Everyone does it, and I'm no worse than them."
 ●●●	*Incrementalism*	"I'll only take a couple of dollars from him this one time."
😊	*Embarrassment*	"I don't want to look foolish in front of my friends for not knowing how to handle this situation."
 ⚖	*Stupid Systems*	"I don't have to do the reading for class because it's not graded."

Figure 6.1   The TRAGEDIES framework. *Source*: Authors Luckman and Gunsalus Product.

have more, *Deception* (self), *Incrementalism* from the cumulative effect of *just one more* over time.

The TRAGEDIES framework sets the stage for the following exercises, offering students an easy way to understand, recognize, and remember where biases or barriers may be getting in the way of their own ethical decision-making. Students can provide examples from their experiences or a lecture can include specific stories related to their contexts. An effective summary of the TRAGEDIES can be tied to students' goals for the reputations they hope to have by the ends of their careers: the TRAGEDIES are the pitfalls, the things *they don't know they don't know*, that can derail them on the path to their ultimate goals.

In the next section, a decision-making exercise that puts these newly articulated values, and the concept of values conflict to work is described.

2 Minute Challenges (2MCs) and the Decision-Making Framework (DMF)

Once students reflect upon and articulate their values, and have an opportunity to explore how they can come into conflict, they practice confronting such conflicts. This requires context-relevant mini case studies that present a values conflict or ethical dilemma with real consequences. Students engage with these case studies through a set series of questions that are designed to elicit the complexities of the situation.

Two Minute Challenges (2MCs) are short case studies, a paragraph or two at most (such that they can fit on a presentation slide) that set up a potential values conflict with consequences (Gunsalus 2012). Examples of 2MCs that may be relevant for undergraduate students can be found in table 6.2.

These case studies can be adapted to any context, and work well in undergraduate classrooms. They can also be expanded from young school-age children to executives by developing new and relevant cases. The authors' examples come from decades of real dilemmas collected from several generations of students and alumni—used with permission—and situations that eventually became research integrity issues.

New examples can be created and tailored to audiences by seeking information from former students or professionals in the relevant field for stories about good or bad ethical outcomes. The goal is to offer a context-situated setup relevant to the group being taught, and allow them to work through the issues systematically, using their own values and goals. Asking an experienced professional, expert in the field, or members of a discipline about ethical dilemmas experienced or seen at work invariably elicits a variety of situations that can then be shaped for a specific audience, expanding the potential impact for this as an educational tool.

Table 6.2   Examples of 2 Minute Challenges

Example A:
It's 2 a.m. and you are out with some friends. You are driving. The roads seem deserted. You come to a stop sign. Do you stop? Why or why not?

Example B:
Your dream company has come on campus to interview. They have decided to award you an *alternate* interview slot, meaning you have the last pick at signing up. They have two openings: one at 2 p.m. and one at 7 p.m. You have conflicts with both. At 2 p.m., you have an exam worth 30 percent of your grade. Your professor is notoriously tough on excused absences, and he does not believe work comes before school. At 7 p.m., you have to attend your best friend's singing performance. You have known this friend since the start of high school, and you two are practically inseparable. Your friend will be moving to California in two weeks. In the past few months, you have also developed feelings for this friend. And, to make things even tougher, your friend says you are always a good luck charm at performances. You must choose two of the three: interview, exam, or performance. What do you do?

Example C:
It is your first job after graduation. You are an accountant for a small firm. One day, your supervisor hands you a set of receipts from a restaurant and lounge, and asks you to process them promptly. He says they were incurred entertaining a client last night. Later, your supervisor's wife stops by to pick him up for lunch and you overhear her telling the receptionist what a great time she had at dinner and dancing with her husband the night before. What do you do?

Example D:
You are an intern for an independent video game development company. Your supervisor asks you to write and post under your name rave reviews for games that are made by your company, regardless of what you think about the games. These reviews will be visible on various websites to people who are considering purchasing the games. When you object to using your name, your boss tells you to make up a new screen name and use that. What should you do?

Source: Authors Luckman and Gunsalus Product.
Note: These 2MC examples are versions of scenarios either adapted for or developed for B101—An Introduction to Business and Professional Responsibility at the University of Illinois Urbana-Champaign. Other examples can be found here https://ethicscenter.csl.illinois.edu/research-ethics-resources/role-specific-re sources/resources-for-instructors/two-minute-challenges/2mcs-for-business/. Versions of scenarios B, C, and D also appear in *The Young Professional's Survival Guide: From Cab Fares to Moral Snares*, written by C. K. Gunsalus, published 2012.

   The process is relatively simple and time-efficient: identify one or more people with experience relevant to the group for whom you want to develop 2MCs. Ask a series of simple and open-ended questions like *What are the temptations and shortcuts that get people into trouble in your line of work/program?* or *When have you had to make a hard choice at work that revolves around personal ethics, or have you observed someone who was faced with one?* The phrasing that includes observed problems of others provides *cover* for those who do not wish to admit to personal dilemmas, although virtually all those who we ask are not only willing, but eager to share past ethical dilemmas they encountered, especially if the result will be anonymized.

Eliciting these stories will reveal some common situations that recur and help to frame 2MCs that can be most useful and relevant to the group being taught. For example, most professions that charge by the hour face dilemmas around attributing time to particular clients, whether that is padding or shaving time. Jobs that pay by the hour can be similar, especially when there is an honor-system for reporting, or a time logging system can be easily circumvented.

Helping friends with private information, discounts, admission, and so on, or pressure from a supervisor to cut corners are common themes. It is important to include both: (1) a dilemma—a situation in which there is no clear *answer* and there are downsides to the obvious choices—and (2) a situation that the group being taught has had or is likely to experience—and for which the relevance to their lives is palpable.

After a case is presented, lead students through applying a systematic Decision-Making Framework (DMF). A DMF accomplishes multiple pedagogical goals. First, it is a fixed set of questions that is easy to memorize, and therefore to use when facing a situation with an ethical dilemma. Second, it is designed to break down the biases and cognitive barriers that typically infect decision-making. The questions help to expose elements of the situation that may lead those in them astray and to explore potential consequences that might not be evident on first consideration.

There are many configurations for a DMF, and the one here is based on trial and error over many years of use. Six basic questions uncover issues that are typically hidden by traditional biases that affect decision-making. Other DMFs exist or can be constructed; there are many choices available. This is one that has been successfully used, and is based on experience and experimentation, meaning it can be revised to fit the context. The DMF, along with probing questions, can be found in table 6.3.

PEDAGOGICAL CHOICES FOR THE 2MC AND DMF EXERCISES

The 2MC and DMF methodologies are flexible and easily adaptable to a variety of contexts. There are a variety of ways to engage students using the 2MCs and DMF. Factors to consider when selecting one include the size of the class, the group chemistry and demeanor of the students, and which elements you wish to emphasize in a discussion. Methods range from debate to discussion to dialogue and can be used to expose differences of opinion so that your teaching can focus on why these matter.

Table 6.3   Decision-Making Framework

	Question	Further Questions
1	What are the issues?	• What is at stake? What are the potential consequences? • What caused the problem? How urgent or serious is it?
2	What rules or regulations apply?	• Institutional regulations? Laws? Unwritten rules? Code of ethics? • What family or community-based expectations are there?
3	What questions do you have or data do you need?	• What is the context? What information do you have? What information you do not have? • What data would shed more light on the issue? How do you get it? • How will others perceive the problem? What if you're wrong?
4	Who, and what, are the resources you have available?	• What were you taught? What does your internal compass tell you? • What do the rules and regulations say? Are there personal values that apply here? • Are there any mentors or reliable confidants you could consult?
5	What are your options?	• What are the consequences of each option? • Who is affected by each option? • Are there any preventative measures you can take to address predictable problems?
6	What will you do? What will you say? How (exactly) will you say it?	• What is your plan of action, including timeline of execution? • What are the pertinent materials you need? What goals will you set? What scripts will you need? • What is the option that best serves a fair and just outcome?

Source: Authors Luckman and Gunsalus Product.

In combination or iteratively, methods using 2MCs/DMF are adaptable so that the methodology can be used repeatedly with the same group, over a class, a semester, or the full college experience.

• *Sequential, class-based*: Write the questions from the DMF on the board. Ask students to respond to the case study and write down the answers to the DMF as they arise in conversation.

- *Selecting from options*: Provide options for how the students could potentially respond to the DMF and ask the students to select which option they would choose. This should elicit different opinions. Then use the DMF to unveil nuanced elements of the decision-making process. At the end of the discussion, ask students to vote again on which option they would choose. Ask a couple of students who changed options and a couple who kept the same option to explain their reasoning.
- *Analyzing options:* Provide a list of options that range from very appropriate to very inappropriate. Ask the students to work in small groups to analyze each option, identifying the consequences of each. Then have groups present their thinking to the rest of the class.
- *Small-group discussion and presentation:* Put students in groups of four and have them go through the DMF together. Ask each group to develop a short skit to demonstrate how the situation could potentially unfold. Have all groups present and discuss the similarities and differences in outcomes.
- *Debate-based*: Ask students to individually write down their initial response to the 2MC. Then divide the students into groups based on these responses. Have the students debate their choices, allowing students to switch sides during the debate if they would like. Keep notes of the points of each side during the debate. After the debate, ask the students to reflect on what they learned and whether the debate helped them to arrive at a *right* answer.
- *TRAGEDIES-based*: Label the career TRAGEDIES that are present in the 2MC. Once the TRAGEDIES have been identified, turn to the DMF and go through the questions to create a plan for avoiding or changing the situation that creates TRAGEDIES.

Time demands are flexible: a complex scenario tying into the topic of class can be interwoven throughout the class period using one or more of the approaches outlined above.

Once the method and elements have been introduced, later class time can be reduced into a 10–12 minutes segment to run through a scenario, apply each element of the DMF, and discuss options. Less time can be devoted if the 2MC is introduced at the end of a session, with the warning the next session will take it up and students should come prepared. Preparation can be assigned as homework, extra credit, or simply used to start discussion in the next session.

These examples demonstrate that the 2MC/DMF approach is flexible and iterative. By making the cases relevant, and then providing various ways to engage with the issues of the case, this approach ensures that students examine the problem from different angles, using different parts of their cognition.

LEARNING OUTCOMES

The values exercises, TRAGEDIES, 2MC, and DMF methods affect students' perceptions of ethical dilemmas and the way in which they respond to these conflicts. Identifying the TRAGEDIES highlights both individual biases and structural barriers that get in the way of ethical decision-making in organizations. The 2MCs with a DMF provides practice and exposure to a range of real-world issues. Even though humans cannot fully remove themselves from their own biases, awareness helps to improve the decision-making progress, and can facilitate moral progress. These are easy to implement in class, and easy for students to internalize, and to remember, increasing the learning impact.

Using these tools, separately or together, one-time or iteratively, serves to address two key steps of the ethical decision-making process: moral awareness and moral judgment. There are elements that help students to understand their own motivations that may differentially influence their own ethical decision-making patterns. Students walk away with (1) a better understanding of the role of values and their own values; (2) a clearer understanding of their own biases, and organizational forces that influence the ethical decision-making process; and 3) an easy to use framework to think through when facing situations with ethical dilemmas. Research shows that behaviors can change, but it takes habit-building to do so (Duhigg 2012).

Habits are built from repetition and routines. Micro goals, or small wins, have been shown to work to successfully change behavior (Amabile and Kramer 2011). The methods here help to build that ethical muscle memory, and increase the chances that when faced with values conflict, those who have practiced will be prepared to do something about it.

STUDENT FEEDBACK

The purpose of these exercises is to encourage students to think about ethical dilemmas more thoughtfully, to finely tune both moral awareness and moral judgment. Gunsalus refers to this as the *inoculation* approach to ethical dilemmas: if a student has thought about his or her own values, has been exposed to a small dose of an ethical dilemma, identified its inherent potential TRAGEDIES, and thought it through, when something similar pops up later, students will be prepared.

While some students reap the benefits of this immediately (rating the effectiveness of the class in providing an understanding of professional responsibility above 85 percent on average), excited about their ability to identify biases and to pay more attention to them in their own decision-making, others realize the value later when they come face-to-face with these types of ethical dilemmas in their professional lives. On student wrote:

> I've begun to appreciate at an entirely different level the personal challenges [the class] put to myself. Perhaps it's the benefit of time, a few years of maturity, or something else entirely, but many of the lessons around reputation, incrementalism, communication techniques, and most of all, taking the time to be thoughtful and prepared stick with me to this day.

The comments that are sent, often years after the fact, are often the most reinforcing and gratifying. This example from a student characterizes the character of that tone. "[The class] helped me choose the person I really want to be, and to continue to be . . . and to choose to be that person on purpose."

CONCLUSION

These exercises work to help students be more thoughtful in their decision-making. They are easy to implement in a range of settings from classrooms to a one-time workshop, can be adapted to a variety of contexts, address research findings on behavioral ethics and ethics education, and are more likely to become habitual because they offer a simple framework to address one's own ethical biases when faced with ethical dilemmas.

ACKNOWLEDGMENTS

We are grateful to Nicholas C. Burbules for his careful reading and suggestions for improvement. Gretchen Winter and Billy Tabrizi were central to the development and refinement of these approaches over many years of working together at the University of Illinois Gies College of Business creating Business 101: *An Introduction to Professional Responsibility* and Business 301: *Principles of Professional Responsibility*. Aaron Robinson contributed to extending, refining, and applying these approaches.

REFERENCES

Amabile, Teresa M., and Steven J. Kramer. 2011. "The Power of Small Wins." *Harvard Business Review* 89 (5). https://www.hbs.edu/faculty/Pages/item.spx?num=40244.

Arce, Daniel G., and Mary C. Gentile. 2015. "Giving Voice to Values as a Leverage Point in Business Ethics Education." *Journal of Business Ethics* 131 (3): 535–42. https://doi.org/10.1007/s10551-014-2470-7.

Bauer-Wolf, Jeremy. 2018. "Study: Students Believe They Are Prepared for the Workplace: Employers Disagree." *Inside Higher Ed.* February 23, 2018. https://www.insidehighered.com/news/2018/02/23/study-students-believe-they-are-prepared-workplace-employers-disagree.

Bazerman, Max H., and Francesca Gino. 2012. "Behavioral Ethics: Toward a Deeper Understanding of Moral Judgment and Dishonesty." *Annual Review of Law and Social Science* 8 (1): 85–104. https://doi.org/10.1146/annurev-lawsocsci-102811-173815.

Bazerman, Max H., and Ovul Sezer. 2016. "Bounded Awareness: Implications for Ethical Decision Making." *Organizational Behavior and Human Decision Processes*, Celebrating Fifty Years of Organizational Behavior and Decision Making Research (1966-2016), 136 (September): 95–105. https://doi.org/10.1016/j.obhdp.2015.11.004.

Chamorro-Premuzic, Tomas, and Becky Frankiewicz. 2019. "Does Higher Education Still Prepare People for Jobs?" *Harvard Business Review*, January 7, 2019. https://hbr.org/2019/01/does-higher-education-still-prepare-people-for-jobs.

Chugh, Dolly, Max H. Bazerman, and Mahzarin R. Banaji. 2005. "Bounded Ethicality as a Psychological Barrier to Recognizing Conflicts of Interest." In *Conflicts of Interest: Challenges and Solutions in Business, Law, Medicine, and Public Policy*, edited by Don A. Moore, Daylian M. Cain, George Lowenstein, and Max H. Bazerman. Boston: Cambridge University Press.

De Los Reyes, Gastón, Tae Wan Kim, and Gary R. Weaver. 2017. "Teaching Ethics in Business Schools: A Conversation on Disciplinary Differences, Academic Provincialism, and the Case for Integrated Pedagogy." *Academy of Management Learning & Education* 16 (2): 314–36. https://doi.org/10.5465/amle.2014.0402.

Dubois, David, Derek Rucker, and Adam Galinsky. 2015. "Social Class, Power, and Selfishness: When and Why Upper and Lower Class Individuals Behave Unethically." *Journal of Personality and Social Psychology* 108 (3): 436–49. https://doi.org/10.1037/pspi0000008.

Duhigg, Charles. 2012. *The Power of Habit: Why We Do What We Do in Life and Business*. Random House Publishing Group.

Einhorn, H J, and R M Hogarth. 1981. "Behavioral Decision Theory: Processes of Judgement and Choice." *Annual Review of Psychology* 32 (1): 53–88. https://doi.org/10.1146/annurev.ps.32.020181.000413.

Giles, Sunnie. 2016. "The Most Important Leadership Competencies, According to Leaders around the World." *Harvard Business Review*, March 15, 2016. https://hbr.org/2016/03/the-most-important-leadership-competencies-according-to-leaders-around-the-world.

Gunsalus, C. K. 2012. *The Young Professional's Survival Guide: From Cab Fares to Moral Snares*. Harvard University Press.

Gunsalus, C. K., and Aaron D. Robinson. 2018. "Nine Pitfalls of Research Misconduct." *Nature* 557 (7705): 297. https://doi.org/10.1038/d41586-018-05145-6.

Haidt, Jonathan. 2001. "The Emotional Dog and Its Rational Tail: A Social Intuitionist Approach to Moral Judgment." *Psychological Review* 108 (4): 814–34. https://doi.org/10.1037/0033-295X.108.4.814.

Haidt, Jonathan, Silvia Helena Koller, and Maria G. Dias. 1993. "Affect, Culture, and Morality, or Is It Wrong to Eat Your Dog?" *Journal of Personality and Social Psychology* 65 (4): 613–28.

Jones, Thomas M. 1991. "Ethical Decision Making by Individuals in Organizations: An Issue-Contingent Model." *Academy of Management Review* 16 (2): 366–95. https://doi.org/10.5465/AMR.1991.4278958.

Kern, Mary C., and Dolly Chugh. 2009. "Bounded Ethicality: The Perils of Loss Framing." *Psychological Science* 20 (3): 378–84. https://doi.org/10.1111/j.1467-9280.2009.02296.x.

Kohlberg, Lawrence. 1981. *Essays on Moral Development. Vol. 1, The Philosophy of Moral Development: Moral Stages and the Idea of Justice.* Harper & Row.

May, Douglas R., and Matthew T. Luth. 2013. "The Effectiveness of Ethics Education: A Quasi-Experimental Field Study." *Science and Engineering Ethics* 19 (2): 545–68. https://doi.org/10.1007/s11948-011-9349-0.

Mazar, Nina, On Amir, and Dan Ariely. 2008. "The Dishonesty of Honest People: A Theory of Self-Concept Maintenance." *Journal of Marketing Research* 45 (6): 633–44. https://doi.org/10.1509/jmkr.45.6.633.

Minnis, William, Michael Abebe, and Dean Elmuti. 2005. "Does Education Have a Role in Developing Leadership Skills?" *Management Decision* 43 (7/8): 1018–31. https://doi.org/10.1108/00251740510610017.

Mueller, Pam A., and Daniel M. Oppenheimer. 2014. "The Pen Is Mightier than the Keyboard: Advantages of Longhand over Laptop Note Taking." *Psychological Science* 25 (6): 1159–68. https://doi.org/10.1177/0956797614524581.

Mumford, Michael D., Shane Connelly, Ryan P. Brown, Stephen T. Murphy, Jason H. Hill, Alison L. Antes, Ethan P. Waples, and Lynn D. Devenport. 2008. "A Sensemaking Approach to Ethics Training for Scientists: Preliminary Evidence of Training Effectiveness." *Ethics & Behavior* 18 (4): 315–39. https://doi.org/10.1080/10508420802487815.

Mumford, Michael D., Stephen T. Murphy, Shane Connelly, Jason H. Hill, Alison L. Antes, Ryan P. Brown, and Lynn D. Devenport. 2007. "Environmental Influences on Ethical Decision Making: Climate and Environmental Predictors of Research Integrity." *Ethics & Behavior* 17 (4): 337–66. https://doi.org/10.1080/10508420701519510.

Pascual-Ezama, David, Derek Dunfield, Beatriz Gil-Gómez de Liaño, and Drazen Prelec. 2015. "Peer Effects in Unethical Behavior: Standing or Reputation?" *PLOS One* 10 (4): e0122305. https://doi.org/10.1371/journal.pone.0122305.

Petrone, Paul. 2019. "The Skills Companies Need Most in 2019 – And How to Learn Them." Linkedin.Com. January 1, 2019. https://learning.linkedin.com/blog/top-skills/the-skills-companies-need-most-in-2019--and-how-to-learn-them.

Prentice, Robert. 2014. "Teaching Behavioral Ethics." *Journal of Legal Studies Education* 31 (2): 325–65. https://doi.org/10.1111/jlse.12018.

Rest, James R. 1986. *Moral Development: Advances in Research and Theory.* Westport, CT: Praeger Publishers.

Schweitzer, Maurice E., Lisa Ordóñez, and Bambi Douma. 2004. "Goal Setting as a Motivator of Unethical Behavior." *Academy of Management Journal* 47 (3): 422–32. https://doi.org/10.2307/20159591.
Schwitzgebel, Eric. 2009. "Do Ethicists Steal More Books?" *Philosophical Psychology* 22 (6): 711–25. https://doi.org/10.1080/09515080903409952.
Sezer, Ovul, Francesca Gino, and Max H Bazerman. 2015. "Ethical Blind Spots: Explaining Unintentional Unethical Behavior." *Current Opinion in Psychology*, Morality and ethics, 6 (December): 77–81. https://doi.org/10.1016/j.copsyc.2015.03.030.
Simon, Herbert A. 1955. "A Behavioral Model of Rational Choice." *Quarterly Journal of Economics* 69: 99–118. https://doi.org/10.2307/1884852.
———. 1978. "Rationality as Process and as Product of Thought." *The American Economic Review* 68 (2): 1–16.
Slovic, P, B Fischhoff, and S Lichtenstein. 1977. "Behavioral Decision Theory." *Annual Review of Psychology* 28 (1): 1–39. https://doi.org/10.1146/annurev.ps.28.020177.000245.
Smoker, Timothy J., Carrie E. Murphy, and Alison K. Rockwell. 2009. "Comparing Memory for Handwriting versus Typing." *Proceedings of the Human Factors and Ergonomics Society Annual Meeting* 53 (22): 1744–47. https://doi.org/10.1177/154193120905302218.
Treviño, Linda Klebe. 1990. "A Cultural Perspective on Changing and Developing Organizational Ethics." *Research in Organizational Change and Development* 4 (2): 195–230.
Wade-Benzoni, Kimberly A., Ann E. Tenbrunsel, and Max H. Bazerman. 1996. "Egocentric Interpretations of Fairness in Asymmetric, Environmental Social Dilemmas: Explaining Harvesting Behavior and the Role of Communication." *Organizational Behavior and Human Decision Processes* 67 (2): 111–26. https://doi.org/10.1006/obhd.1996.0068.

Chapter 7

Ethics and Social Change

Lisa Kretz

Oftentimes, discussions of how to best teach ethics focus on what to do in individual classrooms regarding particular courses. Though such information is invaluable, this chapter is broader in scope. The emphasis in what follows is on curriculum and programming through the design of an interdisciplinary major focused on supporting ethics in practice.

INTRODUCTION

The *Ethics and Social Change Degree* at the University of Evansville bridges theory and action. Intentional curricular design incorporates student-driven pedagogy. Philosophically informed, ethical action is required in two Fieldwork courses, which require substantive, semester-long action projects working on real-world issues with local communities. The degree is inherently interdisciplinary and offers students the ability to select two concentrations to complement the core courses for the major.

The design of the major has far-reaching impacts. For example, it facilitates improving the uptake of philosophical ethics across the disciplines through interdisciplinary design. Additionally, the emphasis on action creates opportunities for students to know their own transformative power as individuals capable of generating positive world change. Finally, there is the opportunity to create strong relationships with community members outside of the university.

Although ostensibly the focus is philosophical ethics, the recommended shifts to pedagogy can be fruitfully employed in ethics courses across the curriculum. Indeed, as will be shown, the design of the major invites conversation and collaboration among disciplines. The intent in what follows is to share the research that grounds the pedagogical and philosophical justification of such a major, and to present the major as a potential model for other institutions.

The layout of the chapter is as follows. The first section identifies dominant methods for teaching philosophical ethics. The second section explores concerns about these methods. The third section outlines additional pedagogical motivation for the major and articulates the design of the degree. The final section discusses the ways in which a major that emotionally engages students through community action can support ethical action.

DOMINANT METHODS FOR TEACHING PHILOSOPHICAL ETHICS

In Book II, Chapter II of the *Nicomachean Ethics*, Aristotle notes,

> "Our present study is not, like other studies, purely speculative in intention; for the object of our enquiry is not to know the nature of virtue but to become ourselves virtuous, as that is the sole benefit which it conveys" (Welldon 1920, 36).

Aristotle's interest in teaching ethics is not limited by a singular focus on theory. Insofar as one agrees with Aristotle, a comprehensive study of ethics should not intend to be purely theoretical, but it should also facilitate the practical wisdom that supports ethical living. Education that fails to support action reflecting the theoretical insights derived from study is ineffectual in terms of moral practice.

Methods for studying philosophy vary. Nonetheless, there are some conventions that remain central to the Western tradition, including the subdiscipline of ethics, which do not fully address what Aristotle articulates. The position advocated in what follows, that teaching philosophical ethics could beneficially support behavior that reflects ethical insights, is a contested one. Exploring common expectations for the teaching of philosophy helps bring into relief the tension between solely teaching theory and teaching both theory and practice. Practice here refers to teaching in ways that support student capacities to enact their reflectively held ethical beliefs.

A useful resource for identifying dominant trends in teaching philosophy is the *American Philosophical Association's Statement on the Teaching of Philosophy*. According to the statement, studying philosophy demands and refines reasoning skills and intellectual abilities (APA Statement). Philosophy education involves grasping philosophical methods, issues, and traditions, and cultivating critical abilities to address various problems, issues, and texts (APA Statement). Students should be able to comprehend philosophical texts and arguments (APA Statement).

Curriculum ought to attend to traditions in philosophy, contemporary developments, and the interests of faculty (APA Statement). There is recognition of the import of experimenting with new courses, methods of instruction, and technology (APA Statement). Although upper level courses that focus on established rubrics and areas of philosophical inquiry are important, alternative special interest courses are also of value (APA Statement). To be sure, content is important, but the way in which students engage with the material is also important.

Tom Cooper's (2019) study of forty professors at U.K. and U.S. campuses to ascertain how moral philosophy is taught is telling here (Cooper 2009, 11). The professors interviewed almost unanimously agreed ethics and moral philosophy ought to be taught as critical thinking and internalized moral reasoning (Cooper 2009, 12). There was disagreement, however, regarding whether instruction should aim to nurture character development or moral improvement—with the group evenly divided on the topic (Cooper 2009, 12).

As for teaching methods, roughly 80 percent of the instructors interviewed used lecture format, nearly 66 percent employed seminars or tutorial formats which emphasize discussion, and approximately 33 percent utilized student-driven formats such as debate and student-led discussion (Cooper 2009, 12). Critical thinking about serious questions was almost unanimously recognized as the core mechanism of ethics pedagogy (Cooper 2009, 23).

The professors who believed ethics instruction might generate moral improvement or character development took their courses to contribute not only to the common goals of education and philosophy but also to correcting injustice (Cooper 2009, 31). The assumption that ethics instruction in the classroom translates to changed behaviors is, however, a contentious one.

It remains an open question whether the agreed upon method (that ethics should be taught as critical thinking and moral reasoning) can facilitate the fostering of moral improvement or character development in the absence of support for bringing to realization practices that reflect the beliefs that result from improved moral reasoning and critical thinking. Certainly, critical thinking coupled with good reasoning generates moral views based on stronger justifications, and, further, such thinking is an essential ingredient to a morally informed and thoughtful populous capable of critical moral reasoning. However, one can still ask, what does such study amount to in terms of actual behavior?

REASONS FOR CONCERN

Multiple sources of evidence suggest that changes in theoretical belief do not necessarily result in changes in behavior that reflect the changes in theoretical belief. This concern is not new. For example, Plato discusses *akrasia*, which occurs when one theoretically knows the right thing to do but fails to do it (Plato). The chasm between belief and action has been a concern for many philosophers in more recent times as well. For example, Elizabeth Anscombe (1958) thoroughly problematizes any form of ethics that fails to make a place for a robust infusion of moral psychology.

In the realm of environmental ethics, Carol Booth (2009) warns of a pronounced rhetoric-behavior gap. Mark Coeckelbergh (2015) contends that rather than focusing solely on environmental thinking, we need to address skilled engagement—engagement that involves habitually acting and thinking in a relational way (97).

Anja Kollmuss and Julian Agyeman argue there is no direct relationship between environmental knowledge and pro-environmental behavior; rather, pro-environmental consciousness is complex which involves emotional involvement, mental knowledge, values, and attitudes which are all embedded in broad personal values shaped by internal and external factors, including personality traits (2002, 256). Emotional involvement, in particular, will be explored in more depth. Although longer education leads to more extensive knowledge of environmental issues, it does not necessarily result in increased pro-environmental behavior (2002, 257).

Numerous empirical studies falsify the knowledge-attitude-behavior model of ethical education wherein it is assumed sharing knowledge inevitably leads to behavior change reflecting the responsibilities associated with this new knowledge (Goralnik and Nelson 2011, 183). For example, Jonathan Haidt's work problematizes the assumed relations between moral emotions/intuitions/judgments and moral reason, illustrating the forceful ways in which moral emotion directs ethical beliefs (Haidt 2001, 823, 830).

The classic argument in Western philosophy about the import of emotion in moral theory is found in the work of sentimentalist philosopher David Hume, who argues that no action is possible without an emotional impetus; without a desire for one thing over another one would be perpetually indifferent to states of affairs (Hume 2002, 265–66). One must therefore take seriously the ways in which emotion influences ethical belief and behavior. This conclusion is reinforced by the fact that measures of reasoning capacity fail "to show a systematic connection to difference in moral conduct" (Railton 2014, 844).

On the dual-process model of the mind, embraced by moral psychologists such as Haidt, for example, system 1 is the affective system, which is a substrate for a distinctive, automatic mode of processing, while system 2 is the higher cortical regions, which serve as a substrate for more controlled and effortful modes of functioning (Railton 2014, 827). Insofar as emotion is taken to be quick and automatic, as opposed to slower and more effortful, the role of conscious thought as the primary or sole director for behavior is called into question. Thus, if supporting moral practice is a goal, the role of emotion in moral theory and practice must be reflected in our pedagogy.

An illustration of the crucial role emotion plays in moral behavior can be found in the literature on unconscious bias. For example, Mahzarin Banaji and Anthony Greenwald note that twenty-five years ago it was widely accepted that human behavior was primarily guided through conscious thoughts and feelings; now, however, the majority agree that "much of human judgment and behavior is produced with little conscious thought" (Banaji and Greenwald 2013, xiv).

Mark Johnson goes so far as to say that one "of the most earth-shattering discoveries to come out of the cognitive sciences over the past three decades is that human thinking and willing operate mostly beneath the level of our conscious awareness, often involving intuitive and highly affect-laden processes" (Johnson 2014, 73). The claims of cognitive science and moral psychology about the hegemony of the affective system do not undermine the relevance of developing moral reasoning skills, but they make clear that developing moral reasoning skills alone will not suffice for facilitating behavior that manifests the findings of reason.

If emotion plays such a powerful role in action, including specifically ethical action, pedagogy that solely focuses on cultivating intellect may not have the behavioral impetus or impact that some ethics educators think it may, or even should. If a teacher is interested in empowering students to enact said students' beliefs through their behaviors—if one agrees with Aristotle that the object of ethical inquiry involves knowing not just what goodness is but how to become good—current modes of teaching philosophical ethics need a critical rethinking. It was with this inspiration that the *Ethics and Social Change* major was developed.

CREATING A GROUNDWORK FOR FACILITATING CHANGE

Paulo Freire's (2012) concern with empowering students so that they can transform the world to make it a place that aims for the humanization of all informs the *Ethics and Social Change* major. According to Paulo Freire, meaningful movement against oppression is rooted in trust and dialogue, and requires both theory and action (2012). This concern with empowerment informs and permeates the *Ethics and Social Change* major. Students are encouraged to engage the world robustly not only as observers but also as participants.

Moral philosophy classes in the Western tradition—as currently taught by philosophy teachers—are often excellent places for honing critical thinking about moral issues, but they fail in other important respects. Notably, such courses often leave much to be desired in terms of supporting ethical practice. The dominant approach as outlined by the APA does not, in many ways, provide for the transformational power of ethics within student lives. If one were to take seriously a need for supporting practical wisdom in the behaviors of students—behavior desired by those students based on their reflectively held and critically grounded beliefs—what might that look like?

Importantly, in what follows, the recommendation is that rather than operating with an assumption of what constitutes ethical behavior, students themselves should define the ethical action in which they wish to participate. For example, volunteer assignments should ensure students select where they want to volunteer and the activity in which they will engage. When students select topics for their Fieldwork, they can choose from existing course offerings or pursue an area that more closely aligns with their interests and career goals. The intent is to widely support various forms of ethical inquiry and application in order to ensure there is no dogmatic imposition of specific agendas.

In 2017, the *Ethics and Social Change* major was introduced at the University of Evansville, a small liberal arts college in Southern Indiana. The degree is designed to bridge theory and action (https://www.evansville.edu/majors/ethicsandsocialchange/). Student-driven pedagogy plays a significant role in the curriculum. Engaging with ethical action is required in two Fieldwork courses, in which students work on real-world issues with local communities that the students have selected. Students take on projects that resonate with them, based on their own moral compass. The degree is also student-focused in that it is meant to reflect each student's career interests and trajectory.

The *Ethics and Social Change* major is inherently interdisciplinary and offers students the ability to select two concentrations from the following areas: Business Administration, Cognitive Science, Communication, Criminal Justice, Environmental Studies, Legal Studies, Gender and Women's Studies, Philosophy, Political Science, Psychology, Race and Ethnicity Studies, Religion, and Sociology or Social Work. The Ethics Committee searched the course catalog to identify areas that are a particularly good fit with the suite of *Ethics and Social Change* core courses. Meetings were held with program directors and department chairs to explore their interest and willingness to contribute to this interdisciplinary major.

At the University of Evansville, these areas of concentration were selected to complement the core courses for the major: *Introduction to Ethics, Social Justice Movements, Complex Systems and Social Change,* two *Fieldwork Courses,* and the *Ethics and Social Change Capstone.* An *Introduction to Sociology* class is also required. The core suite of courses could change from institution to institution, varying according to the areas of specialization of those who are involved, and the level at which there is interdisciplinary complementarity.

Each course provides unique elements. *Introduction to Ethics* provides a philosophical orientation to the study of ethics and volunteer work opportunities, while the *Introduction to Sociology* utilizes a different lens to identify and empirically track the workings of oppression, which, broadly speaking, pertains to the systematic harm of one group by another group which benefits from that harm (Frye 1983, 1–16). *Social Justice Movements* facilitates awareness of how various movements have succeeded and failed, and *Complex Systems and Social Change* enables students to explore the dynamics of social change from a complex systems perspective.

Active components are built into the degree. Philosophically informed, ethical action is required in two Fieldwork courses, which require substantive, semester-long action projects working on real-world issues with local communities. Students themselves identify the issues they wish to work on, and can choose from *Changelab* courses on campus with a social justice orientation or can select organizations off campus to work with in consultation with their Ethics advisor (https://www.evansville.edu/changelab/).

Examples of Fieldwork courses include students working with campus and community organizations to provide services to the homeless—for instance, working on a project to generate *tiny houses* for homeless veterans. *Ethics and Social Change* majors have mentored Queer youth, supported the local human relations commission, created programming to enhance voter turn-out, and provided after school education to financially disadvantaged youth. Other semester-long courses involved supporting a not-for-profit that provides safe housing for primary victims/survivors of sexual or domestic violence and generating accessibility ramps for campus buildings.

There is a reflection required at the end of each off-campus Fieldwork course. Students reflect on their own performance regarding skills in the areas of communication, problem-solving/decision-making, teamwork, self-management, initiative, and relevant technical skills for the area in which they chose to work. They are also asked to articulate what they found to be most useful about the Fieldwork experience, what was most challenging, what could be improved and how to improve it, the most important lessons they learned as a result of the Fieldwork, and to consider how their previous coursework and the Fieldwork experience relate to each other.

The Capstone course empowers students to research an area of interest to them that they see as requiring social change, argue their position, and provide recommendations for how to best address the form of oppression on which they focused. Topics might include, for example, forms of oppression that pertain to people of color, disabled persons, LGBTQ+ persons, nonhuman animals, financially impoverished people, the stigmatization of mental health issues, or environmental issues. In this assignment, students must justify the recommended approach as well as assess the local, national, and global ramifications (if any). Thus, they are invited to be intentional and strategic about how to be most effective at bringing into being hoped-for states of affairs.

Readings for the Capstone course include not only theoretical philosophical material but also material from activists sharing how they cope with, and thrive in the midst of, dealing with what might feel like overwhelming moral issues. For example, students engage with materials that address anxiety. Through addressing such issues, students in the program benefit not only from engaging with theoretical ethical material but also by addressing the emotional fall-out from attending to the ways in which humans are ethically challenged. Readings that engage students with the emotional dimensions of working toward making the world a just and humane place help to support resilience (Kretz 2014, 2017).

The educational opportunities provided by the major have far-reaching impacts. The interdisciplinary approach improves the uptake of philosophical ethics across the disciplines because areas of concentration are brought into conversation with course work in *Ethics and Social Change*. The Fieldwork courses improve the uptake of philosophical ethics throughout society, including nonacademics publics, as students work with local organizations bringing what they have learned in previous classes into their Fieldwork courses.

Additionally, the degree reflects the varied interests of students, weaving *Ethics and Social Change* reflection and action into fields of study in which the students are invested. Importantly, the Fieldwork courses provide a forum for students to richly emotionally engage with the lives of those who are oppressed. The opportunity for students to address more than just theoretical ethics by gaining tools for enacting their beliefs through Fieldwork courses helps students to see firsthand their capacity to transform the world.

COMMUNITY ENGAGEMENT, AFFECTIVE ENGAGEMENT

Community engagement plays a key role in the *Ethics and Social Change* major. In terms of capacity for transformation, Brett Johnson argues that empowerment is facilitated by nurturing civic responsibility, enhancing perceptions of civic efficacy (which makes engagement in civic behavior more likely), developing civic skills, and increasing knowledge about society (which makes the odds in favor of competence better) (Johnson 2005, 49–50). Empowerment involves supporting student-centered active learning as well as student-led social action (and engaging in service learning and community research) (Johnson 2005, 50).

Alternatively, student cynicism and apathy are linked to civic disengagement (Johnson 2005, 44–46). Anne Colby et al. argue that an essential component of higher education involves "coming to understand how a community operates, the problems it faces, and the richness of its diversity and also developing a willingness to commit time and energy to enhance community life and work collectively to resolve community concerns" (Colby et al. 2003, 18). With such an approach, moral problems are explored in particular contexts. Collective action to resolve community problems develops in embodied and embedded ways.

The community-oriented nature of the Fieldwork is meant to reflect the insight of Robert Hironimus-Wendt and Lora Wallace (2009) that "Community-based social engagement represents the most promising pedagogy for helping students develop a sense of empathy *with* diverse others—a sense of connectedness resulting from the sharing of experiences and/or circumstances" (Hironimus-Wendt and Wallace 2009, 79–80).

Abstract presentations of morally salient issues are insufficient. Vivid/concrete presentation of data is more influential than pallid abstract presentation (Horton 2004). Students need to be engaged with communities if they are to care about them in the ways proximity enables, and if they are to be exposed to emotions that can serve to motivate behavior change. The communities identified outlined in the examples of Fieldwork courses are just such communities, composed of folks who are unfairly disadvantaged as well as those that seek to work against the impacts of systematic oppression.

Certain emotions are directly tied to motivation. Martin Hoffman argues that proximity enhances empathy—the suffering of others who are near generates a stronger response than the suffering of distant others. Empathetic biases include the Here and Now Bias, Familiarity Bias, In-Group Bias, Friendship Bias, and Similarity Bias, all of which point to proximity motivating the strength of empathetic response (Hoffman 2000). Working directly with oppressed populations in Fieldwork courses addresses these biases and puts bias to work in establishing relationships in which empathy can grow through proximity.

However, one wants to avoid the false sense of deep understanding from a temporary encounter. As Diane Zorn and Megan Boler point out, it is concerning when students are mere spectators engaging in passive empathy, superimposing their own conceptual framework on another's experience (Zorn and Boler 2007, 142–43; Boler 1999, 161, 184). When students participate in community engagement, it is important to avoid the false "aha" moment in which, due to a limited encounter, one believes they richly understand the phenomenology of oppression (Boler 1999). Likewise, the assumption that contact alone is sufficient must be problematized, because meaningful contact across difference requires intentional design (Paluck and Green 2009).

Beyond empathy, an additional emotion to consider as a bridge from theory to action is hope. If there is no hope for a desired outcome, there is no rational justification for engaging in activities to bring it about. Hope is a precondition for action.

On Charles Snyder's account, hope has an agency component (because it is goal-directed) and a pathway component (because of planning to meet goals) (Snyder 1995, 355). Further, hope can be taught (Cheavens *et al.* 2005, 126). Student engagement with moral issues, where they are empowered to plan remedies for the problems they identify, and execute those plans, while being fortified with hope, can result in an increased sense of responsible behavior, control, and intention to act (Hsu 2004, 41). Hopefulness generates active coping, prevents disengagement from stressful situations, and reduces denial (Braithwaite 2004, 83).

CONCLUSION

Insofar as Aristotle is correct, ethics done right is more than theory—it requires practice. Given the current trends in teaching philosophical ethics, and considering given findings about the limits of such study, emotional engagement can and should be seen as essential to behavior change. The *Ethics and Social Change* major serves as an example of program design, which, in addition to theoretical study of the operations of oppression, seeks to alleviate such oppression through concrete acts that increase proximity to those who are harmed. Such work facilitates the engagement of emotions such as empathy and hope. Cultivating such emotions in the context of responding to real-world harms in areas of genuine student interest provides the opportunity for students to manifest their ethical beliefs in lived practice. The *Ethics and Social Change* major provides an opportunity for students to know their own transformative power as individuals capable of generating positive world change.

The reflection of a graduate from the first *Ethics and Social Change* cohort is illustrative here. As part of the program assessment students were asked a number of questions including the following: "If you had to describe to a friend what a major in Ethics in Social Change will do for them, what would you say?" The student responded: I would say

No matter what your major is, this is the perfect program because it's applicable to anything and everyone needs to learn how to be a better person. The professors are amazing, and the subject matter is super fun to read and discuss. It is well worth it, and any business would be lucky to hire you after you have had this major because you will leave wanting to do good things for the world.

In response to the question, "What was the most useful component of the program for you? Say why," the same student responded,

The experiential learning opportunities were the most useful parts of the program. It allowed me to realize what I want to do, what I'm good at, and what I need to work on. I also developed incredible relationships and realized what I need to do to make myself a better advocate.

Ethics, for this particular graduate, is very much a lived practice.

REFERENCES

Anscombe, Elizabeth. 1958. "Modern Moral Philosophy." *Philosophy* 33(124): 1–19.

American Philosophical Association's Statement on the Teaching of Philosophy (APA Statement). 1995. https://www.apaonline.org/page/teaching.

Banaji, Mahzarin and Anthony Greenwald. 2013. *Blindspot: Hidden Biases of Good People*. New York: Random House Publishing.

Berg, Maggie and Barbara Seeber. 2016. *The Slow Professor: Challenging the Culture of Speed in the Academy*. Toronto: University of Toronto Press.

Bickman, Leonard. 1972. "Environmental Attitudes and Actions." *Journal of Social Psychology* 87: 323–24.

Boler, Megan. 1999. *Feeling Power: Emotions and Education*. New York: Routledge.

Booth, Carol. 2009. "A Motivational Turn for Environmental Ethics." *Ethics & The Environment* 14 (1): 53–78.

Braithwaite, John. 2004. "Emancipation and Hope." *Annals of the American Academy of Political and Social Science* 592: 79–98.

Cheavens, Jennifer, Scott Michael, and Charles Snyder. 2005. "The Correlates of Hope: Psychological and Physiological Benefits." In *Interdisciplinary Perspectives on Hope*, edited by Jaklin Eliott, 119–32. Hauppauge: Nova Science Publishers Inc.

Coeckelbergh, Mark. 2015. *Environmental Skill: Motivation, Knowledge, and the Possibility of a Non-Romantic Environmental Ethics*. New York: Routledge.

Colby, Anne, Thomas Ehrich, Elizabeth Beaumont, Jason Stephens. 2003. *Educating Citizens: Preparing America's Undergraduates for Love of Moral and Civic Responsibility*. San Francisco, CA: Jossey-Bass.

Cooper, Tom. 2009. "Learning from Ethicists: How Moral Philosophy is Taught at Leading English-Speaking Institutions." *Teaching Ethics* 10(1): 11–42.

Costanzo, Mark, Dane Archer, Elliott Aronson, Thomas Pettigrew. 1986. "Energy Conservation Behavior: The Difficult Path from Information to Action." *American Psychologist* 41: 521–28.

Finger, Matthias. 1994. "From Knowledge to Action? Exploring the Relationships between Environmental Experiences, Learning, and Behavior." *Journal of Social Issues* 50(3): 141–60.

Freire, Paulo. 2012. *Pedagogy of the Oppressed*. New York: Continuum International.

Frye, Marilyn. 1983. *The Politics of Reality: Essays in Feminist Theory*. Trumansburg: The Crossing Press.

Geller, E.S. 1981. "Evaluating Energy Conservation Programs: Is Verbal Report Enough?" *Journal of Consumer Research* 8: 331–35.

Geller, E.S., J.B. Erickson, and B.A. Buttram. 1983. "Attempts to Promote Residential Water Conservation with Educational, Behavioral and Engineering Strategies." *Population and Environment Behavioral and Social Issues* 6: 96–112.

Goralnik, Lissy and Michael Nelson. 2011. "Forming a Philosophy of Environmental Action: Aldo Leopold, John Muir, and the Importance of Community." *The Journal of Environmental Education* 42(3): 181–92.

Haidt, Jonathan. 2001. "The Emotional Dog and Its Rational Tail: A Social Intuitionist Approach to Moral Judgement." *Psychological Review* 108: 814–34.

Hironimus-Wendt, Robert and Lora Ebert Wallace. 2009. "The Sociological Imagination and Social Responsibility." *Teaching Sociology:* Special Issue on 50 Years of C. Wright Mills and "The Sociological Imagination" 37: 76–88.

Hoffman, Martin. 2000. *Empathy and Moral Development: Implications for Caring and Justice*. New York, NY: Cambridge University Press.

Horton, Keith. 2004. "Aid and Bias." *Inquiry: An Interdisciplinary Journal of Philosophy and the Social Sciences* 47(6): 545–61.

Hsu, S. J. (2004). "The Effects of an Environmental Education Program on Responsible Environmental Behavior and Associated Environmental Literacy Variables in Taiwanese College Students." *The Journal of Environmental Education* 35(2): 37–48.

Hume, David. 2002. *A Treatise of Human Nature*. Edited by David Norton and Mary Norton. New York: Oxford University Press.

Hungerford, Harold and Trudi Volk. 1990. "Changing Learner Behavior Through Environmental Education." *Journal of Environmental Education* 21(3): 8–21.

Johnson, Brett. 2005. "Overcoming 'Doom and Gloom': Empowering Students in Courses on Social Problems, Injustice, and Inequality." *Teaching Sociology* 33: 44–58.

Johnson, Mark. 2014. *Morality for Humans: Ethical Understanding for the Perspective of Cognitive Science*. Chicago: University of Chicago Press.

Kollmuss, Anja and Julian Agyeman. 2002. "Mind the Gap: Why Do People Act Environmentally and What Are the Barriers to Pro-environmental Behavior." *Environmental Education Research* 8(3): 239–60.

Kretz, Lisa. 2012. "Climate Change: Bridging the Theory-Action Gap." *Ethics & the Environment* 17: 9–27.

Kretz, Lisa. 2013. "Hope in Environmental Philosophy." *Journal of Agricultural & Environmental Ethics* 26: 925–44.

Kretz, Lisa. 2014. "Emotional Responsibility and Teaching Ethics: Student Empowerment." *Ethics and Education* 9: 1–16.

Kretz, Lisa. 2015. "Singing Hope's Praises: A Defense of the Virtue of Hope for Environmental Action." In *Ecology, Ethics, and Hope*, edited by Andrew Brei. London: Rowman & Littlefield.

Kretz, Lisa. 2017. "Emotional Solidarity: Ecological Emotional Outlaws Mourning Environmental Loss and Empowering Positive Change." In *Mourning Nature: Hope at the Heart of Ecological Loss and Grief*, edited by Ashlee Cunsolo Willox and Karen Landman. Montréal: McGill-Queen's University Press.

Kretz, Lisa. 2018. "The Oppression of Nonhuman Life: An Analysis Using the Lens of Karen Warren's Work." *Environmental Ethics: An Interdisciplinary Journal Dedicated to the Philosophical Aspects of Environmental Problems* 40: 195–214.

McKenzie-Mohr, Douglas. 2000. "Promoting Sustainable Behavior: An Introduction to Community-Based Social Marketing." *Journal of Social Issues* 56: 543–54.

Plato. 2005. "Protagoras." *Readings in Ancient Greek Philosophy: From Thales to Aristotle*, edited by S. Marc Cohen, Patricia Curd, and C.D.C. Reeve, 154–80. Indianapolis: Hackett Publishing Company.

Railton, Peter. 2014. "The Affective Dog and Its Rational Tale: Intuition and Attunement." *Ethics* 124: 813–59.

Sia, Archibald, Harold Hungerford, and Audrey Tomera 1985/86. "Selected Predictors of Responsible Environmental Behavior: An Analysis." *Journal of Environmental Education* 17: 31–40.

Snyder, C. R. (1995). "Conceptualizing, Measuring, and Nurturing Hope." *Journal of Counseling & Development* 73: 355–60.

Welldon, J.E.C. 1920. *The Nicomachean Ethics of Aristotle*. London: Macmillan and Co.

Paluck, Elizabeth and Donald Green. 2009. "Prejudice Reduction: What Works? A Review and Assessment of Research and Practice." *The Annual Review of Psychology* 60: 339–67.

Zorn, Diane, and Megan Boler. 2007. "Rethinking Emotions and Educational Leadership." *International Journal of Leadership in Education* 10: 137–51.

Section 4

MORAL REASONING: INSTRUCTIONAL METHODS

Dominic P. Scibilia

Alan Preti and Patrick Croskery return to the place of reason within teaching ethics, learning to formulate moral judgments. In chapter 8, Preti lays out an instructional design for a course in applied ethics wherein students become aware of and sharpen moral reasoning skills. Students practice those rational skills in quest of moral judgments concerning both issues of social import and ethical problems arising during their personal and professional lives.

Patrick Croskery, in chapter 9, designs an instructional model with a commitment to learning *good ethical thinking*. He lays out a moral analytical process in which students draw from the Intercollegiate Ethics Bowl to apply ethical theories to cases—the stress is on rational analysis.

In chapter 10, Cara Biasucci complements learning moral reasoning with substantial attention to behavioral ethics. *Ethics Unwrapped* is a digital instructional model that advances interdisciplinary ethics across all academic fields and trades. Biasucci's greater contribution to teaching ethics, arises from her focus on behavioral ethics—engaging students in a careful consideration of why knowing the right thing does not necessarily lead to taking the right action. The final chapter seeks to confirm that human beings do not become moral social agents by reason alone—teaching and learning ethics should involve the whole person.

Chapter 8

Methods for Developing Moral Judgment at the Undergraduate Level

Alan Preti

This chapter discusses the author's experience teaching undergraduate ethics in an introductory applied ethics course. The course is designed to facilitate the development of a set of capacities that will enable students to form reasonable moral judgments concerning both issues of social import and ethical problems they will inevitably encounter in their personal and professional lives; as such, the overarching goal is the development of moral reasoning.

INTRODUCTION

Methods for teaching ethics at the undergraduate level will naturally depend upon a variety of factors, perhaps most importantly, the aims of the instructor—in the language of current practice, course objectives, and outcomes. Is the course an upper level offering in ethical theory for philosophy majors? Is it a general education course emphasizing current social and moral issues? Does the course focus broadly on ethics in the professions, or is it narrowly tailored for students in a specific pre-professional program?

Students in any given course may best be served by outcomes and pedagogical strategies that are not necessarily appropriate for, or effective in, a different sort of course. Once the goals have been established, the instructor is then well-positioned to develop strategies for achieving these ends. With the increasing emphasis on assessment in higher education, it behooves ethics instructors, both novice and experienced, to make explicit their course goals and consider carefully what methods may best facilitate student attainment of these goals.[1]

COURSE BACKGROUND

The author teaches a course entitled *Ethics and Social Values*. The course is one of several applied or practical ethics offerings through which students can fulfill the General Education (GE) curriculum's *Ethics in Action* requirement. The aim of this area of the GE curriculum is to promote the development of capacities bearing on moral reasoning, namely, moral sensitivity or aware-ness; the understanding, evaluation, and application of fundamental ethical concepts, principles, or theories; and the exercise of sound practical judgment in the making of moral decisions.

As a course that treats of both social and individual ethics,[2] the specific goals of this course are to help students (1) develop skill in the analysis and evaluation of arguments associated with controversial issues such as abortion, euthanasia, genetic engineering, capital punishment, immigration, equality and affirmative action, and so on; (2) develop skill in the analysis, evaluation, and application of ethical concepts and perspectives relevant to the issues; and (3) develop an effective decision-making strategy to address ethical problems in their own lives.

The course is divided into three main sections: synopsis of ethical theories (weeks 1–5), current issues (weeks 6–10), and moral decision-making (weeks 11–15). Below is the portion of the syllabus that identifies the course goals and outcomes:

COURSE GOALS AND OUTCOMES

The overarching aim of this course is to help you attain proficiency in rea-soning about important current moral and social issues, in order to develop consistency and clarity in the expression of your own views on these matters. You will also learn how to address ethical problems in your personal and professional lives.

These goals are central to both the aims of the GE curriculum and the College's mission of fostering in all members of the community open and critical minds and the ability to make reasoned moral decisions. Upon suc-cessful completion of the course, you should be able to:

1. Identify and analyze your own core moral beliefs and their sources.
2. Demonstrate an understanding of various current social and moral issues.
3. Demonstrate an understanding of various moral concepts, principles, and theories.

4. Evaluate a variety of various moral concepts, principles, and theories.
5. Apply a variety of moral concepts and perspectives to the issues examined.
6. Apply a moral decision-making strategy to ethical problems or dilemmas.

The course outcomes are based on those identified on the *Ethical Reasoning VALUE Rubric* (see appendix A), an assessment tool used to evaluate student learning in all courses in the *Ethics in Action* area.[3] The rubric describes ethical reasoning as

> reasoning about right and wrong human conduct. It requires students to be able to assess their own ethical values and the social context of problems, recognize ethical issues in a variety of settings, think about how different ethical perspectives might be applied to ethical dilemmas, and consider the ramifications of alternative actions.
>
> Students' ethical self-identity evolves as they practice ethical decision-making skills and learn how to describe and analyze positions on ethical issues. (AAC&U Ethical Reasoning VALUE Rubric)

The rubric references five capacities: Ethical Self-awareness, Understanding Different Ethical Perspectives/Concepts, Ethical Issue Recognition, Application of Ethical Perspectives/Concepts, and Evaluation of Ethical Perspectives/Concepts. Each capacity is tied to the course outcomes identified above as follows:

- Outcome 1: Ethical Self-Awareness
- Outcome 2: Ethical Issue Recognition
- Outcome 3: Understanding Different Ethical Perspectives/Concepts
- Outcome 4: Evaluation of Ethical Perspectives/Concepts
- Outcomes 5 & 6: Application of Ethical Perspectives/Concepts

In the section that follows, various pedagogical methods employed in connection with each of the course outcomes are discussed.

PEDAGOGICAL METHODS

Outcome 1: Ethical Self-Awareness

Ethical self-awareness, for the purposes of this course, concerns the ability to identify core moral beliefs and their origins, as well as how such beliefs influence the moral decision-making process. During the first week of class, a

Moral Orientation Questionnaire is administered in which students are asked to rank the relative importance of each of the following with regard to their moral decisions: self-interest, religious commands, respecting others' rights, being just or fair, consequences for everyone, doing one's duty, personal character, and empathy/compassion. (See appendix B.)

These choices are representative of the theories covered in the first portion of the course: Egoism, Divine Command Theory, Rights Theories, Justice as Fairness, Utilitarianism, Kantian Deontology, Virtue Ethics, and Care Ethics. For the purposes of this exercise, the theories are introduced via simple slogans that students can presumably relate to, namely, "Look out for #1," "Do what the Good Book says," "Be a good person," and so on. The same exercise asks students to describe briefly their approach to making moral decisions.

Administering the questionnaire at the outset provides a cursory introduction to the moral theories as well as a baseline that is consulted at the end of the semester as part of a pre-post assessment.

The exercise typically, and perhaps unsurprisingly, reveals inconsistencies and contradictions in a number of responses. Many students, for example, will rank *consequences for everyone* as the most important factor in the making of moral decisions, while going on in the written portion to identify *self-interest* as the primary consideration when debating the relative merits of various courses of action with moral implications.

Discussing the results of the questionnaire creates an opening for clarifying the nature of moral theories, principles, and judgments, thus setting the stage for the theory portion of the course.

Outcome 2: Ethical Issue Recognition

What makes an issue or situation ethical? How do we determine that there is a moral dimension present, whether in the setting of individual decision-making or the wider social context? How can instructors help students develop what psychologist James Rest referred to as *moral sensitivity*?[4]

Consider any of the controversial issues canvassed in the course. Students may well have opinions on these issues, but they are unlikely to have been informed by honest reflection and careful analysis about what ethics recommends or possibly requires in such cases.

As might be expected, student beliefs and judgments on social issues are more likely the result of a constellation of values shaped by familial upbringing, early education, unconscious biases, and unreflective intuitions or emotional responses—hardly theirs, in any meaningful sense. At this juncture of their lives, they are more likely to be Kohlbergian conventionalists[5] or subjectivists of some type.

But again, why are such issues characterized as ethical? With a little prodding, students typically respond to the question by capturing what perhaps is the most salient point: they are issues that either affect or can potentially affect individuals (in most cases, significant numbers of individuals) in some way or another that bears on their well-being. The adoption of a course of action or a given policy has the potential to directly or indirectly cause harm, promote some interests at the expense of others, perpetuate or redress an injustice, violate someone's rights, and so on.

Through the Socratic exercise of exploring the question *What makes an issue or situation ethical?* students articulate for themselves the conditions for an issue's or situation's having a moral dimension; the concepts and principles that emerge from these initial reflections, however inchoately, will eventually be seen to be central to ethical theory.

Ultimately, however, the aim is not merely that students succeed in identifying the morally relevant features of various situations or problems, but that they will be able to recognize ethical issues when they are presented in a complex, multifaceted context, and can grasp the cross-relationships that are often found among the issues. Presumably, as the course goes on, in-depth examination of the issues and the relevant concepts, principles, and theories will contribute to a developing moral sensitivity.

The development of moral sensitivity can also be approached through methods that elicit affect. For many instructors, the motive for discussing, say, the practice of district redlining is not simply to highlight its discriminatory impact, but to enable students to literally feel the injustice by imagining themselves as victims of the practice.

Similarly, in covering world hunger and poverty, an instructor can do more than cite statistics, explore root causes, and present the relevant moral arguments; she can also have students assume the perspective of an individual lacking even the most basic of needs to address the complacency that comes from living in one of the wealthiest nations on the planet. Each of the issues covered in a social ethics course is laden with affective significance, and thus particularly well-suited for inducing empathic and emotional response.

A variety of approaches can be used to elicit affect when covering social issues. The fine arts and literature, for example, are common catalysts for empathic and emotional cultivation; film, paintings, fictive and nonfictive narrative, poetry, music, and even the plastic arts can assist in the cultivation of feelings and emotion.[6]

A simple and perhaps obvious case is the use of poignant and disturbing images that immediately capture attention, drawing the student into the world and experience of the subject. *Frontline*'s 2004 documentary *Ghosts of*

Rwanda, for example, succeeds to a much greater extent in this regard than a textbook account of the genocide. Screening this film inevitably makes for a highly charged experience wherein students sit in stone silence afterward; a slow and deliberate debriefing is necessary before discussion can ensue.

The author does not intend to suggest that emotional response is determinative of moral value; indeed, simple subjectivism is canvassed early in the course and found wanting. Nor is it claimed that empathy is necessary for morality. The point is rather that appropriate emotional response is an important dimension of mature moral judgment, and methods for cultivating such responses are not out of place in courses treating of social and moral issues. Minimally, pedagogies eliciting affect often serve well to spark discussion when students might otherwise be disinclined to engage.

Outcome 3: Understanding Different Ethical Perspectives/Concepts

Having completed a general overview of the fundamental concepts and principles that will occupy the class for the rest of the semester, students are next introduced to the relevant moral theories. Note that *ethical perspectives/ concepts* is ambiguous with regard to moral theory; this outcome (as well as outcomes 4, 5, and 6) can certainly be addressed without reference to traditional moral theory.

Indeed, many ethics instructors eschew moral theory entirely in favor of teaching decision-making procedures in order to get right to the business of addressing ethical problems via case analysis (see, for example, Davis 2009 and 2011). There is nothing in principle that mitigates against doing both, as, in fact, is done in this course; the extent to which an approach is implemented depends in part on time constraints, course-related objectives (as noted above), personal predilection, and other factors.

While the relative merits of teaching moral theory in applied ethics courses are contested (sometimes hotly; see C. E. Harris 2009a, 2009b, and Davis 2009),[7] the author unapologetically adopts this approach because he believes it important that students are exposed, however minimally, to the arguments proffered on behalf of the theories by the respective philosophers with whom they are associated.

As the course is offered through the philosophy department at a liberal arts institution, and as the course may well be the only one in which students get a taste of philosophy and its methods, the author is motivated by a self-imposed obligation to provide at least an entrée into the classics and the minds of those important thinkers who produced them.

Each theory is introduced, along with some historical background, and students read excerpts from the relevant philosophers. For each reading, they respond to a series of questions typical of those found in introductory texts which serve as discussion prompts: What is Mill's argument that some pleasures are more valuable than others? Is he right? What does Kant mean by a *good will*? According to Aristotle, what is the aim of all human activity? Do you agree? Why or why not? And so on.

A little role play can be helpful: "You are J.S. Mill. The President of the United States seeks your advice on a policy that would improve the lives of most citizens while negatively impacting a minority group. How do you respond?" A bit simplistic, perhaps. But this type of active exercise is likely to be more effective than the instructor's simply providing the example and moving on.

Of course, creativity on the part of the instructor helps, and such exercises are most effective when implemented regularly and methodically; the more opportunities for students to take an active role in their learning, the more likely it is that learning is taking place.

Concerning this outcome, students are ultimately expected to be able to (1) identify the philosopher(s) responsible for generating a specific theory, (2) identify the fundamental principle of the theory, and (3) explain the theory in some detail.

Outcome 4: Evaluation of Ethical Perspectives/Concepts

The aim of this outcome is to have students identify the assumptions and implications of a given theory or perspective, identify objections, and reasonably defend a theory against such objections. The following criteria are advanced as relevant considerations: (1) consistency with considered moral judgments, (2) consistency with moral experiences, (3) usefulness in moral problem solving (Vaughn 2016, 73–76).

A typical strategy is to have students respond to those commonplace (and by now cliché) scenarios that starkly illustrate various sticking points, whether generated internally or jointly: ticking time bombs, trolley problems, sinking lifeboats, the framing of innocents, and so on. While such scenarios have been mined extensively by ethicists (some might say excessively: witness the seemingly perpetual generation of new iterations of the trolley problem), they remain valuable for how well they reveal the theoretic tensions.

Once the standard objections have been identified (e.g., for utilitarianism: no-rest objection, potential to violate rights or norms of justice, limitations on calculating utility and foreseeing consequences, etc.), students are encouraged to think of at least one possible response to each of the objections (e.g., for utilitarianism's conflict with rights: the *bite the bullet* strategy that emphasizes the importance of the omelet at the expense of the broken eggs).

One particular exercise concerning relativism has students assume the position of an anthropologist and cultural relativist who is observing two cultures: one, a pacifist culture whose members believe that it is morally impermissible to commit a violent act against another human being for any reason, and two, a militaristic slaveholding culture whose members believe that it is morally permissible to invade other cultures and subjugate and enslave their members.

Students are invited to consider what, as the relativist observer, they may consistently maintain about the moralities of both cultures if the second culture invades the first (i.e., can either be criticized or condemned? Are there any obligations to interfere with the invasion?). Several variations of the scenario are examined, and when all is said and done, the inconsistencies of relativism are laid bare.

One of the potential consequences of presenting the theories and objections in the manner described is what Christopher Meyers has called the *roller coaster effect* (Meyers 2018, 32)—once the various objections have been raised against each theory (and regardless of how successful any responses may be), students are left wondering what the point is: if such and such a theory has morally unacceptable implications or faces seemingly insurmountable obstacles, isn't ethics up for grabs?

The experience might only encourage students to embrace subjectivism or relativism (notwithstanding that both have been shown to be particularly problematic), if not complete skepticism about ethics. One way to mitigate this confusion or sense of futility is to emphasize that each theory captures something important about our moral lives (a fact that should be *prima facie* evident), and while none may have *the* answer (despite its original proponent's intentions), together they provide us with the basis for both gaining some clarity on what is at stake in the wider social issues and for a method that can be used to address moral problems—the decision-making model that is introduced in the final portion of the course.

Outcomes 5 & 6: Application of Ethical Perspectives/Concepts.

The application of ethical perspectives or concepts concerns both social issues (outcome 5) and individual decision-making (outcome 6). Regarding the former, the aim is for students to demonstrate how a specific theory can be brought to bear on the issues examined. This is accomplished through two strategies: (1) the application of fundamental principles to a given situation either directly (*the Egoist, Utilitarian, Kantian, Natural Law theorist, etc. would say . . ..*) or by way of their serving as premises in a moral argument (the so-called *top-down* method) and (2) case study analysis (one of several so-called *bottom-up* methods).

The first has fallen out of favor with many ethicists, as its shortcomings are evident: theories' fundamental principles are usually too general to be of help with any but the most general of issues (on which there tends to be wide-ranging agreement anyway). Nevertheless, the direct application of a principle to a concrete situation is a straightforward way of demonstrating a connection between theory and practice. Additionally, understanding how moral arguments work and the ability to construct them on the basis of the conceptual tools that moral theory provides is useful both for students' appreciation of such arguments and the development of analytical skill.

Assignments in which students are to make the case for a particular position on the moral permissibility or impermissibility of X on various theoretical grounds serve in this capacity (e.g., *develop an argument on consequential/ nonconsequential grounds for the moral permissibility/impermissibility of capital punishment*).

Working from the ground up via case study analysis is another valuable method for exploring moral issues and applying theory. Cases can be used to highlight particular moral dilemmas, identify governing principles or rules, stimulate moral imagination, and elicit affective response.

Students typically find case study analysis more interesting and accessible than the more abstract top-down method, particularly when the cases are drawn from contemporary issues relevant to their experience (e.g., the NFL Racial Justice protests, the #MeToo movement). The ultimate aim is to have students become adept at identifying the morally relevant features of the case, indicating which principles are best suited to guiding deliberation on the case, and justifying their position on what ethics recommends or requires regarding the case.

With respect to individual decision-making, a model is utilized for determining the best moral reasons for pursuing a course of action. In recent years, moral decision-making models have proliferated as methods for addressing ethical problems. One of the attractive features of such models is that they integrate the fundamental principles of ethical theory in an intuitive fashion that brings down to earth the ethereal abstractions that students typically struggle with in the theory portion of the course.

In addition, the models explicitly affirm the importance of those principles while denying them the universality claimed on behalf of their classical proponents. In this sense, the moral decision-making model can be said to have its roots in John Dewey's view of ethics as inquiry, namely, that ethics is to be understood as a process of inquiry that seeks to discover the most satisfactory plan of action in the particular, concrete situations in which humans find themselves.[8]

Students are introduced to Dewey's view as a way of setting up the
model. For Dewey, inquiry in ethics is no different than inquiry in other
domains in which solutions are sought to problems; here, the paradigm is
the scientific method, which as a process begins in a condition of uncertainty and ends in a state of equilibrium in which all doubt or ambiguity
has been eliminated.

In broad outlines, initial awareness of a problem prompts a desire to
identify the specific nature of the problem; the problem having been
defined, tentative hypotheses are proposed as possible solutions, implications of the hypotheses are worked out, and the most promising hypothesis is tested in experiment or direct action. The restoration of equilibrium
or harmony serves as a confirmation of the hypothesis; the problematic
situation is resolved.[9]

Such an account acknowledges that the moral life is multidimensional and
messy, and consequently ill-served by the attempt to identify a single and
universal normative principle or set of rules to guide human action within a
uniquely moral domain separate in quality from, and requiring a distinctive
mode of analysis than, the diverse dimensions of human experience.

For Dewey, the claim that one has identified a priori a universal standard of
conduct—whether that of utility, the Categorical Imperative, what the virtuous person would do, and so on—presumes that goods and ends are fixed and
all that need be done is discover what the proposed principle or rule requires.
Such a project has been built upon a narrow circumscription of moral experience that ignores the genuine uncertainty of morally problematic situations
and the possibility that in any such situation there can be (and often are)
plural, competing goods (Dewey 1998 [1930], 315).[10]

All this is not to deny the usefulness of moral principles or rules of conduct; having emerged over the course of history from reflection on human
needs and aspirations, they are indispensable tools for guiding moral inquiry.
Each furnishes us with a point of view from which to appreciate what is at
stake, consider competing demands, foresee how various acts will affect the
interests of all concerned, and determine which action best suits the occasion.
Moral principles thus illuminate rather than dictate.

By introducing Dewey's account of ethics as moral inquiry, and demonstrating how the various principles covered in the theoretical portion of the
course can be brought to bear in very specific ways in solving ethical problems, students can be reassured that the earlier foray into ethical theory has
not been in vain.

Moral decision-making models, however else they might differ, share a similar
framework which consists in becoming aware that a moral problem exists, gathering the relevant facts, identifying alternative courses of action, identifying all

those who would be affected by the decision and how, weighing the alternatives, and choosing the alternative most warranted, all things considered. In the course under discussion, the model takes the following form.

A MORAL DECISION-MAKING MODEL[11]

(See appendix C—A Capstone Assessment Model)

1. Identify the specific problem: the initial identification of the problem, of course, is contingent on a modicum of moral awareness or sensitivity. However deficient students may have been in this regard at the beginning of the course, by this point they should (one would expect) be well-positioned to recognize the various relevant moral features of a given situation and formulate the problem in precise terms.
2. Gather the facts: fact gathering is crucial, as the facts bear on whether the problem is actually one of the moral concerns and, if so, serve to increase the likelihood of an accurate framing of the problem. Of course, it is not only the known facts that are relevant but other facts which, if known, would help frame the issue and guide deliberation. Students are thus encouraged to reflect on both the facts that are known and to consider what unknown facts would be relevant in this connection.
3. Identify all those who may be impacted by the decision: it is important that both primary and secondary stakeholders are considered; it is all too easy to identify the primary stakeholders and thereby narrowly limit the deliberative process. Discussion about all stakeholders can be eye-opening for students, who may not be prone to considering the wider context and scope of individual decision-making.
4. Identify various courses of action: in most cases, this requires more than a simple choice between two alternatives. Students are encouraged to think outside of the proverbial box, with a view to considering creative options that may not be evident at first.
5. Weigh the alternative courses of action based on (1) consequences, (2) deontological principles, and (3) implications for character: the deliberation in connection with this step is what Dewey called *dramatic rehearsal*, and what has been referred to as moral imagination (see Preti 2018, 157–59). While it might be maintained that the entire decision-making process involves the exercise of the moral imagination, this stage is the one which most explicitly consists in an imaginative simulation of the impact of various lines of action on all stakeholders.

6. Determine which action is most warranted: Deliberation ends with the determination of the best available choice, all things considered. In some cases, one set of the criteria identified in Step 5 will be of most obvious relevance, while in others equally powerful considerations will obtain between at least two, and sometimes all three, sets. Ultimately, there will be a point at which the balance falls in one direction, and the decision is made.

It should be noted that the model is not intended as an inflexible decision-procedure, with each step to be executed consecutively in rote fashion; rather, it distills the stages of a fluid deliberative process in which stages can overlap or merge into one another with no clearly defined boundary. Depending on the circumstances, awareness of the problem may precede the identification of relevant facts or it may emerge as facts are gathered; consideration of the alternatives for action may lead to a revisiting of the facts or to a deeper understanding of what is at stake, and so on.

Questions accompanying each step serve as prompts for students to think creatively about alternative solutions and how they might be implemented conscientiously, with post-decision reflection clarifying further the extent to which the action was called for under the circumstances, how attentively it was carried out, and how well it addressed the problem. Granted, unless students are guided through the process thoughtfully and repeatedly, such models can become sterile heuristics; nevertheless, the author has found their potential for assisting in the development of skill in individual moral decision-making invaluable.

ASSESSMENT

Assessment has become part of the institutional fabric of higher education. For better or worse (and there are strident voices on both sides), assessment is here to stay. And while there is a danger that excessive emphasis on assessment—particularly on quantitative methods, which may be of dubious value for ethics courses—may to lead to unrealistic expectations about what it can accomplish, there is little doubt that if approached sincerely and thoughtfully, it can be of great value to educators and their students.

The best teachers have always taken stock of their aims, methods, successes, and failures, making adjustments to their approach as deemed appropriate. Formal assessment strategies can serve to assist them in being more deliberate about the process. In making goals, objectives, and outcomes explicit, specific assignments and pedagogical methods suggest themselves, are experimented with, improved upon, rejected and replaced, all with a view to ensuring as much as possible that students are learning what the instructor wants them to learn.

It was noted earlier that the five assessment criteria for the course discussed in this chapter, namely, Ethical Self-Awareness, Ethical Issue Recognition, Understanding Different Ethical Perspectives/Concepts, Evaluation of Ethical Perspectives/Concepts, and Application of Ethical Perspectives/Concepts are assessed via the AAC&U's *Ethical Reasoning VALUE Rubric.*

There are three levels associated with each of the criteria: benchmark, milestones (itself divided into two levels), and capstone. The levels indicate the degree to which students have met the conditions for each of the criteria. Upon completion of the course, student artifacts are measured against the different levels, and student learning is evaluated accordingly. The results are reported in a standard template together with the faculty member's reflections on the results. Below is the assessment reporting template used for the course:

GENERAL EDUCATION REPORTING TEMPLATE

General Education (GE) requirement area: *Ethics in Action*
Course name/designation: *PHI 0272 Ethics and Social Values*
Semester/year:
Instructor:

1. For each of the objectives below from the rubric governing the GE skill area your course addressed, describe the assignments you gave to teach the students how to master the competencies. (If one assignment covered more than one competency, be sure to explain how. Be prepared to share those assignments with the All-College Assessment Committee, if requested.)
2. What assessment tool did you use to draw *final conclusions* about how well the students mastered each of the competencies? Check all that apply:
   Final paper _____ Final exam _____ Final project_____ Final Presentation_____
   Other (please describe) _____
   (Please include a copy of the instructions sheet or test copy with this template.)
3. What are your conclusions about how well the students learned the General Education criteria? Please describe how you reached those conclusions and supply any other supporting evidence or additional documentation, if necessary.

4. What improvements to the course and its assignments are indicated by the assessment results referred to above? Does the evidence reveal any problems with any specific areas of student learning that should be addressed in future classes?
5. Please provide any other information that you feel is pertinent for understanding the results you observed.

CONCLUSION

As suggested at the outset, the variety of settings and contexts of ethics instruction at the undergraduate level renders it unfeasible to identify a single overarching goal as the ultimate aim of teaching ethics. At the same time, regardless of any other disagreements they may have concerning content and methodology (and there are many), those teaching courses in applied, practical, or professional ethics view the development of skill in addressing moral problems as being of central importance.

How *addressing moral problems* is understood itself depends on various factors, but minimally would seem to include a cluster of related capacities, namely, moral awareness or sensitivity, an understanding of fundamental moral concepts and principles, and skill in moral reasoning or practical judgment. Such capacities can be clarified and further specified through a set of outcomes that serve to indicate success in achieving the stated objectives.

An assessment process is an important means for determining the extent to which such objectives are being met, and for suggesting improvement in course design or pedagogical practices when they are not being met. The author has provided an example of how these elements function in a course on social issues that includes a component on individual moral decision-making. It is hoped that there is something of value in these reflections for both novice and experienced instructors alike.

NOTES

1. The rise of outcomes assessment throughout higher education has precipitated a significant amount of reflection on the goals and objectives of teaching ethics. For an account of common goals and outcomes assessment in "Ethics across the Curriculum" initiatives, see Newton (2001) and Ozar (2018). See Keefer and Davis (2012) for a discussion of outcomes assessment specifically in connection with the teaching of professional ethics.

2. The distinction here is between issues that concern human relations and public policy and those that concern moral decision-making in the context of one's personal and professional life.

3. The Ethical Reasoning Rubric was developed as part of the American Association of Colleges and Universities' (AAC&U) Liberal Education and America's Promise (LEAP) initiative, inaugurated in 2005. "Ethical Reasoning and Action" is included under the broader heading of Personal and Social Responsibility, one of four "essential learning outcomes" for liberal arts education in the "new global century." See Corrigan et al. (2007).

4. Moral sensitivity is the first of four psychological processes in Rest's "Four Component Model of Moral Action," a theoretical account used to explain moral action. The other components are moral judgment, moral motivation, and moral character. See Rest (1986).

5. The psychologist Lawrence Kohlberg identified three stages of moral development, each consisting of two levels, which he believed to be universal among humans. According to Kohlberg, moral reasoning at the conventional level is characterized by the desire to conform to authority and social expectations. See Kohlberg (1984).

6. Martha Nussbaum, for example, has argued at length that the arts (particularly literature) play a crucial role in the development of powers of sympathetic imagination, which she views as a necessary condition for empathy and compassion directed toward individuals and groups whose voices might not otherwise be heard. See Nussbaum (1997, 2010). In a similar fashion, the educational theorist David Carr advocates for the arts as a way of opening pathways to a refinement of one's moral sensibilities, conceiving of moral formation as "an education of the heart as well as the head" (2005, 150). See Boylan et al. for a cross-institutional project implementing fictive narrative in philosophy and ethics courses. Ackerman's contribution in particular speaks to the role of narrative in generating empathy (Boylan et al. 2011, 65–69).

7. This initial debate in the journal *Teaching Ethics* 10, no. 1, led to a spirited exchange among Davis, Harris, and Bernard Gert in a subsequent issue; see *Teaching Ethics* 12, no. 1 (2011). See Englehardt and Pritchard (2018) for additional reflections on the matter.

8. See Preti (2018), where it is argued that the aims of contemporary applied or practical ethics and some of its methodological approaches are indebted to Dewey's view of ethics as inquiry.

9. Dewey's account of inquiry, developed over a number of years throughout a number of his writings, is fully elaborated in his *Logic: The Theory of Inquiry* (1938).

10. It should be noted that exceptions to Dewey's generalization that all moral theories posit a single normative principle can be found in several Scottish Enlightenment philosophers. The nineteenth-century British intuitionist William Whewell and utilitarian Henry Sidgwick also serve as counterexamples.

11. This decision-making model is an amalgam of one found in Hartman et al. (2018, 90–91) and one developed by faculty at Santa Clara University for the Markkula Center for Applied Ethics

(www.scu.edu/ethics/ethics-resources/ethical-decision-making, accessed May 1, 2019).

REFERENCES

Boylan, Michael, F. Nimue Ackerman, G. Palmer-Fernandez, S. Cook Anderson, and E. Spence. 2011. "Using Fictive Narrative to Teach Ethics/Philosophy." *Teaching Ethics* 12, no. 1: 61–94.

Carr, David. 2005. "On the Contribution of Literature and the Arts to the Educational Cultivation of Moral Virtue, Feeling and Emotion." *Journal of Moral Education* 34, no. 2: 137–151.

Corrigan, Robert, R. Crutcher, P. O'Brien, and C. Geary Schneider. 2007. "College Learning for the New Global Century: A Report from the LEAP National Leadership Council." Washington, DC: The American Association for Colleges and Universities. https://www.aacu.org/sites/default/files/files/LEAP/GlobalCent ury_final.pdf. Accessed Jan. 31, 2019.

Davis, Michael. 2009. "The Usefulness of Moral Theory in Practical Ethics: A Question of Comparative Cost." *Teaching Ethics* 10, no. 1: 69–78.

———. 2011. "The Usefulness of Moral Theory in Teaching Practical Ethics: A Reply to Gert and Harris." *Teaching Ethics* 12, no. 1: 51–60.

Dewey, John. 1938. *Logic: The Theory of Inquiry.* New York: Henry Holt and Co.

———. 1998 [1930]. "Three Independent Factors in Morals." In *The Essential Dewey, v. 2: Ethics, Logic, Psychology,* edited by Larry Hickman and Thomas Alexander, 315–20. Bloomington: Indiana University Press.

Englehardt, Elaine, and Michael Pritchard. 2018. "Teaching Practical Ethics." In *Ethics Across the Curriculum – Pedagogical Perspectives,* edited by Elaine Englehardt and Michael Pritchard, 117–30. Cham, Switzerland: Springer.

Gert, Bernard. 2011. "The Usefulness of a Comprehensive Systematic Moral Theory." *Teaching Ethics* 12, no. 1: 25–38.

Harris, C.E. 2009a. "Is Moral Theory Useful in Practical Ethics?" *Teaching Ethics* 10, no. 1: 51–68.

———. 2009b. "Response to Michael Davis: The Cost is Minimal and Worth it." *Teaching Ethics* 10, no. 1: 79–86.

———. 2011. "A Reply to Bernard Gert." *Teaching Ethics* 12, no. 1: 39–49.

Hartman, Laura, J. DesJardins, and C. MacDonald. 2018. *Business Ethics: Decision-Making for Personal Integrity and Social Responsibility,* 4th edition. New York: McGraw-Hill.

Keefer, Matthew, and Michael Davis. 2012. "Curricular Design and Assessment in Professional Ethics." *Teaching Ethics* 13, no. 1: 81–90.

Kohlberg, Lawrence. 1984. *The Psychology of Moral Development: The Nature and Validity of Moral Stages. Essays on Moral Development vol. 2.* San Francisco: Harper & Row.

Myers, Christopher. 2018. "Ethics Theory and Ethics Practice." In *Ethics Across the Curriculum – Pedagogical Perspectives*, edited by Elaine Englehardt and Michael Pritchard, 131–45. Cham, Switzerland: Springer.

Newton, Lisa. 2001. "Outcomes Assessment of an Ethics Program." *Teaching Ethics* 2, no. 1: 29–67.

Nussbaum, Martha. 1997. *Cultivating Humanity: A Classical Defense of Reform in Liberal Education*. Cambridge, MA: Harvard University Press.

Nussbaum, Martha. 2010. *Not for Profit: Why Democracy Needs the Humanities*. Princeton: Princeton University Press.

Ozar, David. 2018. "Identifying Learning Outcomes and Assessing Ethics Across the Curriculum Programs." In *Ethics Across the Curriculum – Pedagogical Perspectives*, edited by Elaine Englehardt and Michael Pritchard, 55–72. Cham, Switzerland: Springer.

Preti, Alan A. 2018. "Developing Habits of Moral Reflection: Dewey, Moral Inquiry, and Practical Ethics." In *Ethics Across the Curriculum – Pedagogical Perspectives*, edited by Elaine Englehardt and Michael Pritchard, 147–64. Cham, Switzerland: Springer.

Rest, James. 1986. *Moral Development: Advances in Research and Theory*. New York. Praeger Vaughn, Lewis. 2016. *Doing Ethics: Moral Reasoning and Contemporary Issues*, 4th edition. New York: Norton.

APPENDIX A

Ethical Reasoning Value Rubric

The VALUE rubrics were developed by teams of faculty experts representing colleges and universities across the United States through a process that examined many existing campus rubrics and related documents for each learning outcome and incorporated additional feedback from faculty. The rubrics articulate fundamental criteria for each learning outcome, with performance descriptors demonstrating progressively more sophisticated levels of attainment. The rubrics are intended for institutional-level use in evaluating and discussing student learning, not for grading. The core expectations articulated in all fifteen of the VALUE rubrics can and should be translated into the language of individual campuses, disciplines, and even courses. The utility of the VALUE rubrics is to position learning at all undergraduate levels within a basic framework of expectations such that evidence of learning can be shared nationally through a common dialog and understanding of student success.

Definition

Ethical Reasoning is reasoning about right and wrong human conduct. It requires students to be able to assess their own ethical values and the social context of problems, recognize ethical issues in a variety of settings, think about how different ethical perspectives might be applied to ethical dilemmas, and consider the ramifications of alternative actions. Students' ethical self-identity evolves as they practice ethical decision-making skills and learn how to describe and analyze positions on ethical issues.

Framing Language

This rubric is intended to help faculty evaluate work samples and collections of work that demonstrate student learning about ethics. Although the goal of a liberal education should be to help students turn what they've learned in the classroom into action, pragmatically it would be difficult, if not impossible, to judge whether or not students would act ethically when faced with real ethical situations. What can be evaluated using a rubric is whether students have the intellectual tools to make ethical choices.

The rubric focuses on five elements: Ethical Self Awareness, Ethical Issue Recognition, Understanding Different Ethical Perspectives/Concepts, Application of Ethical Principles, and Evaluation of Different Ethical Perspectives/Concepts. Students' Ethical Self Identity evolves as they practice ethical decision-making skills and learn how to describe and analyze positions on ethical issues. Presumably, they will choose ethical actions when faced with ethical issues.

Glossary

The definitions that follow were developed to clarify terms and concepts used in this rubric only.

Core Beliefs: Those fundamental principles that consciously or unconsciously influence one's ethical conduct and ethical thinking. Even when unacknowledged, core beliefs shape one's responses. Core beliefs can reflect one's environment, religion, culture or training. A person may or may not choose to act on their core beliefs.

Ethical Perspectives/concepts: The different theoretical means through which ethical issues are analyzed, such as ethical theories (e.g., utilitarian, natural law, virtue) or ethical concepts (e.g., rights, justice, duty).

Complex, multilayered (gray) context: The subparts or situational conditions of a scenario that bring two or more ethical dilemmas (issues) into the mix/problem/context/for student's identification.

Cross-relationships among the issues: Obvious or subtle connections between/among the subparts or situational conditions of the issues present in a scenario (e.g., relationship of production of corn as part of climate change issue) (table 8.1).

Table 8.1 Ethical Reasoning Value Rubric

	Capstone 4	Milestones 3	Milestones 2	Benchmark 1
Ethical Self-Awareness	Student discusses in detail/analyzes both core beliefs and the origins of the core beliefs and discussion has greater depth and clarity.	Student discusses in detail/analyzes both core beliefs and the origins of the core beliefs.	Student states both core beliefs and the origins of the core beliefs.	Student states either their core beliefs or articulates the origins of the core beliefs but not both.
Understanding Different Ethical Perspectives/Concepts	Student names the theory or theories, can present the gist of said theory or theories, and accurately explains the details of the theory or theories used.	Student can name the major theory or theories she/he uses, can present the gist of said theory or theories, and attempts to explain the details of the theory or theories used, but has some inaccuracies.	Student can name the major theory she/he uses, and is only able to present the gist of the named theory.	Student only names the major theory she/he uses.
Ethical Issue Recognition	Student can recognize ethical issues when presented in a complex, multilayered (gray) context AND can recognize cross-relationships among the issues.	Student can recognize ethical issues when issues are presented in a complex, multilayered (gray) context OR can grasp cross-relationships among the issues.	Student can recognize basic and obvious ethical issues and grasp (incompletely) the complexities or interrelationships among the issues.	Student can recognize basic and obvious ethical issues but fails to grasp complexity or interrelationships.
Application of Ethical Perspectives/Concepts	Student can independently apply ethical perspectives/concepts to an ethical question, accurately, and is able to consider full implications of the application.	Student can independently (to a new example) apply ethical perspectives/concepts to an ethical question, accurately, but does not consider the specific implications of application.	Student can apply ethical perspectives/concepts to an ethical question, independently (to a new example) and the application is inaccurate.	Student can apply ethical perspectives/concepts to an ethical question with support (using examples, in a class, in a group, or a fixed-choice setting) but is unable to apply ethical perspectives/concepts independently (to a new example.).

(Continued)

Table 8.1 **Ethical Reasoning Value Rubric** (Continued)

	Capstone 4	Milestones 3	Milestones 2	Benchmark 1
Evaluation of Different Ethical Perspectives/ Concepts	Student states a position and can state the objections to, assumptions and implications of and can reasonably defend against the objections to, assumptions and implications of different ethical perspectives/ concepts, and the student's defense is adequate and effective.	Student states a position and can state the objections to, assumptions and implications of, and respond to the objections to, assumptions and implications of different ethical perspectives/ concepts, but the student's response is inadequate.	Student states a position and can state the objections to, assumptions and implications of different ethical perspectives/ concepts but does not respond to them (and ultimately objections, assumptions, and implications are compartmentalized by student and do not affect student's position.)	Student states a position but cannot state the objections to and assumptions and limitations of the different perspectives/ concepts.

Definition

Ethical Reasoning is reasoning about right and wrong human conduct. It requires students to be able to assess their own ethical values and the social context of problems, recognize ethical issues in a variety of settings, think about how different ethical perspectives might be applied to ethical dilemmas, and consider the ramifications of alternative actions. Students' ethical self-identity evolves as they practice ethical decision-making skills and learn how to describe and analyze positions on ethical issues.

Evaluators are encouraged to assign a zero to any work sample or collection of work that does not meet benchmark (cell one) level performance.

Note: For more information, please contact value@aacu.org

Your Initial Moral Orientation					
How important are each of the following in your life?					
	Extremely	Very	Average	Little	Not at all
Religious Commands					
Conscience					
Self-interest					
Doing what duty demands					
Empathy/Compassion					
Respecting people's rights					
Consequences for everyone					
Being just or fair					
Personal virtues					

In a brief paragraph, please describe how you approach making a moral decision.

_____

_____

_____

_____

_____

Figure 8.1   Administering the moral orientation questionnaire at the start of the course provides a quick overview of moral theories and a baseline for a pre-post assessment. *Source:* Author Alan Preti Product.

APPENDIX B—MORAL ORIENTATION QUESTIONNAIRE*

---

*Adapted from a model developed by Lawrence Hinman. Original Source: http://ethicsupdates.net/index.shtml

APPENDIX C—CAPSTONE ASSESSMENT EXAMPLE

As part of a final examination constituting the capstone assessment piece for the course, students are invited to apply the moral decision-making model introduced in the course to a set of case scenarios. One such example is as follows:

Soon after having taken a course on ethics and social values, you became very interested and involved with the workers' rights of the custodians and gardeners on the college campus. Recently you discovered that the school has increased the cost of the workers' premium and copayments for their health insurance. Now you work for a small local newspaper and think that if you write an article on the insurance cost increases, it might gain the attention of the college administrators who could help the workers' case. However, with the facts and interviews that you have been able to collect, you don't believe the story will be able to persuade those you need to reach. But if you portray a composite character as a real person, estimating her salary and the devastating effect these price hikes would have, you believe your article will have the necessary strength to make an impact. Your actions are not intended to garner praise for yourself; you merely want to help the workers obtain what you believe is their due. Is it ethical for you to employ such tactics?*

Use the ethical decision-making model below to determine what you should do. Answer all questions in as much detail as possible.

1. Define the problem/Identify the specific ethical issue: What is the action or inaction that is the cause for concern?
2. Gather the facts: Do I know enough to make a decision? What facts are not known? Can I learn more about the situation?
4. Identify the stakeholders: Who is affected by the decision?
5. Identify alternative options for acting. Are there any creative options?
6. Weigh the alternative courses of action based on (1) consequences, (2) deontological principles, and (3) implications for character.
7. All things considered, which is the most ethical option for addressing the situation?
8. If I told someone I respect—or told a television audience—which option I have chosen, what would they say?
9. How can my decision be implemented with the greatest care and attention to the concerns of all stakeholders?
10. How did my decision turn out and what have I learned from this specific situation?

---

*Adapted from a scenario developed by the Santa Clara University Markkula Center for Applied Ethics (https://www.scu.edu/ethics/ethics-resources/ethics-cases/).

Chapter 9

Using an Ethics Bowl Competition in the Classroom to Teach Ethical Theory

Patrick Croskery

There are many ways to use the Ethics Bowl productively in the classroom. Here the focus will be on using cases of the Ethics Bowl to help students improve their skills applying ethical theory to cases. Intercollegiate Ethics Bowl (IEB) cases are ideal for this purpose because they have been specifically written to provide a rich foundation for analysis.

INTRODUCTION

The IEB is an activity, sponsored by the Association for Practical and Professional Ethics (APPE), in which teams of students are given cases on a variety of ethical topics. The teams spend several months analyzing the cases, then compete in regional bowls across the country. In the competitions, judges with ethical experience in academia and the broader society evaluate the teams' analyses of ethical topics.

The judges typically evaluate the teams using four criteria: whether the presentation is clear and systematic, whether it avoids irrelevancies, whether it discusses the central moral dimensions of the case, and whether it considers different viewpoints. The top teams from each region compete in a national championship at the APPE annual conference.

Although this discussion makes use of a particular approach to teaching ethical theories called the *tri-level model* developed by Mark Dixon and Patrick Croskery, the suggestions made here can be readily adjusted for any of a variety of ways of using ethical theories. The tri-level model starts with the familiar division of ethical traditions into the consequentialist, deontological, and virtue-theoretic. On this model, each theory is applied on a *first-pass basis* to a different level of analysis. Consequentialism is applied at the institutional level, deontology at the role level, and virtue-theory at the individual level.

The institutional level is *a big picture* perspective, asking what results will follow over the long-term if institutional structures are critically considered. The role level is more intermediate. It takes as given the roles participants have agreed to and asks what the implications are for taking the responsibilities of those roles to others seriously. The individual level is more personal, looking at the particularities of the context, including one's character and the specifics of the relationships they are engaged in.

The course design calls for each theory to be explored separately as students move from the most abstract understanding of a theory to the most concrete exploration of how it relates to a topic that shows up in everyday life. Topics and arguments are selected with care so that the theory they are exploring at that point has meaningful things to say about the subject they are discussing.

LOGISTICS

At the start of the term, students are provided with a selection of IEB cases, typically the most recent set of championship or regional playoff cases (https ://appe-ethics.org/cases-rules-and-guidelines/). The students rank the cases in terms of their interest in the topic (they will be working on the cases all term). Then they are each assigned to a team. Each team of four players is assigned four cases, with each member of the team *taking the lead* on one case.

At the end of each section of the class, when the students have been using the theory in question for a while, they are given the assignment to analyze the ethics bowl case they took the lead on using the ethical theory the class has covered. They then meet in the teams and compare analyses. Because the students are responsible for the quality of the ethics bowl analysis for all four cases, they have a strong incentive to improve each other's understanding of the ethical theory. Because they are analyzing different cases, they must utilize the resources that theory makes available.

Toward the end of the term, the participants have worked with all three ethical theories. At this point the students must determine how their overall ethics bowl analyses will integrate the considerations raised by each theory. At this point the criteria used in the evaluation of IEB presentations are relevant. (The full criteria are accessible here: http://appe-ethics.org/wp-content /uploads/2017/05/2017-2018-Judges_Guidelines.pdf)

Thus, some of the considerations raised by the theories help the team "clearly identify and thoroughly discuss the central moral dimensions of the case" as highlighted in criterion 2. Others help the team "indicate both awareness and thoughtful consideration of different viewpoints, including especially those that would loom large in the reasoning of individuals who disagree with team's position" as found in criterion 3.

Even though the IEB criteria are not formally evaluated as Learning Objectives (LO) for assessment purposes, there are several ways of using them in this fashion. The first is simply to link them to the LOs for the course. Since these capacities are so fundamental, they are likely to connect with any LOs that involve thoughtful ethical analysis. A second way is to link them to existing LOs that have been more fully developed for assessment purposes. The link to the AAC&U's ethical reasoning outcome, for example, is particularly strong (rubric accessible here: https://www.aacu.org/ethical-reasoning-value-rubric)

During the last week or two of the term, the class holds the Ethics Bowl itself. For each match, the students who are not participating serve as judges using the standard judging score sheet and rubric. The scoresheet (accessible here: http://appe-ethics.org/wp-content/uploads/2017/05/2017-2018-IEB-J udge's-Score-Sheet.pdf) guides the students through the process of evaluating the presentations just as it does the judges at the IEB. The scoresheet tracks the evaluation of the presentation according to the rubric allowing for consistent scoring. The full set of criteria are applied to the initial presentation.

A commentary on the presentation by the other team follows. As the rubric for the commentary emphasizes, the commentary is not a rebuttal, a key contrast with debate. Rather, the goal of the commentary is to advance the analysis, whether that involves agreeing and raising additional concerns or disagreeing and raising considerations to support that disagreement.

Even though these scores determine the winner of the match, they have no impact on a student's grade. Grades are based on an evaluation of a portfolio of materials: (1) the initial applications of each theory that they produced through the term; (2) the outline produced in preparation for the Ethics Bowl; (3) the instructor's observations during the Ethics Bowl itself (because most students do not lead a presentation on the case they took the lead on, this factor is relatively small); and (4) a final write-up where the students are given an opportunity to strengthen their accounts based on what transpired during the Ethics Bowl.

An Example

To illustrate the analysis, let's consider Case 3 from the 2013 APPE IEB Championship (this case was used in the Championship match):

Case 3

For six years, Charles Darwin Snelling cared for Adrienne, his wife of 61 years, after she was diagnosed with Alzheimer's disease. An essay Snelling had written about the richness of caring for Adrienne since her diagnosis was published online in the *New York Times Life Report* December 7, 2011. In the essay, Snelling stated that caring for his wife was not a sacrifice or a noble act: "What I am doing for her pales beside all that she has done for me for more than half a century."

In March 2012, Snelling killed Adrienne, and then took his own life.

According to the *Washington Post* (March 30, 2012), Adrienne Snelling wrote a letter to her children three years after her diagnosis. In that letter, she told her children that she and their father had decided that neither of them wanted to continue living after hope of the wonderful life they had shared with each other and their children was gone.

The day following their parents' death, the Snelling children released a statement that acknowledged their shock, despite knowing their parents' end of life wishes. They confirmed, however, their conviction that their father had acted out of deep love and devotion.

On April 2, the *New York Times* reported that public opinion was mixed but largely sympathetic to Snelling's despair. One reader called Alzheimer's "a slow horror show." Others criticized Snelling's actions, arguing that no one has the right to decide that another person's life is not worth living.[1]

It should be evident that all three ethical theories apply in a reasonably direct fashion to this case. As noted earlier, students are using the tri-level model, so for each ethical theory they are focusing on a particular level of analysis.

At the integration stage, the first step is to decide which level to start with. Often this depends on the perspective the case encourages one to take. On the topic of assisted suicide, for example, a case could focus on institutional, role, or individual levels. The way this particular case is written encourages starting with the individual level. The particular details included in the case description lead the reader to identify with Snelling as an individual and to struggle with the decision he had to make.

According to the tri-level model, virtue theory provides a helpful first pass approach to analyzing a case at the individual level. Even if an instructor does not use the tri-level model, it should be clear that this case is a rich one for virtue theory. Thus, starting with Aristotle, one may begin by showing how the doctrine of the mean can be used to zero in on the particulars the virtuous person is responsive to when feeling pleasure and pain "at the right times, with reference to the right objects, towards the right people, with the right motive, and in the right way."[2]

Aristotle's doctrine of the mean holds that for most virtues there is a vice on either side. Courage is the mean between cowardice and foolhardiness, for example. Students can see this more clearly if they consider extreme vices first—extreme cowardice showing up if Snelling is simply afraid to live up to his wife's standard. Extreme foolhardiness would involve recklessly pursuing those goals without any attention to context. A subtler vice of cowardice, meanwhile, would be failing to focus on the values he and his wife shared, while a subtler vice of foolhardiness might involve failing to incorporate a relevant element of context.

Through this back-and-forth process students can come to appreciate what the virtue of courage calls for in this setting. By applying the doctrine of the mean in this way to several other virtues that pull in different directions, such as justice and love, the students can get the nuances of the challenge Snelling faces at this critical stage of his relationship to his wife.

On the tri-level model, students apply deontological considerations at the role level. Students focus on Kantian approaches that emphasize autonomy, respect, and consent. The students *back off* a bit from the relationship between Adrienne and Snelling and focus more on the nature of the agreement between a husband and a wife. What responsibilities does Snelling have to Adrienne? What was the exact agreement between them? Was it binding on Snelling under the particular circumstances? Was Adrienne competent to make the agreement? The more deeply the students think about the nature of autonomy, respect, and consent, the greater their insight into the case.

Finally, the tri-level model suggests that consequentialist considerations apply best on a first-pass basis to the institutional level. Even though the way this case is written does not initially encourage students to look at the issues at the institutional level, a bit of reflection makes them realize that the challenge Snelling is facing is part of a larger complex of problems. The students look at the suffering that Snelling and Adrienne face and wonder if the background institutions could be changed to reduce the suffering of the many people who face such circumstances.

To draw these points out, one can focus on a rule or institutional version of utilitarianism that brings out the strategic structure of institutions. Such an approach becomes particularly relevant as the students consider the potential unintended side-effects of permitting assisted suicide. Moreover, as it shifts the focus away from questions about culpability, for example, whether an agent is less blameworthy because of the impact of institutional forces, this forward-looking approach helps students appreciate the fact that ethics and ethical thinking have a larger scope than judgments about actions (e.g., whether they are right or wrong) and agents (whether they are blameworthy or admirable, for example).

While there is, of course, much more to be said about the application of the ethical theories to this case, these points illustrate how examining a powerful case like this one help provide reality and complexity to students' thinking about ethics. The particular approach an instructor takes would depend on the ethical theories that they wish to illuminate. The richness of IEB cases supports a wide range of pedagogical approaches.

The team then faces an important challenge—how to bring the insights the'y've gleaned by applying a variety of ethical theories together into a single account. In the final section of this chapter participants explore some of the deeper philosophical issues this topic raises, but for now they simply note that different teams can coherently come to different conclusions about how to bring together the various insights.

What they cannot do is simply adopt a relativistic stance. If the students have learned to apply the theories correctly, they feel the genuine pull of the considerations that each one raises in the case. They may try to harmonize the results, holding that the theories support a common conclusion, or they may decide that, for example, the deontological considerations trump the consequentialist ones for this particular case (or vice versa, of course).

In any case, that students find themselves struggling with these competing values is one of the most significant benefits of the ethics bowl. It's also a reason to emphasize the importance of teams having to "indicate both awareness and thoughtful consideration of different viewpoints, including especially those that would loom large in the reasoning of individuals who disagree with the team's position" (IEB evaluation criterion 3). The competition between the theories (and, not infrequently, between different applications of the same theory) is a valuable resource for this criterion of evaluation.

The tri-level model provides students with a structured way to move from one theory to another and to identify the sources of tensions between the accounts. Thus, for example, a consequentialist can be thought of as looking at rules *from above* as entities that must be designed to generate optimal outcomes. Deontological theories, on the other hand, look at rules *from below* as products of the agreement of free individuals. In a similar fashion, it can be said that while deontologists look at roles *from above* as positions we enter into, virtue theorists see them *from below* as built out of the relationships that constitute our identity.

DEVIATIONS FROM THE STANDARD IEB

An instructor might run a full-fledged Ethics Bowl, following all the rules of the IEB. Certainly, this would be good preparation for developing teams for the competition. However, in this section attention focuses on ways of modifying the standard practice of the IEB for pedagogical and practical reasons. One might not choose to embrace these modifications; the important thing to realize is that the Ethics Bowl is a tool that can be shaped to different purposes.

When starting to use an Ethics Bowl in class an instructor may be tempted to proceed as if she were coaching all the teams. For fairness reasons, coaches in the IEB must let the students discover their own path through the cases—they cannot make significant suggestions to the teams as to factors that should be considered. Thus, if an instructor were to give the guidance one normally gives in class—sometimes challenging students, sometimes illustrating or even suggesting factors to consider—she might think that she has slipped up. However, done properly, this sort of guidance does not dictate the response of the students, it significantly increases their ability to understand the theories.

That suggests that thinking of oneself as a coach one would be using the wrong framework. A solid IEB team has already gone through the work of learning how to tackle any case that comes at them. In the class suggested here, students aren't in that position, they are at a much earlier stage in that process. It's best not to use coaching standards when talking to all the teams. Be an instructor who uses all the resources available to maximize the pedagogical value of the exercise. Among other things, this means that one should allow students to wander off on pathways that aren't promising—good guidance leaves a great deal of room for learning through errors.

This point connects to another important point. It's best not to make much of a fuss about winning and losing. It's not necessary to have playoffs, an overall winner, or prizes. Experience with student responses has shown that the simple fact of being judged by their peers is enough to motivate them to put appropriate care into their analysis. Indeed, it helps to deemphasize the importance of winning.

If students serve as judges in the matches where they are not participating, which is a good idea (more on this in following pages), make it clear to them that an instructor may not always agree with the results. That way students will feel less stress (and be less upset by questionable scores) and be more open to treating the overall process as worthwhile—a valuable discussion.

While it's a good idea to deemphasize winning, completely eliminating the competitive aspect would sacrifice some significant benefits. The extra excitement of the competition increases the energy level of the final few weeks of class, as well as the motivation to analyze the cases using the theories throughout the term.

Using the students as judges is a significant deviation from the IEB. It is, however, valuable for students to adopt a judge's point of view. By applying the standards of evaluation to another team, they glean significant insight into what they mean when applied to their own case.

In addition, because an important part of what the students have in common is the ethical theories, they are able to recognize how those theories

allow them to systematically articulate values and concerns that are otherwise difficult to express. When a team uses a theory well, the judges see
its power; when a team uses a theory poorly, the judges enhance their own
understanding by imagining how the theory could have been used more
effectively.

The final deviation to be considered here emerges from an appreciation
of the value of all roles—presenter, commentator, and judge. Such appreciation can emerge as one deals with unexpected consequences. For example,
thinking that suspense might heighten the excitement of the competition, one
might have students draw from a hat both the teams and the cases for a round
of competition. Unfortunately, that may lead to cases often being repeated,
some students not getting much input, and an unwelcome level of frustration,
because students don't like uncertainty, especially at the end of the term.

Lessons learned from that sort of misfire may lead to the development of
a new system. For a class of twenty-four there are six teams of four. There
are six cases; each team only covers four cases, but there is an overlapping
pattern that allows an instructor to have any two teams compete. When they
get close to the end (once they have their case presentations ready to go), an
instructor tells students what teams are going on which cases which day.

At that point they still do not know whether they will present or comment
on a case, but they know their role: for the case that the student takes the lead
on they are either lead presenter, lead commentator, or lead judge. All cases
are done, and each case is done only once. Every student participates in a
meaningful way, and they are in a position to see how these different roles
interact.

The deviations discussed here are, of course, based on particulars that
vary—a particular teaching style, semester plan, and typical student. An
instructor may find it more valuable to have suspense about which team will
compete on any given day or to have students develop responses to the cases
with no guidance. A teacher might equally consider other deviations from the
standard IEB. Experimentation and modification are a hallmark of the IEB
itself, and should be a part of its use in the classroom as well.

CONCLUSION: USING MULTIPLE THEORIES

In closing, let's return to a point that was touched on briefly earlier. Given
that the three ethical traditions provide different foundations and resources
for analyzing cases, how do students reconcile the differing results? Do they
take one theory to be true across the board? Do they choose different theories
for different cases? Do they attempt to use one theory to absorb the insights
of the other two? Do they create a hybrid theory that combines the insights?

This issue of reconciliation arises repeatedly in the IEB itself. It is common to see teams simply run through applications of the three ethical traditions and consider that a complete analysis. The teams often selectively use applications that allow the three theories to support a single consideration. Stronger teams use the competing theories to "indicate both awareness and thoughtful consideration of different viewpoints, including especially those that would loom large in the reasoning of individuals who disagree with team's position" (Criterion 3). Even these teams, however, face the problem of explaining why the theory they favor should be chosen over the competing theory.

This challenge is a feature not a flaw in the IEB. Why? Because, properly appreciated, it represents an important feature of good ethical thinking. Experience has shown that analyzing a problem using a single ethical theory, one inevitably leaves out important considerations. That strongly suggests that it is better to move between the perspectives provided by the three ethical traditions in order to unpack the underlying issues involved in any particular topic.

A universal approach to reconciling the resulting insights has proved elusive. Discussion of competing ideas and tentative approaches is beyond the scope of this project. But this much can be said. One of the most stimulating parts of teaching ethics is that one sees that there is still much important work to be done; reconciling the power of the three ethical traditions is a task for students and teachers of ethics alike. It is a challenge that they should happily share.

NOTES

1. © Association for Practical and Professional Ethics 2013.
2. Aristotle, Nicomachean Ethics (translation, W. D. Ross), Book II Section 6.

Chapter 10

Integrating Behavioral Ethics with Ethics Unwrapped

Cara Biasucci

No matter what discipline or trade students chose to study, ethics education is an integral part of their preparation for their adult and professional lives. Many colleges, universities, and vocational schools wish to infuse ethics into their curriculum and are grappling with how to do so effectively and efficiently.[1] This chapter provides an overview of *Ethics Unwrapped*, a new model of pedagogical instruction that propels interdisciplinary ethics forward across all academic fields and trades. It is a free, online educational program which merges ethical theory and behavioral ethics with a media-driven approach that appeals to students and supports a variety of classroom formats and sizes.

INTRODUCTION: ETHICS TODAY

Ethical decision-making has a positive impact on the world. Today people work with a diverse set of stakeholders in a global context that requires trust and sustainability to function and flourish. Indeed, the interplay between ethics and leadership, global political stability, and economic prosperity is obvious and critical. Ethical leadership is essential for meeting society's needs now, and for fulfilling our responsibility to future generations tomorrow.

Students face an array of ethical issues that have never been broached before, such as human cloning, genetic engineering, and artificial intelligence. With the increasing influence of climate change, mass migration, and technologies that disrupt the ways in which people live, work, and govern, it is likely that new pressures will present ever more challenging ethical issues in the future, too. Add to that the social pressures that students face with the outsized role of social media in their lives, and it is clear why learning ethics today is as important as ever.

Every student, no matter the subject he or she studies, needs to have a well-developed sense of acting with integrity, as well as the skills to navigate ethical dilemmas as they arise. It is helpful, too, to know the ways in which people get tripped up in their moral decision-making, so these pitfalls can be avoided. Few instructors, if any, would object to meaningful conversation in the classroom regarding ethics; these discussions can prepare students for future roles as participants and leaders in their workplaces and their communities.

So, while the fundamental need for ethics education in all disciplines and trades is clear, experience shows that in a wide variety of situations—in business, politics, sports, media, medicine, mechanics, performing arts, and in our personal lives—human beings often make poor ethical decisions.[2] Around the world, people witness ethical lapses in organizations of all kinds. In fact, ethical missteps are common. They are often demoralizing and, importantly, can carry significant negative consequences for society.

Indeed, society faces complicated, interconnected global problems today—situations where nations, businesses, politics, religions, technology, nature, human health, and a multitude of communities coexist and (often) collide. It is essential that students become engaged, informed, global citizens to cope with the world they are inheriting. Every student must learn to make sound ethical judgments, and to know how to act with integrity amid the many pressures of the modern world.

With the right guidance and resources, students can learn to recognize national and global issues for the complex ethical dilemmas that they are. They can develop the skills to talk about these tough issues productively in peer-to-peer discussion, and in classroom conversation. This dialogue can foster moral awareness and encourage students to develop moral imagination and moral courage. Everyone wants to avoid the ethical missteps that harm individuals, families, communities, institutions, and governments. We all feel the impact, even if indirectly, as cynicism and mistrust ripple throughout our organizations and society at large.

CHALLENGES TO TEACHING ETHICS

The classroom can be a tinderbox of opinions in an ever-changing landscape of topics to explore (or avoid) depending on student learning goals and a teacher's tolerance for challenging conversation. Initiating an ethical discussion and managing it in the classroom is a skill; it can be learned. It often requires a comfort level with messy conversation, one where there are often no clear right or wrong answers. Humanities' instructors may be more comfortable in this milieu. Facilitating this kind of classroom conversation may run contrary to disciplines where students expect a clear "right" answer, such as they might find in a chemistry lab, under the hood of a car, or on a math problem.

Teaching ethics in any field can be a challenging proposition. Often, instructors who are asked to incorporate ethics into their courses are not experts in ethics. Teachers have limited time, if any, to read or research. Significantly, instructors often feel uncomfortable teaching outside their area of expertise and may shy away from teaching ethics when given the opportunity to do so.

Traditionally, ethics has been taught in philosophy and religion courses where students learn through lectures, and by reading ancient, classical texts. Traditional ethics education does not resonate with many students' skills level. Studies show that slightly more than one-third of high school seniors read at or above proficient levels.[3] Dense philosophical and religious texts are often not a good fit for the average college student and are unlikely to spur lively discussion in the average classroom.

Indeed, GenZers spend more than half their waking hours on a screen of some sort.[4] As such, media-based teaching and learning seems a more natural fit for many of today's students. To teach ethics effectively today across disciplines and trades, in fact, it seems essential to have captivating educational media that is entertaining and emotionally resonant while also being academically sound.

Often, ethics is added to a course to fulfill an institutional or departmental requirement; it is not something that the instructor choses to incorporate. Importantly, teachers recognize that unless ethics content is in some way relevant to the course content, it can feel like an after-thought, tacked on and lacking integration with the rest of the coursework. On the other hand, meaningful integration of ethics can suffuse a course with significant new content, and support student learning in a way that makes ethics relevant (and important) to understanding the course content fully.

So, while it seems obvious that ethics has a far-reaching impact on the world, the question is how to best prepare students to act with integrity? How can students learn to make sound ethical judgments and decisions despite the many forces that can pull them off course? Studying behavioral ethics—ethics at the nexus of psychology, neuroscience, evolutionary biology, and economics—is one promising route. *Ethics Unwrapped* offers behavioral ethics content that is research-based and easily integrated into a wide range of subjects and settings.

BEHAVIORAL ETHICS

The lessons of behavioral ethics apply across the board—to all human beings—regardless of the academic discipline or trade being studied, or the type of educational institution offering the ethics instruction. Students of all stripes can benefit from the practical and versatile knowledge nurtured by the study of behavioral ethics, which offers a revealing look into how and why humans make the choices that they do.

Many unique insights come out of behavioral ethics research. For example, most people assume that when a person has the desire to do the right thing, and knows what the right thing to do is, she will do the right thing. But behavioral ethics shows that between a person's intention, and her action, there is a huge chasm. In other words, knowing the right thing to do does not guarantee doing the right thing. Reading or listening to the news occasionally will verify this disappointing reality.

Why the gap? In the same way that the brain can be fooled optically and aurally, the brain can be fooled morally. Indeed, the research in behavioral ethics over the past decade points to one overwhelming finding: most people act unethically every day, generally in minor ways, while at the same time thinking of themselves as good people.[5] So, while most people generally aspire to do the right thing (and expect others to do so too), how people actually end up behaving is often very different than their aspirations and expectations.

Too often, ethical lapses occur due to unpreparedness in the face of an array of internal psychological biases, external social pressures, and situational factors that are often beyond our recognition or control. Lacking awareness of these biases and pressures, most people operate reflexively and out of their own past conditioning. Unless people are familiar with the human propensity toward self-delusion through rationalization, it is difficult (if not impossible) to address the biases and pressures that influence moral decision-making and actions.

ETHICS AND MORAL EMOTIONS

Ethics is as much a matter of the heart as it is of the head. Research in behavioral ethics shows that ethical decision-making is largely emotional, even though most people believe that they make moral decisions based on rationality and facts. But in truth most decisions, including moral ones, are made quickly, intuitively, and largely unconsciously with little cognitive processing going on.[6] When a person thinks that she is reasoning to an ethical conclusion, often what she is really doing is rationalizing a decision that has already been made instinctively and emotionally.

Many scholars believe that moral intuitions are the underpinning of moral judgments.[7] While scholars disagree regarding the extent to which emotion factors into moral intuitions, it is clear that "gut feelings" and other affective, automatic processes underlie most of our moral judgments. In fact, as a social species, our emotions have evolved to do important work: "[w]e modulate our morals with signals from family, friends, and social groups with whom we identify because in our evolutionary past, those attributes helped individuals to survive and reproduce."[8]

For example, other-praising emotions, such as gratitude, can encourage people to act ethically. If someone has been kind to us, our gratitude for that kindness often spurs us to be kind in return. Self-conscious emotions, such as guilt and shame, encourage people to follow the group's moral standards. On the other hand, other-condemning emotions, such as anger and disgust, are feelings that people often experience when they see other people violate moral norms. Other-suffering emotions, such as sympathy and empathy, can cause us to take prosocial action or to help others in need.

THE ROLE OF INTERNAL BIASES
AND EXTERNAL PRESSURES

Psychological biases—such as the self-serving bias or the overconfidence bias—can interfere with people's ability to spot ethical issues. For example, when a person is looking out for #1, it can be easy to overlook moral issues that affect other people. In fact, unless people actively keep ethics in their frame of reference, they may miss ethical issues until it is too late.

To illustrate how these biases work, consider the concept of *framing*, which speaks to the fact that context counts a lot! What a person *sees* in a situation is often influenced by how that situation is *framed*. In one study, for instance, people would rather buy a hamburger labeled 75 percent fat free than a hamburger labeled 25 percent fat, even though the two burgers are made with the same meat. In fact, the 75 percent fat-free burger seemed to taste better, even though the burgers were identical.[9]

Cognitive biases, social and organizational pressures, and situational factors can combine themselves in not so great ways, too. For example, research shows that financial gain changes people's frame of reference, often significantly.[10] Money is not the only factor that influences human decision-making, but it is a very powerful one.[11] For instance, in a job where profit maximization is a key metric, a person can easily overlook an ethical issue in the service of being a loyal employee and doing their best at work.

In one study, people were asked to judge the morality of a company that sold a drug that caused unnecessary deaths when its competitors' drugs did not. Ninety-seven percent of people said it would be unethical to sell the drug. Then, researchers placed other people into groups, and asked the groups to assume the *roles* of the company's directors. When asked whether or not it was moral to sell the drug, all of the fifty-seven groups decided it was okay to sell the drug.[12] As company directors, people framed the issue as a business decision in dollars-and-cents terms, and ignored the harmful impact their decision would have on others.

The concepts and principles of behavioral ethics can help students design organizations, and processes within organizations, that support better moral decision-making and behavior, too. Most people have good intentions and believe that they will act with integrity when faced with social and organizational pressures inside companies and other organizations. But often, people make suboptimal ethical decisions without knowing that they are doing so. This is especially true when confronted with unhelpful circumstances such as unrealistic deadlines or big bonuses that encourage cutting ethical corners.

Teaching about the many influences of behavioral ethics can help students discern their own subconscious biases, recognize social and organizational pressures, and take note of the factors that might cause them to miss ethical issues, or make unethical choices. Every student will be better equipped to guard against the unhelpful rationalizations that support these influences. As students become aware of rationalizing, they can look more carefully at the situation, and make different (and hopefully better) choices. In these ways, behavioral ethics offers real tangible benefits to students now, and in their futures.

ETHICS UNWRAPPED VIDEO SERIES AND EDUCATIONAL PROGRAM

Ethics Unwrapped is a unique educational tool for anyone wishing to learn about or teach behavioral ethics and moral decision-making. It combines cutting-edge research in behavioral ethics with today's high-tech learning environment to meet students where they live and put every instructor in a position to teach ethics effectively. The award-winning program was launched in 2012 at The University of Texas at Austin (UT Austin), and is created and produced by the author for the Center for Leadership and Ethics at McCombs School of Business. All of the program's resources are freely available at www. EthicsUnwrapped.utexas.edu.

Ethics Unwrapped was developed to provide primary or supplementary teaching materials for instructors; it is designed to meet a variety of instructional needs. For example, if an instructor is new to teaching ethics, the program can provide expert content and bring the instructor up to speed. On the other hand, if an instructor is an expert in ethics, the program can provide fresh, engaging classroom materials to supplement the existing curriculum. Broadly speaking, the program's innovative teaching resources are readily integrated into any academic discipline, vocational training, or leadership program.

The goal of *Ethics Unwrapped* is to increase every student's awareness of behavioral ethics and to improve students' moral reasoning and decision-making skills. The resources offer an opportunity to transform students' experience of ethics education in the classroom, and to expand the conversation about ethics and integrity. Many students seem to prefer watching captivating images on a screen; the program leverages this mode of media-driven communication with engaging videos that teach students about ethics through a blend of expert knowledge and creative storytelling.

Ethics Unwrapped videos, and their accompanying teaching resources, can nudge the discussion of ethics forward in the classroom. With the glossary videos, students gain the vocabulary to discuss ethical challenges productively. The focus on behavioral ethics expands students' understanding of how people make decisions. This can, in turn, increase students' introspection and self-awareness regarding their own moral choices. Indeed, classroom discussions can flourish as students and teachers alike glean a more complete understanding of how people make ethical (and unethical) decisions through the study of behavioral ethics.

CONCEPT-BASED EXPERIENTIAL LEARNING

Ethics Unwrapped videos package complex ethics concepts in an entertaining, accessible, powerfully visual way by featuring a unique blend of animation, expert content, and student experiences. Overall, the videos explain ethics concepts. Teachers can use this concept-based modular video content to build a solid foundation of ethical inquiry for their students.

Ethics concepts can be made into discrete content modules that integrate seamlessly with course content to enhance student learning and improve learning outcomes. Each *Ethics Unwrapped* video is a unit of stand-alone content that can be easily combined with other *Ethics Unwrapped* videos, case studies and teaching resources from the website, or other course materials to form an educational module. These modules can be tailored to fit an instructor's curricular goals, regardless of classroom size. The modules are especially useful in blended learning environments and online courses.

Instructors do not need special expertise in ethics to use *Ethics Unwrapped*, facilitating easy adoption by a large network of teachers of all disciplines and trades. Equally important, *Ethics Unwrapped* videos harness experiential learning—learning through the process of reflection—that is accessible to every student regardless of their chosen subject matter. Peer-to-peer discussion seems to be important for students to assimilate ethics in their lives, too, and the videos open the door to this kind of conversation.

As a natural extension of peer-to-peer learning, many of the videos include interviews with students who share personal stories and reflect on their experiences of the ethics concept at hand. The students' stories are universally relatable, and students in the classroom quickly compare these experiences to similar situations in their own lives. In addition, students learn by watching students in the videos wrestle with, and reflect on, their ethical (and unethical) choices and actions.

FLEXIBLE CROSS-DISCIPLINARY TEACHING TOOLS

Ethics Unwrapped resources were developed with an eye toward versatility for use across disciplines and platforms. The research-based videos are self-sustaining with an indefinite shelf-life on the *Ethics Unwrapped* website (http://www.ethicsunwrapped.utexas.edu/) and on YouTube. The abundance and variety of videos makes teaching ethics with *Ethics Unwrapped* easily scalable. The videos easily support flipped classrooms, online environments, traditional seminars, and lecture-based courses.

Currently, *Ethics Unwrapped* has more than 130 videos and 80 case studies with accompanying teaching materials. All of the videos, and most of the resources are available in English and Spanish; the website is offered in both languages, too. The videos are close-captioned for the deaf and hearing impaired, and some of the videos are described for the blind and visually impaired. Those videos are freely available through the *Described and Captioned Media Program*'s website (https://dcmp.org/).

Ethics Unwrapped case studies are strategically paired with *Ethics Unwrapped* videos. For example, a concept video on role morality, which includes its own discussion questions, teaching note, and bibliography, is linked to a case study that explores the concept of role morality in a real-life situation. The case study also has its own set of discussion questions and a bibliography for further reading and research. Some case studies include an ethical insight or related videos as well. Ethics concepts can be reviewed in the video glossary, which also includes related terms to help students develop a network of behavioral ethics concepts.

Ethics experts from across the country contribute to *Ethics Unwrapped*'s content. In addition, more than fifty case studies were developed in partnership with faculty from seven colleges at UT Austin. These *Cases* include a range of academic disciplines, including liberal arts, fine arts, communication, natural sciences, medicine, and business. The case studies cover a wide variety of topics, such as journalism ethics, research ethics, free speech, foreign policy, politics, digital downloads, educational testing, offshore drilling, consumer purchases, privacy issues, medical decision, and more.

The multidisciplinary collaboration, and the interdisciplinary nature of behavioral ethics, means that *Ethics Unwrapped*'s resources are truly applicable across a wide range of fields. On the UT Austin campus, the program has become a meaningful part of the undergraduate curriculum in such varied academic areas as fine arts, natural sciences, liberal arts, business, communications, social work, computer science, and education. The effort to integrate ethics across the campus has been successful, in large part, because these resources offer both flexibility and scalability.

Indeed, based on the steady increase of traffic to the *Ethics Unwrapped* website, frequent use of materials by more than 1,500 colleges and universities, and unsolicited feedback from faculty and other instructors, it seems that colleges and universities across the country (and around the world) have been able to successfully integrate *Ethics Unwrapped* into a wide variety of courses.

However, based on faculty surveys and conversations at conferences, there are instructors who have a strong interest in using *Ethics Unwrapped* resources but do not know which videos (or teaching resources) to select, or how to integrate behavioral ethics into their coursework. To help provide guidance, and to make navigating the available resources easier, many of the resources have been curated for general topic areas on a special section of the program's website (https://ethicsunwrapped.utexas.edu/ethics-topics).

CURATED RESOURCES FOR EASY ACCESS

For those who are not familiar with *Ethics Unwrapped*, or with teaching ethics in general, the *Curated Resources* section is a helpful tool to more readily and easily select suitable videos and case studies. Many of the materials (but not all of them) are sorted according to nine broad topic areas or categories; these nine areas are a simple way to group and explore the bulk of the program's content. It has been an effective approach for instructors who want to either sample the materials and/or explore them through the lens of their own discipline.

The *Curated Resources* offers nine categories (or big buckets) that sort much of the program's content. The topic areas are:

- Intro to Ethics Unwrapped
- Behavioral Ethics

- Law & Policy
- Leadership
- Media, Arts & Culture
- Organizational Ethics
- Professional Ethics
- Science, Medicine & Research
- Sustainability & CSR

Each of the nine categories begins with an overview of the ethics themes and concepts covered in that topic area. There is also a *Start Here* section that features three videos and case studies. Additional videos and case studies that are also relevant are listed separately. Case studies are sorted by academic discipline for quick access by instructors who are looking for materials specific to their field.

The *Intro to Ethics Unwrapped* category offers an overview of the entire program and a sampling of each video series. Instructors who are not familiar with *Ethics Unwrapped* will get a feel for the program's resources as well as an introduction to each of the video series. Importantly, many of the ethics concepts operate in tandem with each other. Consequently, the more *Ethics Unwrapped* videos and case studies people review, the greater their understanding of behavioral ethics; the clearer the relationship becomes, too, between the concepts and their own moral choices and actions.

TESTING ETHICS UNWRAPPED AT THE
UNIVERSITY OF TEXAS AT AUSTIN

The cross-campus integration of *Ethics Unwrapped* into seven colleges on UT Austin campus may be a helpful guide for those who wish to infuse ethics across the curriculum, as well as instructional for teachers who want to incorporate ethics in their courses.

UT Austin reaffirmed its commitment to ethics education in 2009 through the ambitious *Ethics and Leadership* flag program (EL), whereby all undergraduates entering the university are expected to take at least one course that emphasizes ethical analysis and decision-making before they graduate. To meet the demand of more than 38,000 undergraduates on campus, more than 175 EL courses were flagged and offered across campus.

However, five years later, full implementation of the requirement had not been realized because of the difficulty of teaching practical ethics to students within courses designed to teach disciplinary knowledge. Indeed, instructors from colleges such as natural sciences, computer science, fine arts, engineering, and so on are not trained as practical ethics experts, and often have difficulty drawing out the ethical issues implicit in their course content.

With the support of the Provost's Office and the Teagle Foundation, *Ethics Unwrapped* partnered with the EL flag program and embarked on the *Ethics Integration Initiative* (EII). The EII was a two-year project to add ethics to the undergraduate curriculum across campus in significant academic areas like fine arts, liberal arts, communications, natural sciences, education, and business. In addition, the EII gathered assessment data on the efficacy of *Ethics Unwrapped* videos for teaching and learning ethics from students and instructors.

Like many universities, UT Austin is required by the Texas Higher Education Coordinating Board to demonstrate student learning in the areas of personal and social responsibility. All undergraduates are also required to meet *Basic Education Requirements* in ethics for the University to retain its accreditation through the Southern Association of Colleges and Schools. The surveys and assessments from the EII helped to support institutional demands and goals related to such compliance and accreditation.

ETHICS INTEGRATION INITIATIVE: AN OVERVIEW

The EII focused on one-on-one integration techniques with instructors with an eye toward creating high-quality ethics content and sustainable program resources. Over two years, accessible, functional materials that could easily be adopted by other instructors (at other institutions) were developed and tested on the UT Austin campus. The initiative worked, in large part, because *Ethics Unwrapped* resources offered both flexibility across disciplines, and scalability across various classroom formats and methods of instruction.

Over five semesters—from 2014 to 2016—*Ethics Unwrapped* was integrated into classes in the liberal arts, fine arts, natural sciences, business, education, and communication studies. Examples follow in this chapter. The courses that were selected for the project included core courses that might be taught at other universities, such as business law and business ethics, as well as courses that were undergraduate requirements and popular electives on campus.

An expansive partnership across campus between professional staff and faculty helped to identify and develop additional teaching resources to fill the gaps in program content. Colleagues worked across disciplines on faculty ethics committees to share best teaching practices (and failures) and help develop teaching resources. In total, the EII involved thirty-four instructors and eighty-eight teaching assistants across thirty classes, as well as five staff members and several graduate students.

Beginning in the fall of 2014, five videos were used across eight different classrooms. In spring of 2015, twenty-eight videos were integrated across eight new classrooms. In the second year, forty-five videos were integrated across twenty-six classes in the College of Liberal Arts, College of Fine Arts, College of Education, Moody College of Communication, College of Natural Sciences, and McCombs School of Business. Except for four instructors and four courses, all of the courses developed in the first year were repeated in the second year. In the first year alone, the EII reached 3,200 undergraduates. In year two, it reached more than 7,800 undergraduate students.

To assist faculty with the integration of ethics into their coursework, professional staff (trained in ethics) consulted with instructors to select appropriate concepts and ethics content. After funding for the EII ended, it was not possible to sustain one-on-one consultations. So, in an attempt to replicate the type of one-on-one assistance that instructors had received during the project, *Ethics Unwrapped* materials were curated according to nine of the most common topic areas (see "Curated Resources for Easy Access" section).

The survey tools developed for EII were deployed in all of the courses where the curricular resources were used. The primary objective was to assess how effective the videos were for students' understanding of ethics concepts. The secondary objective was to gauge whether the teaching materials were truly flexible and effective across disciplines. Over two years, approximately 8,600 undergraduates were surveyed. Students also assessed their confidence levels in identifying and dealing with ethical issues. Assessments expanded the second year to include faculty who were using *Ethics Unwrapped* as part of the EII.

The first year was key to developing a foundation that would measure the efficacy of *Ethics Unwrapped* videos as teaching and learning tools. A fruitful collaboration in the first year between the assessment team in the School of Undergraduate Studies and the EL Flag Committee helped to create the necessary survey tools and deploy them strategically during the initiative.

THE SURVEY SAYS . . .

The student surveys used post- then pre-retrospective questioning methods designed to account for any propensity toward overestimation of prior knowledge on the part of the students. Specifically, the EII measured the impact of the videos on students' abilities to identify and discuss the ethical concepts presented, to apply a process of ethical reasoning, and to engage in decision-making around the concept. Some courses underwent additional evaluation and analysis by trained EL staff to assess students' ethical analysis and reasoning skills. Post-course evaluation measures were used in all the courses.

Overall, the collection and evaluation of student survey data, with direct assessment of samples of student work, offered some insight into student experiences and gains in ethical skills development. The three-pronged assessment methodology targeting students, instructors, and video-views gave a comprehensive picture of the efficacy of *Ethics Unwrapped* resources and allowed for strategic improvements in the delivery and development of this content·during the second year.

The assessment surveys generated tangible findings during the first year, and those findings were repeated in the second year. Overall, they showed that a well-integrated ethics program yields significant benefits to student learning. Moreover, survey data showed that using *Ethics Unwrapped* videos is an effective way to introduce students to ethics concepts. The videos improved both students' understanding of these concepts as well as their confidence in spotting ethical issues and discussing them.

Specifically, of the 8,600 students on campus who were surveyed, 90 percent found *Ethics Unwrapped* videos *helpful* or *very helpful* for explaining ethics concepts (figure 10.1).

Student confidence levels for dealing with ethics topics rose greatly with video instruction, too (figure 10.2).

More than half of students reported being *not at all confident* or *minimally confident* in their ability to identify, explain, discuss, or apply ethics concepts *before* viewing a video. Of the students who were uncertain, 79 percent

Survey Question: "How helpful was this video for explaining the concept of … ?"

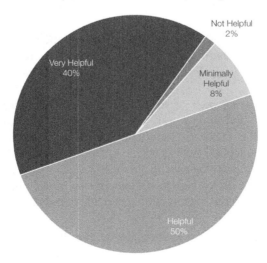

Figure 10.1 Survey. *Source*: Ethics Unwrapped Survey sourced by Biasucci.

Aggregate of Student Confidence Levels

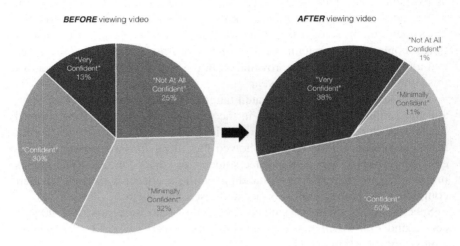

These charts summarize the results in Figures 3 and 4, showing how well students
understand ethics concepts before and after viewing an Ethics Unwrapped video.

Figure 10.2   Survey. *Source*: Ethics Unwrapped Survey sourced by Biasucci.

reported becoming *confident* or *very confident* in their abilities to recognize, discuss, and apply ethics concepts *after* viewing a video (figure 10.3).

Indeed, the need for ethics education became starkly clear after the EII was completed. Assessments of thousands of undergraduate students across a range of colleges showed that more than half of students said they were not confident in spotting ethical issues, explaining ethical concepts, or making informed decisions involving these concepts. Similar results were found in a *Leadership and Ethic Institute Survey* on the UT Austin campus in 2016 (figure 10.4).

During the second year of the project, the assessment results from the video surveys were subject to a thematic analysis of student comments. Approximately 8 percent of students surveyed offered comments of any kind. From these comments, seven thematic categories emerged. More than half the student comments—approximately 55 percent—offered general praise, constructive feedback, or demonstrated a deeper engagement with the ethics concepts covered in the videos. Students made comments such as:

- "The animations kept me really engaged and the student comments made me feel that the issues being discussed were pertinent to today's society and everyday issues."

Survey Question: "Think back to how well you understood this concept **BEFORE** viewing the video. How confident are you that you could have done the following?"

■ Identified issues involving …
▣ Clearly explained the concept of …
▨ Engaged in a conversation about …
■ Made an informed decision based on …

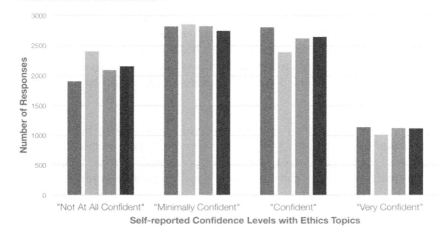

Figure 10.3 Survey. *Source*: Ethics Unwrapped Survey sourced by Biasucci.

Survey Question: "**AFTER** viewing the video, how confident are you that you could now do the following?"

■ Identify issues involving …
▣ Clearly explain the concept of …
▨ Engage in a conversation about …
■ Make an informed decision based on …

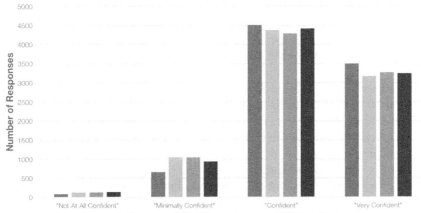

Figure 10.4 Survey. *Source*: Ethics Unwrapped Survey sourced by Biasucci.

- "I really enjoyed how different people were able to give their perspectives and discuss their thoughts on the subject."
- "Spend a little more time on the vocab/names of each type of ethical dilemma and less on the student perspectives, although the life examples were helpful to connect ideas."
- "This has really opened up my eyes to my own practice of relativism and now I feel better about how I express myself on certain issues."
- "This video is engaging but superficial. It does not give any indication of how one would adjudicate serious conflicts between competing values in a way that would yield a definitive resolution and not just be a recourse to 'relativism.'"

In the second year, an instructor survey gauged how helpful *Ethics Unwrapped* resources were in the classroom to teachers. While this assessment was a relatively small sample of approximately forty faculty, clear trends emerged. Namely, the videos and supporting materials offer a versatile resource for teaching ethics across a wide range of disciplines, class sizes, and instructional formats, including traditional seminars, blended learning, and online courses.

While the majority of faculty used *Ethics Unwrapped* videos and teaching resources in traditional in-person seminars or lectures, approximately one-quarter of instructors used the materials in either online or blended learning environments (figure 10.5).

Regardless of classroom format, the videos served various functions: as the primary tool to teach ethics concepts; as a supplemental teaching tool; to initiate classroom discussion; to introduce a course topic; to prompt student writing assignments; to illustrate case studies in class.

Ninety-five percent of faculty members surveyed found the videos *helpful* or *very helpful* for teaching and learning, and 91 percent found the accompanying teaching resources *helpful* or *very helpful* (figures 10.6 and 10.7).

Instructors also indicated which supplemental resources they had used in addition to videos (figure 10.8).

More than 80 percent of faculty members intended to use *Ethics Unwrapped* videos in future courses, and 85 percent said they would recommend *Ethics Unwrapped* resources to colleagues. Indeed, nearly half of the instructors surveyed had learned about *Ethics Unwrapped* from a colleague.

Feedback from faculty members and teaching assistants revealed that case studies are a critical resource to effectively teach ethics topics in a tangible, discipline-specific manner. Consequently, a concerted effort to develop additional case studies across many different disciplines has been an ongoing project for *Ethics Unwrapped*. Instructors also suggested making the ethical

Survey Question: "How did you use Ethics Unwrapped video(s)?

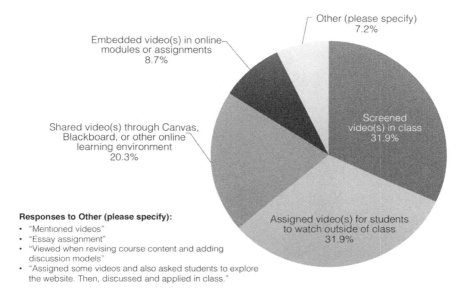

Other (please specify)
7.2%

Embedded video(s) in online modules or assignments
8.7%

Shared video(s) through Canvas, Blackboard, or other online learning environment
20.3%

Screened video(s) in class
31.9%

Assigned video(s) for students to watch outside of class
31.9%

Responses to Other (please specify):
- "Mentioned videos"
- "Essay assignment"
- "Viewed when revising course content and adding discussion models"
- "Assigned some videos and also asked students to explore the website. Then, discussed and applied in class."

Figure 10.5   Survey. *Source*: Ethics Unwrapped Survey sourced by Biasucci.

Survey Question: "How helpful did you find these videos for teaching and learning in your class(es)?"

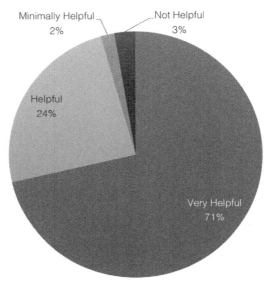

Minimally Helpful
2%

Not Helpful
3%

Helpful
24%

Very Helpful
71%

Figure 10.6   Survey. *Source*: Ethics Unwrapped Survey sourced by Biasucci.

Survey Question: "How helpful were these resources for teaching and learning in your class(es)?"

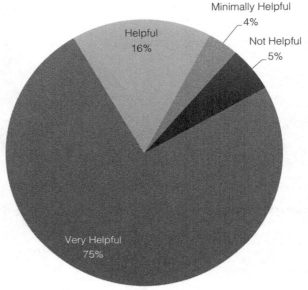

Figure 10.7   Survey. *Source*: Ethics Unwrapped Survey sourced by Biasucci.

Survey Question: "In addition to the video(s), what other teaching resources did you use from Ethics Unwrapped? Check all that apply."

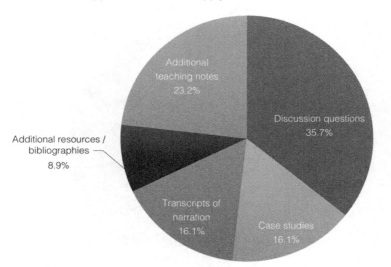

Figure 10.8   Survey. *Source*: Ethics Unwrapped Survey sourced by Biasucci.

concept embedded in case studies explicit. This suggestion, too, was incorporated into subsequent program resources.

Overall, both the student and faculty surveys suggested a well-integrated ethics program yields significant benefits to student learning and supports teachers in the classroom. The data also suggest that using *Ethics Unwrapped* videos is an effective way to introduce students to both behavioral ethics and basic ethics concepts. Importantly, the videos are an engaging teaching tool that resonate with students today. Indeed, because a diverse student population is keen on watching (rather than reading) to learn, their responses to *Ethics Unwrapped* videos have far exceeded expectations.

The EII was a successful initiative on the UT Austin campus because it targeted large undergraduate core courses that continue to repeat every semester, as well as courses that form the backbone of specific programs within popular disciplines. In this way, the effects of the EII have continued well beyond the timeline of the two-year project and serve as a model for other institutions wishing to develop similar initiatives.

EXAMPLES OF ETHICS UNWRAPPED
IN THE CLASSROOM

Infusing ethics into the curriculum across campus magnified the utility of *Ethics Unwrapped* and made the integration of ethics into undergraduate curricula on the UT Austin campus more sustainable (and available) in non-traditional areas of study, such as computer science, music, and art education. In general, instructors said that integrating Ethics Unwrapped resources brought ethics to the forefront of their classroom in a positive manner and sparked lively classroom discussion.

To support the development and integration of sustainable and replicable ethics curricula across a variety of academic disciplines, professional staff at UT Austin worked closely with instructors to develop and pilot courses. Dedicated faculty also took creative initiative to produce their own courses, often building on *Ethics Unwrapped* resources to do so. What follows are two examples from two disciplines—natural sciences and liberal arts—and two additional examples of ethics integration with Ethics Unwrapped from other universities.

COLLEGE OF LIBERAL ARTS—UT AUSTIN

In College of Liberal Arts, *GOV 312L: Issues and Policies in American Government/US Foreign Policy* was selected for the EII because it is a large online class that fulfills a general education requirement. This course is offered three times a year and typically enrolls 800 to 1,300 students each during the long semesters. With the assistance of the EL staff, Professors Robert Moser and Patrick MacDonald developed and taught this course the first year of the EII; various faculty have taught the course in subsequent years.

Ethics Unwrapped videos and supporting curricula were integrated into lectures, student assignments, and online resources to emphasize the role that various behavioral ethics concepts and ethical theories have played in historical events in American history and foreign policy. For example, in the first ethics module for *GOV 312*, students were asked to watch the *Ethics Unwrapped* video on *Systematic Moral Analysis*. Then, students read an *Ethics Unwrapped* case study, *Pardoning Nixon*, on President Gerald Ford's pardon of Richard Nixon. Finally, students were asked to write a brief essay based on the class and lecture material, the video, and the case study. In the essay, students were instructed to:

- Identify any harms caused.
- Note the responsible moral agents.
- Discuss values conflicts.
- Consider alternative perspectives and respond to those arguments.
- Evaluate whether President Ford's decision was justified on ethical grounds.

COLLEGE OF NATURAL SCIENCES

In the College of Natural Sciences, *CH 372C: Chemistry Peer Mentors in Research and Teaching* was developed by Professor Stacey Sparks to train approximately seventy-five of the best chemistry students to become laboratory teaching assistants and student mentors. The class is a two-semester professional development course that follows a flipped classroom format where students learn content outside of the classroom and use class time for discussion.

Professor Sparks began the first online module with a brief introduction of behavioral ethics. Then, students watched the *Ethics Unwrapped* video *Introduction to Behavioral Ethics*. Next, Professor Sparks posed a hypothetical scenario familiar to students (involving cheating or some similar academic transgression) that invoked one of the behavioral ethics concepts covered in the video. Then, she asked students, "What would you do?" Students were instructed to write out their responses and bring them to class to discuss.

Other questions in the online module asked students to identify ethical concepts using a multiple-choice format, and to put themselves in the shoes of students in the video who had shared ethical dilemmas. Professor Sparks asked, "How would you have responded?" Again, students were asked to write down their thoughts to the open-ended questions and come prepared to discuss their responses in class. Classroom discussion was informal and conversational. The students' stories in the video helped to normalize ethical dilemmas for the chemistry students; classroom discussions were unusually frank, revealing, and self-reflective.

Based on the success of the first ethics modules in the first year, Professor Sparks added additional online modules the following year drawing from the *Giving Voice to Values* video series on *Ethics Unwrapped*. Her course also served as a model for training student mentors in other departments in the College of Natural Sciences, such as the Biology Department, and in other schools on campus such as the School of Engineering.

ETHICS UNWRAPPED AT THE
UNIVERSITY OF ILLINOIS

The Gies College of Business and the Grainger College of Engineering at the University of Illinois have integrated *Ethics Unwrapped* resources in some of their courses. Professor Gretchen Winter, who teaches in both schools, uses *Ethics Unwrapped* videos with undergraduate business minors as well as with computer science engineering students who are doing professional internships in Chicago.

In the business school, Professor Winter assigns five videos from either *Ethics Defined* or *Concepts Unwrapped* and asks students to pick two or three additional videos that appeal to them. Students watch all the videos, answer a question for each video from a list of questions Professor Winter provides, and then write journal entries responding to what they have seen. She also asks students to provide examples from their own lives that might fit with the ethics concept explained in the video. As a fully online course, this writing reflection exercise helps students process the information they have viewed, as well as apply the ethics principle to their own lives.

The course in the School of Engineering is a required class for all students in the college and focuses on professional responsibility and ethics. It is a small in-person seminar course. Professor Winter asks students to look at the *Ethics Unwrapped* website and pick three to five videos from the *Concepts Unwrapped* series that appeal to them. Students watch the videos outside of class and answer the video's discussion questions from the *Ethics Unwrapped* website. The written responses are turned in as a homework assignment.

In the same course, Professor Winter assigns groups of students case studies from the *Scandals Illustrated* series. The teams are asked to watch the short video together, read the case study, and discuss it as a group. Individually, each student writes a response to watching the video, and answers the discussion questions on the *Ethics Unwrapped* website provided with the case study. Then, student teams lead group discussions in class. Professor Winter engages each team with additional questions, including inquires such as, "Would you have handled this in the same way?"

Overall, Professor Winter finds that *Ethics Unwrapped* videos help students understand ethics concepts more fully because students tend to understand things when they are related to their own lives. Additionally, by asking students to peruse the website and chose what appeals to them from certain video series, she finds that students tend to review much more content on the website than if she assigned them particular videos. Students are exposed to, and investigate, more ethics concepts than the relatively few concepts she assigns to the class as a whole.

ETHICS UNWRAPPED IN GEORGE MASON UNIVERSITY LEADERSHIP COURSES

Ethics Unwrapped resources have also been folded into leadership programs at George Mason University. Nick Lennon, Director of the Leadership Education and Development Office, created a course to help students develop as ethical leaders. Entitled *Ethics and Leadership: Lessons from the Holocaust*, the course uses a learning laboratory format where student groups travel to Germany, Poland, and the Czech Republic to see and study the locations where Jews and others were incarcerated and killed during World War II.

The experiential learning allows students to connect theoretical concepts to real world experiences and explore ethical questions such as, "How are values and ethics established in individuals, groups, and organizations?" "What are the responsibilities of followers and bystanders?" "Why do ordinary people behave unethically?" The course is composed of readings, site visits, class discussions, a reflection paper, and a multimedia presentation.

Because access to the Internet can be patchy during their trip, Professor Lennon provides students with a course book to read and study throughout their travel. In it, he excerpts the narration from several *Concepts Unwrapped* videos, such as *Fundamental Attribution Error, Obedience to Authority, and Conformity Bias*, to introduce students to these behavioral ethics concepts. In addition, he includes discussion questions from the website to initiate group conversation and touch on key points during their morning discussion groups. Once the group returns to campus from Europe, Professor Lennon encourages students to watch the *Ethics Unwrapped* videos to help them prepare for their final reflection paper and presentation.

TIPS ON USING ETHICS UNWRAPPED
IN THE CLASSROOM

As these examples indicate, *Ethics Unwrapped* supports a subset of activities that individuals or groups can work on to unpack ethical dilemmas and apply ethics concepts to course content and real world situations. Additionally, this section shares some tips for instructors who wish to incorporate *Ethics Unwrapped* resources into their curriculum.

Teachers can show a video in class, assign a video to watch outside of class, or embed a video in an online learning module such as Canvas. Then, the teacher can prompt conversation in class by asking students to answer the video's discussion questions. They can ask students to reflect on the issues raised by the students in the video, inquire as to how students would navigate these situations, and ask what pressures they might face when doing so. To wrap up the conversation, teachers could encourage students to brainstorm how they might manage these ethical challenges if they faced them individually, and as a group.

Ethics Unwrapped videos also make good writing prompts. After students watch a video, an instructor can ask them to apply the ethics concept from the video to a topic or dilemma covered in the course. As students learn more ethics concepts, ask them how the concepts relate to each other; challenge students to provide examples of how these interrelated principles manifest in the subject matter they are studying. Instructors can also ask students to dig deeper by reading the related case study (or a current event in the news) and answer the case study questions on the program's website.

For group projects, teachers can select a case study from the *Cases* series and ask students to reason through the ethical dimensions with their team members. Then, the team can explore any parallels that emerge between the case and the content covered in the course. Many teachers encourage students to brainstorm possible solutions to the ethical dilemmas presented in the case, and to identify best practices that could be applied to the issues that surfaced. As a follow up, teachers can ask students to commit to practical steps to support ethical decision-making around this issue, and to track their own progress toward this goal.

All the case studies include bibliographies and allow instructors and students to explore the details of each case in more depth. In addition, each case study has its own set of discussion questions on the website that can be used to prompt conversation in the classroom or be assigned as part of the coursework or homework. Many cases have additional ethics concepts, videos, or ethical insights that are included with the teaching resources. All these activities can be turned into stand-alone online content modules to support flipped and online courses, as well as offered as exercises and group activities in seminar and traditional in-person courses.

CONCLUSION

As an educational resource that is universally available at no cost for all who wish to teach ethical decision-making and behavior, the potential impact of *Ethics Unwrapped* is boundless. Instructors at every level, regardless of their discipline or trade, can use these tools to create a bridge for students to move from good intentions to tangible ethical awareness. Indeed, the program can positively impact undergraduate education today, and the world tomorrow, by sending ethically aware students into organizations and communities across the globe.

Even if only a few instructors from every degree-granting college or vocational school offer behavioral ethics education, this would be an important contribution to the overall goal of practical ethics education for all. To build the capacity for citizens of the world to work collaboratively, and to foster the integrity and creativity necessary to face the enormous challenges of our time, we need to trust one another and work well together. Trust enriches local communities and is necessary for economic health; it is built through honest, transparent relationships, and by doing no harm.

Ethics Unwrapped can help all of us understand our weakness as humans—both individually and collectively—and raise our awareness of the many subtle ways in which we overlook the harm we do to others and to our environment. This ethical awareness—and the recognition of the pernicious influences described by behavioral ethics—is key to having productive relationships, and to building trust within our organizations, our communities, and the world at large.

NOTES

1. National Ethics Project. 2019. Research project to assess ethics education in higher education nationwide and share effective ethics pedagogy and tools. https://nationalethicsproject.org/.

2. *Scandals Illustrated*. 2019. Ethics Unwrapped Program, McCombs School of Business, The University of Texas at Austin. https://ethicsunwrapped.utexas.edu/series/scandals-illustrated.

3. U.S. Department of Education, Institute of Education Sciences, National Center for Education Statistics. 2015. *National Assessment of Educational Progress (NAEP), 2015 Reading Assessments.*

4. Hawkins, B. Denise. "Here Comes Generation Z. What Makes Them Tick?" *NEA Today*, July 13, 2015.

5. Ariely, D. 2009. *Predictably Irrational: The Hidden Forces That Shape Our Decisions*. New York, New York: Harper Perennial.

6. Kahneman, D. 2011. *Thinking, Fast and Slow*. New York, New York: Farrar, Straus and Giroux

7. Sauer, H. 2017. *Moral Judgments as Educated Intuitions*. Cambridge, MA: MIT Press.

8. Shermer, M. 2012. "The Alpinist of Evil." *Scientific American* 307(6): 84.

9. Levin, I.P. and Gaeth, G.J. 1988. "How Consumers Are Affected by the Framing of Attribute Information Before and After Consuming the Product." *Journal of Consumer Research* 15(3): 374–78; Levin, I.P. 1987. "Associative Effects of Information Framing." *Bulletin of the Psychonomic Society* 25(2): 85–86.

10. Shermer, M. 2015. *The Moral Arc*. New York, New York: Henry Holt and Company.

11. Piff, P.K. 2013. "Does Money Make You Mean?" TED talk. https://www.ted.com/talks/paul_piff_does_money_make_you_mean?language=en.

12. Armstrong, J. S. 1976. *"The Panalba Role-Playing Case."* Retrieved from http://repository.upenn.edu/marketing_papers/129.

ETHICS UNWRAPPED PROGRAM OVERVIEW

Ethics Unwrapped is attractive to colleges, universities, and vocational schools that need high-quality educational resources to teach ethics and leadership in their courses and programs. Many schools have some ethics offerings, but very few have instructional budgets to create ethics courses or to hire ethics experts to develop cross-disciplinary ethics content. There is no cost associated with using any of the *Ethics Unwrapped* videos or teaching resources such as case studies, teaching notes, and discussion questions.

All of the research-based videos and associated teaching resources are written by ethics experts, and based on the latest studies in behavioral ethics as well as on the most recent ethics pedagogy. The videos have won fifteen awards for academic and filmmaking excellence; the program won the prestigious Reimagine Education Award—Bronze in Business Education for educational innovation in 2019.

Ethics Unwrapped videos are engaging: short, entertaining, accessible, and often featuring student interviews and animation. They are also effective tools for teaching and learning. A survey of approximately 8,600 undergraduate students who used the videos in courses across the University of Texas at Austin campus found that 90 percent of students said the videos were helpful to understanding ethics concepts. Additionally, 95 percent of faculty said the videos (and accompanying resources) were helpful for teaching ethics to their students.

All of the program materials may be accessed through the Internet at https://EthicsUnwrapped.utexas.edu/. The videos can also be found on

YouTube. Some of the video series are available on DVD for those who cannot access the Internet.

Viewership has been doubling every year since the program's launch; new milestones are being reached at faster rates. To date, more than 2,000 universities from 170 countries have accessed the website, and more than 80 percent of top research universities worldwide use the resources. The videos have had more than 3 million views on YouTube, and are being used on teaching platforms such as PBS Learning Media (https://www.pbslearningmedia.org/collection/confronting-bias-ethics-in-the-classroom/) as well as by trade associations, local and federal government agencies, large and small businesses, and a multitude of companies and organizations including AT&T, the United Nations, and the U.S. Navy.

In addition to its focus on behavioral ethics, *Ethics Unwrapped* offers a full range of ethics content. For example, video topics include basic ethics concepts and theories such as deontology, hedonism, virtue ethics, fundamental moral unit, moral philosophy, and so on. Principles of moral character, such as altruism, integrity, and justice, are also included along with values-driven leadership principles and important ancillary concepts such as fiduciary duty, sustainability, and the veil of ignorance.

The *Ethics Unwrapped* website includes an ethics blog, a section of curated resources to navigate the content more readily, an ethics glossary, and social media channels including Facebook, Twitter, LinkedIn, and Instagram. The blog, which is shared on social media, often examines current events through an ethical lens and also offers ethics-related book reviews. Social media outreach and the Internet make availability and scalability of *Ethics Unwrapped* resources not only possible, but easy as well.

The social media channels often highlight current events related to ethics concepts that are explained or explored in *Ethics Unwrapped*. In this manner, current events supply an additional source of teaching material that is both timely and relevant. Free ethics resources from other organizations and institutions are shared through the program's social media channels, too, so instructors can find a variety of teaching materials for ethics by following *Ethics Unwrapped* on social media.

VIDEO SERIES OVERVIEW

There are more than 130 videos across five videos series in *Ethics Unwrapped*. Many videos are accompanied by case studies, teaching resources, and bibliographies. This section describes each videos series briefly. All of the series and teaching materials are available on the program's website: www.ethicsunwrapped.utexas.edu.

ETHICS DEFINED GLOSSARY SERIES

More than fifty short animated videos define key ethics terms and concepts in 2 minutes or less. Many of the terms focus on behavioral ethics, such as Ethical Fading, Framing, Group Think, and Moral Emotions, although a significant number of glossary terms cover basic ethics principles and ethical theories such as Deontology, Justice, Moral Philosophy, and Virtue Ethics. New terms are added at regular intervals. This is the program's most popular series, and can be found here: https://ethicsunwrapped.utexas.edu/glossary.

Ethics Defined is a useful tool for students and instructors to develop a shared vocabulary that can support rich classroom discussion. The glossary is a helpful primer for students to learn about the basics of behavioral ethics. It is an excellent study tool to prepare students for readings, exams, and classroom discussion. Related glossary terms are shown in the *Ethics Defined* sidebar to help students connect the dots between concepts and to develop a framework of interrelated ethics concepts.

Here is a list of essential concepts from *Ethics Defined*: Bounded Ethicality, Conflict of Interest, Conformity Bias, Ethical Fading, Framing, Moral Equilibrium, Overconfidence Bias, Self-serving bias, and Rationalizations. To build on that foundation, add Altruism, Corruption, Diffusion of Responsibility, Groupthink, Incrementalism, In-group/Out-group, Integrity, Moral Muteness, Obedience to Authority, Prosocial Behavior, and Role Morality.

CONCEPTS UNWRAPPED VIDEO SERIES

Thirty-six videos of approximately 5-minutes each include a more detailed explanation of these important ethical concepts, and include students' reflections on these ideas. Largely devoted to the concepts of behavioral ethics, this video series highlights the cognitive biases, social and organizational pressures, and situational factors that can make it difficult for good people to do the right thing although general ethics concepts are also included in this series, too, such as Fundamental Moral Unit, Relativism, and Systematic Moral Analysis. This series can be found here: https://ethicsunwrapped.u texas.edu/series/concepts-unwrapped.

Interviews with undergraduate and graduate students are intercut with animations and the professor's expert narration that defines and explains the ethics concept. The students' experiences illustrate the ethics concepts in specific, measurable ways that are meaningful to students. The videos include discussion questions, teaching notes, additional resources, and a case study with its own set of discussion questions and a bibliography.

The behavioral ethics concepts in this series include many of those mentioned in the glossary series, and many others including some general ethics concepts: Causing Harm, Incentive Gaming, Legal Rights & Ethical Responsibilities, Representation, Cognitive Dissonance, Fundamental Attribution Error, Implicit Bias, Moral Myopia, and Moral Imagination.

IN IT TO WIN VIDEO SERIES

A 25-minute documentary features disgraced super-lobbyist Jack Abramoff, who went down in flames (along with high-profile politicians) and explores the biases and pressures that lead to his professional downfall and subsequent incarceration. Students can learn from his poor ethical decisions. The documentary is supplemented by six short videos that explain how Abramoff's situation illustrates several key behavioral ethics concepts, including: Framing, Moral Equilibrium, Overconfidence Bias, Rationalizations, Role Morality, Self-serving Bias.

The documentary includes a lengthy case study with discussion questions, teaching notes, and a bibliography; each short video has its own set of discussion questions and teaching notes with additional resources for further exploration. The series can be viewed here: https://ethicsunwrapped.utexas .edu/series/in-it-to-win.

GIVING VOICE TO VALUES (GVV) VIDEO SERIES

Eight videos, approximately 7 minutes each, introduce the seven principles of values-driven leadership outlined by Professor Mary Gentile in her book, *Giving Voice to Values: How to Speak Your Mind When You Know What's Right*. Mary Gentile narrates this *GVV* series, which offers a practical guide for students who want to learn how to speak up for the right thing and to do so effectively.

Each video in the *GVV* series includes discussion questions, teaching notes, and additional resources. All the videos are paired with a single case study with its own set of discussion questions and a bibliography. Mary Gentile offers additional free resources to teachers through the *Giving Voice to Values Curriculum* website (https://www.darden.virginia.edu/ibis/initiatives/ gvv), a link to which can also be found in the *Ethics Unwrapped* teaching notes for this video series, which is found here: https://ethicsunwrapped.u texas.edu/series/giving-voice-to-values.

SCANDALS ILLUSTRATED VIDEO SERIES

Thirty videos of approximately 1-minute each use a graphic-novel style animation to summarize recent scandals in the news. Each video concludes with a concept that appeared to play a role in the scandal, either by bringing the scandal into being, or by escalating a single wrong deed into a major blunder. This series is available here: https://ethicsunwrapped.utexas.edu/series/scandals-illustrated.

Students not familiar with the ethics concept teased out in the *Scandals* video will find the concept explained in *Ethics Defined* and/or *the Concepts Unwrapped* video series. Each *Scandals Illustrated* video is accompanied by a detailed case study of the scandal, discussion questions, and a bibliography so instructors and students can do further research. Every video also includes an ethical insight that explains how the ethics concept relates to the case at hand.

Authors' Biographies

Cara Biasucci is creator of Ethics Unwrapped and director of ethics education for the Center for Leadership and Ethics at the University of Texas at Austin. For more than a decade, she made films for (among others) American Public Television, Discovery Times, the New England Patriots, the National Gallery of Art, and Johns Hopkins.

Sandra L. Borden, PhD, is professor of communication and director of the Center for the Study of Ethics in Society at Western Michigan University.

Michael D. Burroughs, PhD, is director of the Kegley Institute of Ethics at CSU Bakersfield and president of the Philosophy Learning and Teaching Organization (PLATO). Michael is coauthor of *Philosophy in Education: Questioning and Dialogue in Schools* and founding editor of *Precollege Philosophy and Public Practice*. More information on his work can be found on his professional website: https://www.michaeldeanburroughs.com/

Dennis Cooley, PhD, is professor of philosophy and ethics at North Dakota State University, where he also serves as the director of the Northern Plains Ethics Institute, the secretary general of the International Academy of Medical Ethics and Public Health, and secretary general and coeditor of Springer's International Library of Ethics, Law, and the New Medicine.

Patrick Croskery, PhD, was a professor in the Department of Religion and Philosophy at Ohio Northern University, where he specialized in ethics and social and political philosophy and served professional organizations such as the Association for Practical and Professional Ethics and its Intercollegiate Ethics Bowl.

Ronald L. Dufresne, PhD, is an associate professor in management and the director of the Leadership, Ethics and Organizational Sustainability Program at Saint Joseph's University (Philadelphia, Pennsylvania).

Elaine E. Englehardt, PhD, is the distinguished professor of ethics at Utah Valley University and president of the Society for Ethics across the Curriculum.

C. K. Gunsalus, PhD, is the founding director of the National Center for Professional and Research Ethics (NCPRE) at the University of Illinois at Urbana-Champaign.

Lisa Kretz, PhD, is an associate professor of philosophy and the director of the ethics program at the University of Evansville (Indiana).

Elizabeth A. Luckman, PhD, is a clinical assistant professor of business administration at the Gies College of Business, University of Illinois Urbana-Champaign, where she teaches at both the graduate and undergraduate levels.

Alan Preti, PhD, is an associate professor of philosophy and the director of the Institute for Ethical Leadership and Social Responsibility at Rosemont College (Pennsylvania).

Dominic P. Scibilia, PhD, is a faculty emeritus of Saint Peter's Preparatory School (Jersey City, New Jersey).

David S. Steingard, PhD, is an associate professor and associate director of the Pedro Arrupe Center for Business Ethics at Saint Joseph's University (Philadelphia, Pennsylvania).

Daniel E. Wueste, PhD, was founding director of the Rutland Institute for Ethics at Clemson University where he is a professor of philosophy. He is a member and treasurer of the board of directors of the Association for Practical and Professional Ethics as well as member of the executive committee of the Society for Ethics across the Curriculum.

Made in United States
North Haven, CT
29 April 2023

36049996R00114